Former scientists Alan and Jackie Gear, Britain's ⟨…⟩ gardeners, were directors of the Henry Doubleday Research Association (now called Garden Organic) for many years, where they were instrumental in making environmentally friendly gardening mainstream.

They set up Ryton Organic Gardens, the Vegetable Kingdom visitor centre, developed the Heritage Seed Library, created National Potato Day, presented Channel 4's ground-breaking series *All Muck & Magic?*, and ran many campaigns, including 'Grow Your Own Organic Fruit and Vegetables' – the first initiative in the country-wide trend towards producing home-grown food. Celia Haddon, writing in *The Daily Telegraph*, said 'At the heart of Jackie and Alan Gear's message lies a great truth – that to change the world for the better a person can, and should, start in their own back yard.'

In 2003 they were awarded Honorary Fellowships by the Royal Horticultural Society, and MBEs for ⟨…⟩ horticulture. They are authors of the highly respected *Organic Gardening: The Whole Story*, published by Watkins in 2009.

Alan and Jackie are passionate fruit and vegetable growers on their garden and allotment in north-west ⟨…⟩.

ORGANIC
VEGETABLE & FRUIT

GROWING & PRESERVING
MONTH BY MONTH

ALAN & JACKIE GEAR

WATKINS PUBLISHING

LONDON

This edition published in the UK 2011 by
Watkins Publishing, Sixth Floor, Castle House,
75–76 Wells Street, London W1T 3QH

Text Copyright © Alan and Jackie Gear 2011

1 3 5 7 9 10 8 6 4 2

Designed and typeset by Paul Saunders

Printed and bound by Imago in China

British Library Cataloguing-in-Publication Data Available

ISBN: 978-1-906787-92-9

www.watkinspublishing.co.uk

For past and present staff of the Henry Doubleday Research Association (working name Garden Organic)

Contents

Illustrations

Acknowledgements

This book draws on the expertise and experiences of many more people than we are able to mention here. Were it not for Lawrence D. Hills, the acknowledged leader of the organic gardening movement in the early days, we wouldn't have written it at all. He personally passed on much knowledge when we trained with him in the 1970s at HDRA, the charitable research organization he founded. As directors of HDRA between 1986 and 2003, we also learned an enormous amount about growing fruit and vegetables organically from the gardeners, advisers and scientists who worked there. We have also taken advantage of invaluable research done at that time by what was then called the National Vegetable Research Station, now part of the University of Warwick. There is nothing quite like sharing experiences to broaden your outlook, and we freely acknowledge the role of the many HDRA members, friends and other keen gardeners we have chatted to over the years, who have generously passed on their tips and advice.

Our thanks also go to Bob Sherman, Director of Horticulture at Garden Organic, and one of the country's leading experts on organic fruit growing, for checking what we have written about fruit in Part 3. We are also indebted to Dr Bill Blyth, originally a research microbiologist and Chairman of HDRA for many years, for looking over the information contained in Chapter 2.

To Michael Mann at Watkins, our gratitude for commissioning the book, and for allowing us free rein to develop it as we saw fit. We'd also like to thank Penny Stopa, our editor Alison Bolus, Paul Saunders for his illustrations, and our indefatigable agent, Jane Graham Maw. Any mistakes in the text are, we fear, entirely down to us.

Finally, we would like to acknowledge the constant support of family and friends during the past six months, particularly Gray and Sue, Betty and David, Anne and Brian, Heather, Graham, Sylvia and Norman. They must have asked the question 'How's the book going?' thousands of times!

Alan and Jackie Gear, Snettisham, Norfolk, Easter 2010

Introduction

This is the perfect book whether you want to start growing your own produce for the very first time or if you're an experienced grower who would like all the details of yearly cultivation laid out concisely and clearly in a handbook you can pop into your pocket for easy reference.

So, if you want to eat healthily and cheaply and enjoy the wonderful taste of freshly harvested produce, as well as help the environment by avoiding chemical pollution and unnecessary 'food miles', read on! You're in good company, for it seems that just about everyone is using whatever space they can find – from their patios to allotments – to 'grow their own'. Flowerbeds up and down the country are being dug up in favour of fruit and vegetables, and even the Queen now has heritage vegetables growing in the former flowerbeds of Buckingham Palace.

This book will show you how to produce fresh, sweet-tasting peas, mouth-watering tomatoes and luscious strawberries. It will guide you through the gardening calendar, from sowing to harvesting, with a comprehensive list of jobs for each month of the year. And it's backed up with detailed descriptions of how to grow more than 80 different vegetables, herbs and fruit, ending with advice on all the many ways in which you can preserve and store what you have grown.

Its philosophy is unashamedly organic, because we care about the food we put into our bodies and, more importantly, we care about the environment, so we avoid chemical pesticides and fertilizers, concentrating instead on building up a rich population of soil organisms. When fed by the composted organic matter we add to the soil, they convert it into a range of nutrients to feed our plants to make them healthy. We also encourage a rich diversity of beneficial wildlife, which helps us to cope with any plant pests and diseases.

Our thinking is based on how we have been gardening for the past 35 years, ever since we gave up conventional jobs as scientists to work for Lawrence Hills, the legendary organic gardening guru, and founder of the horticultural research organization, the Henry Doubleday Research Association (HDRA). In 1986 we took over as joint directors of HDRA, and during the next 17 years we and its gardeners, scientific researchers and educational advisers built it into the largest organic horticultural research and demonstration organization in Europe. Much of the information and many of the growing techniques in this book were discovered and developed by our team at HDRA. Its important work continues to this day, as Garden Organic, its new working title.

Unusually in a gardening book, we have included information about human nutrition, because, as much as we all enjoy our food, its role is to nourish us. Put simply, we are what we eat, and research from trials around the world has shown that organically grown produce contains greater amounts of phytochemicals than conventionally produced food. These plant chemicals play an important role in protecting the body against cancer, heart disease and other degenerative conditions, and so we list the major phytochemicals, minerals and vitamins contained in each fruit and vegetable in the book. Certain of them, usually the brightly coloured ones, are so rich in vitamins, minerals and phytochemicals that they are called 'superfoods'. We have selected the top 20, so that you can take these into consideration when you're planning what to grow, although, as we emphasize in the book, you can't really go wrong if you eat a balanced diet containing a rich variety of fresh fruit and vegetables – five a day at the very least!

Before you begin the book proper, we'd like to wish you every success with your crops, especially if this is your first attempt. You're sure to have some failures – the weather will see to that, if nothing else – but, if you follow the advice we've given, you'll enjoy success after success. And the satisfaction that comes from eating your own food is hard to put into words. You'll just have to have a go yourself and see what we mean!

How to use this book

Part 1, The Basics, covers a practical introduction to gardening, and a brief but detailed description of healthy food. The first part will be of special interest to people who are new to gardening, or to organic growing, and deals with all the main gardening techniques. The second is simply an easy-to-read crash course in nutrition, with an emphasis on the vitamins, minerals and phytochemicals present in fruit and vegetables, which are so important to our wellbeing.

Part 2, The Gardening Year, takes an in-depth look at the gardening year, season-by-season, month-by-month. Each month includes an invaluable checklist of tasks. This is followed by a series of special features on subjects that are particularly appropriate for that time of the year. You will find a cross-reference next to some of the tasks, which directs you to additional information contained in one of the seasonal features, or in the crop-by-crop section, that you might find useful. Where one of the tasks involves several crops, you can just go straight to the individual crop relevant to you.

Part 3, A Crop-by-Crop Guide, is an in-depth, alphabetically arranged, crop-by-crop compendium that gives you individual details on how to grow a wide range of vegetables, fruits and herbs. The text covers sowing, planting, cultivation and harvesting, plus dealing with pests and diseases, as well as the key nutritional information (including the glycaemic index, or GI) of each crop.

Part 4, Preserving the Harvest, tells you all you need to know about making the best use of your home-grown produce. Individual features cover storing, freezing, drying and bottling, as well as making jams and jellies, pickles, relishes and chutneys, sauces and ketchups, juices and syrups, flavoured oils and vinegars.

Finally, the Resources section provides suggestions for additional reading, organizations to join and other sources of further assistance. We have also included the names of companies who, between them, can supply all the seeds, plants and products we have mentioned. Many of them are known to us personally, or have been recommended by others.

In this book we have concentrated on the practical 'nuts and bolts' of organic fruit and vegetable growing, but if you would like to know more about the organic philosophy and how it has evolved over the years, read our earlier book, *Organic Gardening: The Whole Story*, which was published in 2009 by Watkins Publishing.

PART 1

The basics

CHAPTER 1

Gardening basics

Right, let's get started! In this chapter we're assuming that you're growing fruit and vegetables for the first time. Maybe you have a large garden, with plenty of space to grow a wide range of crops, or you've taken on an allotment. At the other end of the scale, perhaps you have only a pint-sized patch, or a patio – but even so, you'll be surprised at how much you can produce and enjoy.

The gardening year

In a nutshell, this begins in the winter (December, January and February), when you decide where and what you are going to grow and how you are going to grow it. It's the time to tidy your shed, get your tools ready and prepare your plot for sowing. In the spring (March, April and May), you're busy sowing and planting. In the summer (June, July and August), you need to get the weeds under control and deal with any pests and diseases, while also making sure that your crops have enough water and nutrients. This is a busy time, but at last you're eating your very own delicious, fresh produce. During the autumn (September, October and November) you are fully occupied harvesting, storing and preserving your crops to enjoy over the winter and beyond. Of course, in reality it's a little more complicated than this, but it's actually great fun learning all the tricks of the trade along the way.

Where to put your fruit and vegetable plot

Few of us have the luxury of choice when it comes to siting our plot. If you live in a newly built house, the chances are that your garden will be tiny. The soil might even be thin and mean, overlying a compacted seam of builders' rubble. More mature gardens bring different difficulties – a tall *Leylandii* hedge casting deep shadows over your plot, perhaps, or a tangled mat of perennial weed roots. Alternatively, you may have been given an allotment that's covered in brambles. These are just some of the problems that gardeners have, but they can all be overcome one way or another.

Whatever the constraints, your vegetables and fruits should be given the best possible chance to thrive, so don't tuck them out of sight on impoverished soil, in a shady and neglected part of the garden. Instead, give them pride of place, possibly incorporating them, potager-style, in with the flowers. Stay away from hedges, whose shallow roots make digging difficult and suck water from the soil, and avoid hollows, where frost can linger and damage sensitive vegetables and early flowering fruits.

Don't forget to think upwards, too! Every wall, fence, pergola and post can support something, be it a fan-trained cherry, a grape vine or a clambering cucumber (to name but a few). And whilst some fruits are delicate, and should be planted against a south-facing wall, others will grow successfully even if they never see the sun full on.

If you want to enjoy your garden to the full, you need to think about the style and design of your plot. The best time to do this is during winter, when nothing is growing, the days are short and there is not a lot you can do, apart from digging occasionally when the weather allows. Garden structures, such as a garden shed, wooden compost bin, tripods for climbing plants and netted frames to keep flying pests off your crops can be bought or made in a variety of styles. You can even paint them all the same colour if you wish – a look that is especially good for small gardens. (These days there are dozens of shades of safe water-based paints on offer, from sage-green to mellow-yellow!) You should also leave space for a small pond somewhere – it will give you pleasure and provide a habitat for wildlife. Even bees, which are essential for pollinating crops, get thirsty like the rest of us! If you have pets or small children, you will need to cover the pond with mesh for safety. A small dog might decide that this is the perfect place to play in, thereby disturbing any wildlife, and a child could drown in just a few inches of water.

What to grow on your plot

Once you've decided on the best place for your plot, and the overall look of it, you need to plan what's going where. This is when we gardeners come into our own! We look forward to the new season, poring over seed catalogues and dreaming of bounteous harvests to come. There is a huge temptation to buy more seeds than you have the space to grow, so try not to get carried away at your first attempt. You can always get more next year.

You may already have a good idea of what you want to eat. Some people opt for basics, such as carrots, parsnips and potatoes; some for more Mediterranean crops, such as tomatoes, peppers and basil; and others for high-value vegetables, such as asparagus and sweet potatoes. Few people, as yet, base their decision on nutritional content, although this will hopefully change in future, as the health-conferring properties of certain 'super' fruits and vegetables become better known. In the meantime, grow a wide variety of brightly coloured fruit and vegetables, including plenty of greens, and you can't go wrong!

A lot will depend on the size of your plot. A traditional apple orchard is wonderful if you have a spare half-acre, but most of us have to make do with a dwarfing fruit tree or two in our gardens. Some people will be unable to find space even for these, in which case it is easy to fit a pot-grown peach or apricot somewhere – even on a small patio. Likewise, you can usually squeeze in a grow-bag of tomatoes or a tub of salad leaves. Turn to page 68 for more on container-grown fruit, vegetables and herbs.

Geography may also prevent us from growing everything that we would wish. We are all at the mercy of the weather to a certain extent, but if you live in the north of the UK, you are going to find it difficult, if not impossible, to raise some of the more tender crops unless you have a glasshouse or some other sort of protection from the elements.

Having decided what to grow, you must then select the individual varieties. One of the great pleasures of leafing through a seed or nursery catalogue is the enormous choice you find. It can, however, be somewhat overwhelming if you're a first-time gardener, so we've included our own personal selection of some of the best varieties on offer to help you choose, based on qualities such as flavour, pest- and disease-resistance, hardiness and continuity of picking. They range from newly minted F1 hybrid seeds to old favourites, dating back a hundred years or more. Another way of finding out which plants and varieties are good ones to grow is to talk to keen gardening neighbours, who will invariably be willing to share their knowledge of what does well in your area.

When you first begin to garden, it's a good idea to start a diary, noting down the names of the crops and varieties, and when and where they're planted. Later in the season you can comment on how they have performed. Once you're hooked, you'll want to do this every year, because you'll find it a great help to look back at previous successes and failures, and the reasons behind them.

Grouping vegetables that belong to the same botanical family to grow together as part of a crop rotation is an important part of this winter planning exercise, because it helps to prevent pests and diseases from building up in the soil. You can find out more about this on page 51.

How to grow your vegetables

Early on, you must decide whether you're going to grow vegetables in long rows across the plot, in traditional allotment fashion, or whether you're going to create a series of individual beds, linked by narrow paths. There's no hard and fast rule saying how big a bed should be, but a typical size is 90cm–1.2m (3–4ft) wide and 3–4m (10–13ft) long, separated by paths that are 45–60cm (18–24in) wide.

Bed gardening has many merits, which is why it's become so popular in recent years, especially 'raised beds', in which the soil is contained within an enclosure edged with timber or other materials. You can easily construct raised beds from scrap timber (re-used decking planks, or scaffolding boards are ideal) or you can buy self-assembly kits made from wood or recycled plastic that simply slot together. There's a lot to be said in favour of raised beds, but you can just as easily make beds on the flat, without the edging (which is how we garden ourselves).

Beds allow you to put compost and manure exactly where you want it, not wasting it on paths, and as you will not be treading on the soil, compaction is eliminated, especially when the ground is wet. Another advantage is that plants can be put closer together, so you can reach them from either side of the bed, and therefore you don't need to allow space for walking between the rows.

Paths can be made of almost anything. Some people lay lengths of old carpet, or a weed-excluding polypropylene mulch covered with woodchips or gravel; others prefer a more permanent, paved way. Grass paths look attractive, but they must be mown and edged and they persistently encroach onto the beds. Cheapest of all are paths made of beaten earth, but they can become muddy. The choice is yours.

Tools

Every gardener needs tools, but some are more useful than others. A spade and a fork for digging are essential, and if you purchase wisely, from a reputable manufacturer, they should last you a lifetime (but it is also worthwhile asking friends and family for any they no longer want). You can take a look at stalls at car boot sales too, or check out the Freecycle website (see Resources, page 304). Apart from the obvious cost saving involved, the quality of materials and workmanship of recycled tools is frequently superior to their modern equivalents.

The spades and forks may all look much the same, so examine the materials carefully. Do they have wooden or plastic handles? High carbon steel or stainless-steel blades and tines? Try out the different styles of handle, and compare the length of the shafts, which can vary considerably. How do they feel? Not too heavy? Remember that you could be digging for hours at a stretch, so your spade has to be comfortable.

You'll also need a rake, to create a fine tilth and a level seed bed, and a hoe or two. Hoes come in various designs, but the most useful are a 'swan-necked' draw hoe for marking out seed drills and earthing up, and a Dutch hoe, with a flat, angled blade, for general weeding. Having said this, our own favourite is a Swiss oscillating hoe, which has a push-pull action, and combines the qualities of both.

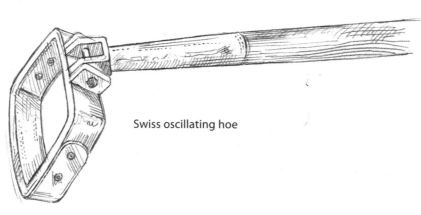

Swiss oscillating hoe

A proper garden line makes marking out rows far easier than using a piece of string tied to a couple of sticks; and a steel-tipped dibber comes in handy when planting larger seeds and leeks. You should also get a hand trowel for planting – ours is pointed and made of bronze – a bit expensive, but it slices effortlessly through the hardest of soils. Pair it with a hand fork for delicate weeding and other close-up work.

Wheelbarrows come in all shapes and sizes, but a robust builders' barrow with a pneumatic tyre does for most jobs, being built to withstand considerable wear and tear. A good, general-purpose, galvanized steel watering can, holding 9 litres/2 gallons, is needed too, for watering individual plants. Equip it with fine and coarse roses that fit onto the spout to regulate the flow. It's also worth getting a much smaller watering can, with a narrow spout and extra-fine rose, for watering seeds and seedlings.

When working with fruit, you need a pair of secateurs – buy the very best you can afford (or ask for a pair for Christmas!). Get some that can be sharpened easily and have a replaceable blade. The branches of mature fruit trees and bushes will be too thick to be cut with secateurs, so loppers or a pruning saw will be needed as well.

Complete your garden tool kit with a soil thermometer. As you become more experienced, you'll know when the time is right to sow seeds, but in the beginning you can save yourself a lot of disappointment (if they fail to germinate) by checking the soil temperature first.

If, after all this outlay, you still have money left in the kitty, spoil yourself by investing in a really good plant propagator, to germinate your seeds in the warmth, and give your plants an early start to the season.

Feeding the soil

What is your soil like? Ideally, for growing vegetables, it should be easy to dig, water-retaining and rich in nutrients. But don't worry if yours isn't like this when you start, because it can always be improved. You often hear gardeners refer to their soil as being 'heavy', if it contains a lot of clay, or 'light', if it's sandy. Each type has its own strengths and weaknesses, and on page 46 we explain what these are and how you can work out the composition of your garden soil. We also explain the importance of soil pH, which is a measure of its acid/alkaline balance, and how it affects what you can grow.

We organic gardeners believe that the healthier the soil, the healthier the plants that grow in it, so our soil is given a rich diet of natural compost (decomposed weeds and other plant wastes), manures and other organic materials. These are broken down by the countless billions of bacteria and other microorganisms that live in the soil, releasing nutrients that feed the plants. Compost also acts as a soil conditioner, binding sandy soils together, improving water retention and lightening clays, making them more work-able. It's easy to make in the garden, but if you have a really poor soil, such as you can find on new housing estates, one of the quickest ways of improving it is to buy a lorry load of compost from your local authority. This is made from composted household 'green waste' and is a rich source of organic matter – just the thing to mobilize moribund microorganisms. Composting is the key to successful organic gardening, but more about that later (see page 47).

A few soils are inherently short of particular minerals and need to be supplemented with ground rock fertilizers to correct any deficiencies. Other minerals, such as ground limestone or dolomite, are used to 'sweeten' acid soils. Organic fertilizers, such as bonemeal and hoof and horn, are also useful, as are concentrated manures (e.g. chicken manure pellets), and plant residues such as seaweed and processed sugar beet. These act faster than rock-based fertilizers and provide additional nutrients to soils in which winter 'greens' and other demanding crops are growing – see page 48.

Plants growing in containers can also become short of nutrients, which is why organic gardeners supply them via natural liquid feeds. One of the best, and cheapest, is made from comfrey leaves. Every gardener should try to find space for half a dozen of these incredibly useful plants in their garden (see page 69).

Dig this!

The first thing to do when you begin gardening is to dig the soil thoroughly. Ground preparation can be done at any time of the year, but it usually takes place during the cold winter months, except when the ground is frozen. At one end of the plot you intend to dig, you need to take out a trench as deep as the blade of your spade (a spit) and twice as wide as the spade's width, barrowing the soil you've removed to the other end of the plot, where you will use it later to fill the final trench you dig. Then push your fork as far as it will go into the bottom of the trench, rock it back and forth, and twist the tines one way and then the other to break up the soil. This will shatter any pan (compacted soil) that might be there, which would otherwise prevent roots from reaching deep into the subsoil. While you are digging, remove the roots of couch grass, bindweed and other perennial weeds (see page 90), which frequently flourish on neglected land, and pick out any other rubble or rubbish that is there.

If you have a supply of compost or well-rotted manure, spread it across the bottom of the trench. Now dig the next trench adjacent to the first (one spit wide and deep), throwing the soil on top of the compost in the first trench, and mixing it with a fork. Loosen the soil at the bottom of the second trench with a fork, as already described. Continue in this way, working backwards across your plot, until you reach the far end – where the original soil from the first trench will go into the last trench. The ground that has been dug will now be higher than the surrounding soil, but it will gradually settle over the coming weeks. 'Double digging', as this is called, involves a lot of work, so you'll be relieved to hear that you shouldn't need to do this more than once every three or four years. A light forking over of the ground in between times is usually sufficient. There is also a system of growing called 'no-dig' gardening, which you can find out about on page 53.

Aim to have most of your winter digging finished, and the land cleared of weeds, by the middle of March. In some years, spring comes early, so don't be caught napping!

Time to sow

Many gardeners begin to sow seeds in March, but it's risky to sow outside then, because they frequently fail to germinate, and can perish if the weather takes a turn for the worse. At this time of year, it's safer to start seeds off under cover, in a glasshouse or polytunnel or on a windowsill indoors, giving them the best possible start by sowing them in specially formulated growing media. These are available from garden centres and other retailers, in brightly coloured plastic sacks, marked 'seed compost', 'potting compost' and 'multipurpose compost'. The use of the word 'compost' in this context often causes confusion, because it's not the same as the compost you make at home, which is too rich to sow into. We prefer to call them 'growing media'.

A decade or so ago, growing media used to be mainly based on peat, but concern over the environmental damage caused by its extraction has led to the gradual substitution by coir (coconut fibre) and other recycled wastes. Most products on the market are fortified with chemical fertilizers, but you can buy peat-free organic growing media, which contain additional nutrients from accredited sources. We usually use an organic multipurpose mix, which is fine for most situations.

Sowing in 'modules' (moulded plastic trays, subdivided into individual cells) to produce small plants, or 'plugs', is an increasingly popular way of raising plants. Each cell holds a single seedling, where it remains until it's planted out into its final position, or is 'potted on' into a larger cell, or plant pot. You can also use seed trays or pots, instead of modules, but you'll have to 'prick out' (transfer) the seedlings into individual pots when they're large enough to handle. The great advantage of plugs is that the roots aren't disturbed when they're transplanted, and competition between seedlings is eliminated. Not all plants grow well in modules, however – crops with sensitive tap roots, such as carrots and parsnips, rarely prosper. You can overcome this difficulty by using deeper modules, called 'root trainers', which have hinged sides. They're also useful for sowing bigger seeds, like broad beans and runner beans.

Most plugs are planted out as soon as ground conditions permit, which early in the spring usually means waiting until the soil has dried out and warmed up sufficiently. But, first, they must be acclimatized to the cooler

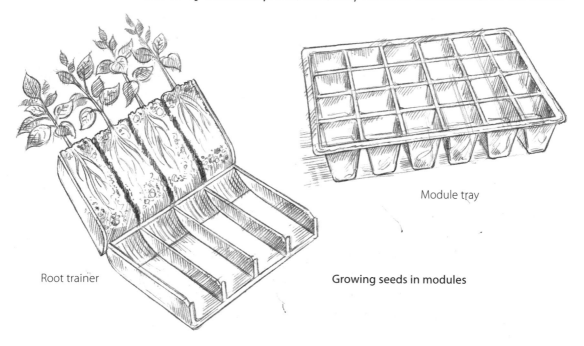

Root trainer

Module tray

Growing seeds in modules

outdoor temperatures – a procedure known as 'hardening off'. One of the best ways of doing this is to transfer them to a cold frame, then you can open the lid during the day for an increasing length of time over a two- to three-week period, and close it at night. For more information on seed-raising techniques, see page 67.

Crops under cover

Apart from its role in hardening off seedlings, you can also use a cold frame to grow crops such as melons and cucumbers, which will only do well outdoors in a good summer. There's only a limited amount of space in a cold frame, however, so if you want to grow peppers, tomatoes, aubergines or sweet potatoes successfully, you'll need to invest in a glasshouse or a polytunnel. Both are incredibly useful and allow you to extend the seasons considerably – starting crops earlier in the year and continuing well into the winter. Some crops, such as oriental salad leaves, will even crop all year round.

Protective cloches, which come in all shapes and sizes, provide many of the benefits of polytunnels and glasshouses at a fraction of the cost. They're invaluable in the garden, protecting plants at vulnerable stages in their lives, such as immediately after planting. Some, like glass or plastic bell-shaped cloches, enclose individual plants. Others cover a complete row or bed, and are made from polythene stretched over a series of plastic or metal hoops that are pushed into the ground. Often, these are designed so that netting, to protect plants from pests or to shade them, can replace the polythene later in the year. There's nothing stopping you from making your own cloches, and you can find some ideas, and more information about protected cropping, on page 70.

Grow some fruit

If you plan to grow any fruits, March is the latest time to buy bare-rooted trees, bushes, canes and vines, which must be planted during the winter, when they're leafless and dormant. This doesn't apply to plants supplied in pots (container-grown), which can go in at any time, but you'll have far fewer varieties to choose from. Apples, pears, peaches, plums and cherries are usually called 'top fruit' or 'tree fruit'. Raspberries and blackberries (also known as 'cane fruit'), blackcurrants, blueberries, gooseberries and red and white currants (also known as 'bush fruit') and strawberries are collectively known as 'soft fruit'.

Fruit has somehow acquired the reputation of being difficult. Perhaps people are put off by the thought of pruning, or the length of time before trees crop, but whatever the reason it's a pity, because growing your own fruit brings rewards out of all proportion to the effort involved. Fruit trees took up a lot of room in the past, but the development of dwarfing root-stocks (onto which trees are grafted) now means that they can be squeezed into the smallest of spaces, and, as previously mentioned, some peach and apricot trees will even grow in tubs. By linking together apple trees that have been trained to produce a single horizontal branch at little more than ankle height ('step-over' trees), you can create a stylish, yet productive, border edging.

Even pruning is not as difficult as you might imagine, and it can become seriously addictive, once you get the hang of it. For the first few years you'll need to concentrate on building up the shape of the tree, and the best person to tell you how to do this is your supplier. In subsequent years, the chief purpose of pruning is to maximize fruit production. Some trees bear their fruit on short stubby branches (spurs), built up over time, others on shoots that are only a year old (see the descriptions of individual fruits in Part 3). After a while, you'll easily spot the difference between older and younger wood, and between those buds that will develop into new shoots and those that will go on to form fruit.

If you're still not convinced, start with soft fruit, and ease yourself in gradually. Raspberries and currants are no trouble at all, and pruning is simple, although you will have to cover the plants with netting at certain times of the year, especially when the fruits ripen, to protect them from hungry birds. Strawberries are even easier, and have the virtue of cropping within a year of planting. They, too, are ideal for patio culture as they can be grown in pots, specially designed strawberry barrels or even hanging baskets.

Making the most of small spaces

If your garden isn't huge, one of the most productive ways of making use of its limited space is by growing 'baby salad leaves'. Sow the seeds much closer than usual and cut them when they are only 10–15cm (4–6in) tall, leaving a short stump. After a few weeks, they'll have re-grown and you can cut them again. With luck, you should even get a third helping. If you're unsure of exactly what to grow, seed companies advertise single varieties and seed mixtures suitable for 'cut-and-come-again' (CCA) or 'seedling' crops. Check out saladini, misticanza and mesclun in catalogues.

CCA crops are great for containers and pots on patios and windowsills, and they can also be sown outside, in the gaps in the rows between widely spaced plants. This multi-cropping technique is called 'intercropping' and it's frequently used in between tall brassicas such as Brussels sprouts. Other fast-growing vegetables, such as lettuces or radishes, can also be used for intercropping– anything, in fact, that can reach maturity without interfering with the growth of the main crop. Sweet corn plants, which grow tall but cast little shade, provide another opportunity to harvest two crops from the same patch of ground by allowing ground-covering plants, such as marrows and pumpkins, to scramble underneath, in a technique known as 'undercropping'. If you have land that has been cleared of one crop but won't be needed for the next few weeks, sow rocket, baby salad leaves and other fast-maturing 'catch crops'. As you become more experienced, and experiment for yourself, you'll come up with your own multi-cropping combinations.

By June, you should be enjoying freshly picked vegetables and delicious fruits in a garden full to overflowing. The last of the frosts has gone and a hot, sunny season beckons (in your dreams!). But there's no time to relax: weeds are threatening to overrun your plot, pests and diseases are poised to strike and, if it really does stay hot and dry, there are plants to be watered. Summer has arrived!

Dealing with weeds

It is one of the great ironies of gardening that, even if the vegetables in your garden may be performing poorly, you can always depend on weeds, which compete with and can smother our crops, to do well. Invariably, they are the first seeds to germinate in spring, and by mid-summer they'll be growing with the speed of the proverbial beanstalk. Even in winter, tough little weeds can be seen clinging grimly to the soil. So, how do we get rid of these stubborn survivors? Happily, many can be dealt with simply by hoeing. These are the annual weeds that only live for a season, and it's important to kill them promptly, using a hoe to slice them just below soil level, before they're able to shed their seeds. Delay, and they join other weed seeds, lying undisturbed in the soil for years without germinating, until they burst into life when brought to the surface during digging. Not for nothing does the old saying go 'one year's weed, seven years' seed'.

Perennial weeds, which can live for many years, are a different matter entirely. These are much more difficult to eradicate. Most have extensive root systems, against which the hoe is helpless; indeed it makes things worse, because each piece of chopped root, no matter how tiny, has the potential to grow into a new plant. If you have couch grass, bindweed or ground elder in your garden, be prepared for a struggle in which you must be equally tenacious. With effort they can be overcome, using a mixture of techniques that includes thorough digging and laying a smothering, light-excluding mulch. Turn to page 90 for more on outwitting weeds.

Beat those pests and diseases

In summer time, the biggest concern of first-time gardeners is what to do about pests and diseases. What are the choices? Chemical pesticides kill indiscriminately – garden friends and foes alike – and despite official assurances regarding their safety, the long-term effects on human health of eating food contaminated with pesticide residues remain alarmingly uncertain. Fortunately, we don't have to worry that the experts might be wrong, because there are many non-chemical ways of controlling pests and diseases, which have been developed by organic gardeners over the years.

Health is the birthright of all plants, as we've already said, and if they're grown on fertile land that has had lots of compost added to it to feed the soil's microorganisms, they have the best possible chance of withstanding attack. However, danger still lurks, so it's best to have some solutions to rely on.

Outwitting the pests

One of the tricks of the trade has been to study a pest's lifecycle, to find out when it's most vulnerable. For example, you can foil the wingless female winter moth, as she makes her way painstakingly up apple trees to lay her eggs on the branches, by wrapping a sticky paper band around the trunk. Flying pests, like the pea moth, carrot root fly and all types of aphid can be prevented by completely covering your crops with fine-meshed netting. Barriers and traps, like these, are highly effective in foiling pest attacks, and you can discover more examples on page 87 and within the individual crop descriptions in Part 3.

Crop rotation

Some pests spend the winter in the soil, having dropped from plants at the end of the growing season. If you have planted the same crop there again, when the pests emerge in springtime, they will have a ready food source. Similarly, fungal diseases produce spores that can remain dormant in the ground for years at a stretch until triggered into life by their host crop. That's why gardeners should never grow the same crop in the same place for two consecutive years, preferably not returning to the original patch of ground for at least another four years. This is called 'crop rotation', and you can find out more about it on page 51.

Growing disease-resistant varieties

Growing fruit and vegetable varieties that are 'resistant' to diseases is one of the main ways in which organic gardeners combat these foes. They are most useful in countering weather-dependent diseases, such as potato blight, which can strike even the healthiest plants without warning. Fortunately, thanks to a concentrated research effort in recent years, breeders have developed varieties that are resistant to blight, mildew, rust and many of the other serious diseases that can affect fruit and vegetables. We have made a point of including the names of these in the crop-by-crop guide (see Part 3).

Making gardens wildlife friendly

All pests, in turn, have their own natural enemies – the predators and parasites that prey on them. Or, as the saying goes, 'Great fleas have little fleas upon their backs to bite 'em; and little fleas have lesser fleas and so *ad infinitum*'. We can tilt the balance in favour of these unpaid helpers by making our gardens wildlife-friendly – a job to look forward to, ideally, in the quieter autumn months. Building a pond then, for example, will attract slug-devouring frogs and toads; a stack of logs beneath a hedge makes a fine home for predatory ground beetles; and a small patch of nettles in an out-of-the-way part of the garden will host nettle greenflies – one of the earliest aphid species to arrive in the spring – which provide a welcome snack for hungry ladybird beetles fresh from their winter slumbers. These and other strategies, put into place in the autumn, will have a noticeable effect on pest levels the following year.

The larval stages of some beneficial insects, like hoverflies, lacewings and various tiny parasitic wasps, feed on aphids and other pests, so it's a good idea to encourage them into the garden. The best way of doing this is to grow flowers that have plentiful, and easily accessible, nectar and pollen, close to your fruits and vegetables. Then, if you can induce these beneficial insects to visit, they should lay their eggs on the crops nearby. Flowers with showy, open centres, or those with large umbels, such as dill and fennel, are particularly good attractant plants, but there are many others too, some of which are mentioned on page 109.

Introducing biological pest controls

You can take the principle of encouraging natural enemies one step further by actively introducing your own biological pest controls. Outside, this may take the form of introducing ladybird and lacewing larvae to the leaves of plants to eat aphid pests. Under glass, there are insects you can use to control red spider mites, whiteflies and mealybugs. More and more of these useful little creatures are being made available to gardeners, including a remarkable class of organisms called nematodes, which are invisible to the naked eye but live as parasites on or within some of the most destructive garden pests, such as slugs, vine weevils and codling moth larvae. One of the great attractions of using biocontrols such as these is that they affect only the target organisms, leaving everything else unharmed. Find out more on page 88.

Companion planting

Planting French marigolds in glasshouses, alongside tomatoes, peppers and cucumbers, is an effective method of keeping whiteflies at bay, because they are repelled by the scent given off by the flowers. This is an example of 'companion planting', and it also happens to be one of the few examples that actually work (although only when the marigolds are in flower). Over the years, we and our former colleagues at the Henry Doubleday Research Association have carried out many companion-planting experiments, but, try as we might, the results were inconclusive in almost every case. So, if you come across the subject elsewhere, have a go by all means, but don't be too disappointed if it doesn't work.

Natural pesticides

In coping with any particular pest or disease, it's not unusual to adopt several different strategies simultaneously. In dealing with slugs and snails, for example, you might set beer traps, erect copper barriers (see page 87), encourage beetles and hedgehogs into the garden or drench the soil with millions of parasitic nematodes. Ninety-nine times out of a hundred this does the trick, but on rare occasions (early in the season, when friendly predators are thin on the ground, for example), it won't be enough, and you might resort to the handful of natural pesticides that are authorized for use by organic growers. These are mostly made from minerals, plant extractions and oils, which break down quickly in the environment and pose a minimal threat to wildlife (see page 88). We hope that you will agree with us that pesticides, even approved organic ones, should only be used *in extremis*.

Watering

As well as weeding your plot, one of the main summer preoccupations is watering your plants. Some require more than others. Quick-growing leafy vegetables, such as spinach, lettuce and other salad crops, need the soil to be permanently moist if they are to reach their full potential. Others, such as Florence fennel, flower prematurely and fail to mature properly if conditions are dry. When plants don't get enough water, they can no longer suck up nutrients from the soil efficiently. A lack of the mineral calcium, for example, leads to conditions such as splitting and blossom end rot in tomato fruits.

Root crops, and other plants with deep roots, are less vulnerable to water stress. Interestingly, the roots of crops grown in organically managed soil tend to grow downwards in search of nutrients, and are better able to access underground water reserves than conventionally grown crops, which develop relatively shallow rooting systems in response to the chemical fertilizers applied at ground level.

It's much better to give plants a thorough soaking every few days than to water little and often. Trickle irrigation systems, in which water drips out over several hours through a length of deliberately 'leaky' pipe laid amongst the crop, are one of the best ways of achieving this, and they're far superior to overhead sprinklers, which are extremely wasteful of water. Most are designed to operate off the mains, but they can be adapted for use with water butts without too much trouble.

You can cut down the evaporation of water from the soil by laying well-rotted compost, straw, wilted grass mowings and other organic materials on the ground as a mulch. As a bonus, they also help to suppress weeds. This is especially useful in preventing water loss from soils in which soft fruits are growing. Most fruit trees will be able to tap into water underground, except in the worst of droughts, but many soft fruits are surface rooting, just like vegetables, and need regular watering. See page 92 for more advice.

As summer draws to a close, your garden will be at its most productive, overflowing with wonderful fresh fruit and vegetables. Then, as autumn begins, your main focus turns to preserving and storing for future months. This will be a frenetic time of freezing, bottling and making jams, chutneys and other preserves. Amidst all this abundance, it's easy to forget that you also need to be sowing and planting now, if you're to enjoy fresh winter 'greens' and salads throughout the long winter months ahead. And, as the leaves turn coppery and fall from the trees, make sure that you collect and convert them into soil-enriching leaf mould (see page 105), which will benefit your land for years to come.

CHAPTER 2

Healthy food basics

There is now an official consensus of opinion that eating five portions of fruit and vegetables a day is good for us. Many of us already believed this, but now it is backed up by research studies that have demonstrated definite links between the food we eat and our health, showing that certain plant foods may actively reduce the risk of cancers, heart disease, stroke and other serious illnesses.

Poor diet is thought to be implicated in a third of all cancer cases; and people with a high intake of fruit and vegetables have been shown to have a correspondingly decreased risk of getting cancer and other degenerative diseases. Eating fruit and vegetables may even help to protect us against Alzheimer's disease.

What do they contain that could be responsible for these protective effects? Until relatively recently, the nutritional value of any foodstuff was thought of chiefly in terms of its carbohydrate, protein, fat, mineral, vitamin and dietary fibre content. Fruit and vegetables contain these, although they are typically not rich sources of carbohydrate, protein and fat. However, research carried out mostly over the last decade or so has drawn attention to the important role that lesser-known substances known as phytochemicals (where 'phyto' means 'plants') play in combatting diseases by bolstering the body's protective mechanisms, and we will be looking at these in more detail later.

Carbohydrates

Carbohydrates supply us with energy – think of them as fuel. They are found in two forms in our food – as 'sugars' or 'starch' – which are both broken down in the body into glucose. Over-refined, or sugar-rich, foods, such as white bread and sugar-laden soft drinks, release their glucose quickly, creating rapid insulin surges in the body, which can lead to diabetes. By contrast, wholefoods, and the starch found in vegetables such as potatoes and sweet corn, are broken down much more gradually, as is the fructose (a form of sugar found in fruits).

Foods can be ranked according to the speed with which they are broken down to glucose. This is expressed as the Glycaemic Index (GI) – see Part 3 for a complete listing. Most fruits and vegetables have a low GI, so we can eat as much of them as we like without rapidly increasing our blood-sugar level, but some, like parsnips and broad beans, have a high GI and so need to be eaten in moderation.

Proteins

Proteins are the building blocks of the body, needed for body structures and organs, including the muscles. Proteins are made of amino acids, some of which are essential, because we can't make them in our own bodies. The only vegetables that contain a significant amount of protein are peas and beans. Eaten fresh, peas and broad beans outperform other beans, but dried beans, such as haricots and butter beans, are also an excellent protein source.

Fats

We need fats as another source of energy, and they are essential in carrying out many of the body's metabolic processes, but these days we eat far too much. Fat provides around 40 per cent of our total daily calorific intake, whereas a desirable level is half this amount. Most fruits and vegetables are low in fats, and those they do contain are unsaturated, rather than the less-healthy saturated fats that we are continuously being advised to cut down on.

All fats are made up of fatty acids, and some vegetables (as well as whole grains, rapeseed and linseed oil) contain 'essential' omega 3 fatty acids, which are important for brain development. Pumpkin seeds are a very good source of fatty acids, which are also found in sweet potatoes and a number of green vegetables. Oily fish contain the most omega 3, and there is some suggestion that the fish version may be more nutritionally beneficial than the omega 3 found in plant sources.

Fibre

Although fibre is not really a nutrient, as such, it plays an important role in aiding digestion: pushing food along our alimentary system and helping to control blood-sugar levels. The more efficiently this happens, and the quicker the passage of food through our system, the better, since the risk of cancer of the colon is lessened. High-fibre fruit and vegetables include broad beans, many brassicas, parsnips, dried figs and prunes.

Minerals

Minerals are necessary for bone formation and for the day-to-day functioning of our bodies. Some are needed in relatively large quantities, whereas others, although essential, are required in only tiny amounts, hence their name – 'trace elements'. Most vegetables contain a broad spread of minerals (there are fewer in fruits), but these are often present in relatively small amounts. Modern methods of food production and its distribution have been responsible for an alarming drop in the levels of minerals and trace elements. To take just one example: fruit and vegetables have lost more than half their copper, iron and zinc content during the past fifty years, and selenium levels have also diminished considerably in our diets. It's hardly surprising, then, that, according to the UK National Diet and Nutrition Survey 2008/09, children aged 11–18 are not getting enough magnesium, potassium, iron and selenium. Growing your own fruits and vegetables organically at home is one way that you and your family can overcome this significant mineral deficit.

Some of the more important minerals are as follows:

- Calcium helps to build bones and teeth and regulates muscle action. It may also help to lower blood pressure and protect against colon and breast cancer. The best fruit and vegetable sources are spinach, kales and rhubarb; however, oxalic acid, which is also present in these three, limits calcium uptake.

- Copper is required for the production of hormones and blood cells. The best fruit and vegetable sources are blackcurrants, grapes, broad beans and Jerusalem artichokes.

- Iron is the key element of the blood pigment, haemoglobin. Women require more than men, because of blood loss during menstruation. Deficiency results in anaemia. The best vegetable sources are leafy greens, such as spinach, kales, broccoli, legumes and garlic.

- Magnesium helps to turn our food into energy, is a vital constituent of bones, and plays a critical role in many of the body's metabolic processes. The best vegetable sources are leaf beet, broad beans, kales, spinach and sweet corn. Blackberries and raspberries contain more magnesium than other temperate fruits.

- Manganese is essential in bone formation and plays a role in making and activating enzymes. The best fruit and vegetable sources are blackberries, beetroot, kales and spinach.

- Phosphorus is an essential nutrient in bone and teeth formation, and in metabolizing food. The best vegetable sources are broad beans, peas and garlic.

- Potassium controls fluid balance and plays an important role in transmitting nerve impulses. The best vegetable sources are beetroot, Brussels sprouts, garlic, kales, parsnips and spinach.

- Selenium plays an important role in many metabolic processes, and is a key part of the body's antioxidant defence system. There have been claims that selenium can reduce the incidence of various cancers; however, most fruit and vegetables contain only traces.

- Zinc is involved in many metabolic processes, including building new cells, processing food and maintaining the reproductive system. The best vegetable sources are asparagus, broad beans, peas and spinach.

Vitamins

Vitamins are required by the body for a wide range of metabolic processes, including: breaking down and utilizing food; building and repairing bone, tissue and skin; forming and renewing blood cells; and the effective working of the body's defence mechanisms.

Vitamins are essential nutrients, and if we don't have enough, we experience deficiency diseases, like the sailors of old who contracted scurvy from a shortage of vitamin C. There are officially recommended daily allowance figures (RDAs) for vitamins (see page 115), which are designed to prevent deficiency diseases, but there is a growing consensus that, in some cases, greater amounts are even more beneficial – promoting good health and preventing and fighting diseases. We know that vitamins A, C and E, for example, have antioxidant properties (see below), which help in the prevention of degenerative conditions. The vitamin B complex and vitamin C are water-soluble, and need to be replenished daily; but vitamins A, D, E and K are fat-soluble, and can be stored in the body.

- Vitamin A is an antioxidant. It's important for healthy eyes (particularly night vision), tissues, bones and organs. It also builds resistance to respiratory infections. We make, and store, vitamin A in the body and get a healthy proportion from the carotenes found in fruits and vegetables. The best sources are plums, carrots, pumpkins, cabbages, Hamburg parsley, kales, spinach and sweet potatoes.

- Vitamin B complex. The B vitamins work better together, and we need more of them during periods of illness and stress.
  - Vitamin B1, or thiamine, assists digestion and plays an important role in the nervous and circulatory systems. The best vegetable sources are peas and leeks.
  - Vitamin B2, or riboflavin, aids growth and reproduction, benefits vision, and is important in the metabolism of food and the elimination of toxins. The best fruit and vegetable sources are blackcurrants, brassicas, new potatoes and French beans.
  - Vitamin B3, or niacin, is involved in metabolizing food, growth, and making new red blood cells. The best fruit and vegetable sources are peaches, strawberries, broad beans, peas, swede and sweet corn.
  - Vitamin B5, or pantothenic acid, releases energy from carbohydrates,

produces anti-stress hormones, and maintains the nervous and reproductive systems. Broad beans contain by far the most B5, but Brussels sprouts, mangetout peas and sweet corn are all other good vegetable sources.

- Vitamin B6, or pyridoxine, is involved in food metabolism, blood and haemoglobin formation, and helping to prevent various nervous and skin disorders. The best vegetable sources are Brussels sprouts, garlic, leeks, potatoes and spinach.
- Folate, or folic acid or vitamin B9, works in conjunction with vitamin B12 to form red blood cells, and is vital in children's growth. Deficiency during pregnancy can result in spina bifida in infants. Folate is widely found in vegetables, but the best sources are asparagus, beetroot, Brussels sprouts, Hamburg parsley, kales and spinach.
- Vitamin B12, or cobalamin, is needed for the generation of red blood cells, maintaining a healthy nervous system, metabolizing food, and improving concentration, memory and balance. Fruit and vegetables do not contain any B12, but it is found in liver, eggs and dairy products.

- Vitamin C, or ascorbic acid, is an antioxidant and plays a vital role in the body's immune system. It's integral to the growth and repair of tissues, teeth, bone and skin. It decreases blood cholesterol, prevents viral and bacterial infections, acts as a natural laxative, reduces the risk of blood clots in veins, and prevents scurvy. According to the eminent scientist Linus Pauling, large daily doses (in excess of 3g) help to significantly decrease infections and fight cancer (though this is regarded with scepticism in many quarters). Vitamin C occurs widely in fruit and vegetables, but the best sources are blackcurrants, lemons, strawberries, Brussels sprouts, broccoli, kales and peppers. Rose hips are the best wild source.

- Vitamin D is a fat-soluble vitamin, essential for bone growth and metabolizing food. There is none in fruit and vegetables, but we can manufacture it ourselves when sunlight strikes our skin.

- Vitamin E, or tocopherol, is also fat-soluble, and has antioxidant properties, to assist the body's defence mechanisms. It prevents and dissolves blood clots, helps to supply the body with oxygen, and can lower blood pressure. The best fruit and vegetable sources are blackberries, blackcurrants, aubergines, leafy greens, parsnips, pumpkins and tomatoes.

■ Vitamin K is another fat-soluble vitamin, which is essential for blood clotting, bone formation and maintenance. We can synthesize it in the gut, through the action of friendly bacteria living there. It's widely found in fruit and vegetables, the best sources being leaf beet, Brussels sprouts, cabbages, Hamburg parsley, kales and spinach.

■ Biotin is also called vitamin H. It's essential to normal growth and development, and is involved in many of the body's complex metabolic processes. Raspberries and blackcurrants are the best fruit sources. There are small amounts in most vegetables, but the best sources are broad beans, mangetout peas, cauliflower, leeks, onions and sweet corn.

Antioxidants

Antioxidants counteract the harmful 'oxidative stress' in the body that can trigger cancer and other degenerative diseases. This oxidative stress is caused by excessive amounts of what are known as 'free radicals' – unstable molecules (very often oxygen), which, in an attempt to become stable, 'steal' an extra electron from another molecule, which then does the same thing, and so on, in a chain-reaction involving hundreds of thousands of reactions at a cellular level. This process continues unabated unless checked by antioxidants, which donate electrons without becoming unstable themselves. Once an antioxidant has neutralized a free radical, however, it is rendered inactive, which is why we need a continual supply.

Free radicals are continually being produced during the course of the many oxygen-related reactions that go on in our bodies, and we are exposed to millions of free-radical 'hits' every day. Although we produce enzymes that help to control free radicals, we also rely on the protective activity of dietary antioxidants in our food. As we get older, however, our enzyme activity can reduce, so we need to obtain more antioxidants from our food.

In addition to free radicals being produced routinely in our bodies, we may make things worse by taking in potential carcinogens through smoking cigarettes, eating food contaminated with pesticide residues, eating starchy foods cooked at high temperatures (such as potato crisps), which produces acrylamides, or breathing in bonfire smoke. Even excess polyunsaturated fat in our bodies will increase the number of free radicals.

Phytochemicals

As we have already mentioned, vitamins A, C and E act as antioxidants, but many phytochemicals exhibit strong antioxidant capacities, too, as well as other protective effects. Scientific discoveries linking particular phytochemicals with degenerative disease-protecting benefits are being made all the time.

Phytochemicals play vitally important roles in the lives of plants. They assist them to attract insects and birds to help pollination and seed dispersal; offer protection, if needed, from the powerful rays of the sun; defend themselves against attack by bacteria, viruses and fungi; or deter harmful predators. They also give plants their characteristic colours, flavours and odours. There are thousands of different phytochemicals, with new ones being discovered all the time.

As already stated, their antioxidant properties help to protect us against disease: they can generally stimulate our immune systems, be anti-cancer, anti-inflammatory, anti-thrombotic, anti-bacterial and can lower cholesterol. They can help to prevent cancer at all stages of its development, from tumour initiation onwards, and regulate inflammatory conditions such as arthritis and heart disease. They can also relax blood vessels, influence hormones and balance gut bacteria.

A four-year EU study in 2008, involving a team of international researchers, reported that organically grown carrots, apples and peaches contained up to 40 per cent more antioxidants than those grown on conventional farms. Its co-ordinator, Professor Carlo Leifort of Newcastle University, said that the health benefits were so striking that switching to organic produce was equivalent, in health terms, to eating an extra portion of fruit and vegetables a day. In addition, a ten-year study by researchers at the University of California, Davis, which ended in 2006, found double the amount of flavonoids (see page 30) in organic tomatoes compared with those that had been grown conventionally.

It is convenient to group phytochemicals, according to their chemical composition, into:

- terpenes
  - carotenoids
  - saponins
  - limonene
  - phytosterols
  - oleanolic acids
  - ursolic acids

- phenolic compounds, of which flavonoids are the most numerous, with more than 5,000 discovered to date

- organo-sulphur compounds and their derivatives

- protease inhibitors

- betalains

- fructo-oligosaccharides

Terpenes

Carotenoids are pigments that give plants their red, orange and yellow colours. Green plants can have them too, but their hues are masked by the green pigment, chlorophyll. Fifty or so carotenoids appear to be beneficial to us, and they are found in broccoli,* carrots, spinach, sweet corn, and many other brightly coloured fruits and vegetables.

Many studies have identified a connection between people with diets that are rich in carotenoids, and a lower mortality rate from a range of chronic illnesses. Carotenoids act as antioxidants, efficiently reducing free-radical damage and enhancing the immune system, with different carotenoids being associated with a reduced risk of cardio-vascular disease, cancer, Alzheimer's disease and dementia, type-2 diabetes, rheumatoid arthritis, cataracts, and age-related macular degeneration (AMD) – the commonest form of blindness in old age.

Carotenoids seem to work most efficiently with each other, and when other antioxidants, such as vitamins C and E, are present. One research study has suggested a more than 50 per cent reduced risk of strokes if carotenoids are consumed twice a month; whilst another study of elderly people found that those who consumed carrots or squash every day had a 60 per cent less chance of heart attacks, compared with people who ate less. High carotene intake has also been linked with a 20 per cent reduction in post-menopausal breast cancer, and a 50 per cent reduction in cancers of the larynx, oesophagus, bladder, cervix, prostate and colon.

The six best-understood carotenoids, which are known to be important for human health, are three carotenes (alpha-carotene, beta-carotene and

---

* This is not an all-inclusive list. See Part 3 for more details.

lycopene) and three xanthophylls (zeaxanthin, lutein and cryptoxanthin). The carotenes and cryptoxanthin are converted into vitamin A in the body, but beta-carotene is most efficient at this – it has twice as much vitamin A activity as the others.

Alpha-carotene has antioxidant properties. It prevents low-density lipoprotein (LDL or 'bad') cholesterol from oxidation, which can lead to restricted blood flow to the heart. One study found that people with the highest alpha-carotene level in their blood had a lower risk of angina, compared with those who had the lowest levels. It would also appear to help to prevent cancer – in a study on cervical dysplasia, which can lead to cancer of the cervix, women with higher levels of alpha-carotene were thought to be less likely to develop the disease. Other research shows a possible link between Alzheimer's disease and low alpha-carotene intake. Alpha-carotene is found in butternut squash, carrots, pumpkins, sweet corn and red peppers.

Beta-carotene has strong antioxidant properties, and is one of the most potent free-radical scavengers. It is protective against several diseases, including cataracts and AMD, and it helps night vision. Carrots contain far more beta-carotene than any other type of vegetable, which perhaps explains the old saying that carrots help you to see in the dark. Consumption of significant levels of beta-carotene is also linked with reducing the risk of rheumatoid arthritis and certain cancers, such as lung cancer. Conversely, it would seem that consuming low amounts of beta-carotene might actually increase the risk of cancer and heart disease. Beta-carotene is found in carrots, kales, spinach and sweet potatoes.

Lycopene is mostly found in tomatoes and is also a potent antioxidant. It is linked with reducing the risk of cancer: one large American study found that men who consumed tomato products ten or more times a week had a 35 per cent lower risk of developing prostate cancer. Even eating two portions lowered the risk to some degree. Lycopene also seems to help to protect against stomach, colon and rectal cancer. Another piece of research showed that men with high lycopene levels in their bodies had half the risk of heart attacks, compared with those with low levels – perhaps because lycopene has known anti-inflammatory properties. Yet another study found that those who had been diagnosed with diabetes had a lower level of lycopene and other carotenoids in their blood than those without the disease. Lycopene is also present in carrots and sweet potatoes, and is one of the few phytochemicals that benefit from being processed, being released more effectively when heated.

Zeaxanthin is one of three types of xanthophylls: phytochemicals that are usually yellow pigments. It has antioxidant properties, and it appears to work closely with lutein to protect the eyes from age-related macular disorder (AMD). One study found that people who consumed spinach, or other xanthophyll-containing leafy greens, five or more times a week, had a 43 per cent lower risk of contracting the disease, compared with those who consumed the least. The report suggests that even if you already have AMD, eating spinach may improve your vision, if it is consumed regularly. Sweet corn is the best source of zeaxanthin, but it is also found in broccoli, French beans, spinach and peas.

Lutein also helps to protect the eyes from cataracts, caused by free-radical damage to the lens. Two very large studies showed that people with the highest consumption of lutein-rich foods had a 20 per cent reduction in the risk of cataract extraction, compared with people with the lowest consumption. Evidence is also emerging that regular consumption of leafy green vegetables, which are rich in lutein, can lead to a reduced risk of cancer in, for example, the mouth, stomach, breasts, lungs and colon. Kales have the highest antioxidant properties of all the leafy greens. Yet another traditional saying, the plea of mothers to their children everywhere – 'eat your greens, they're good for you' – is proving to be correct. Lutein is also present in rhubarb, turnip greens, sweet corn and leaf beet.

Cryptoxanthin has been linked to protection from heart disease, such as a reduced risk of angina. It occurs in peaches and pumpkins, and a significant amount is found in red peppers.

Other terpenes

These include saponins, found in asparagus and garlic, which help to prevent the multiplication of cancer cells and which help to reduce the level of LDL cholesterol in the blood. They also include limonene, found in cherries, celery and many herbs, which helps to increase the production of enzymes that may counter potential carcinogens; and phytosterols, found in aubergines, parsnips and tomatoes, which may help to prevent cancer of the colon.

Phenolic compounds

Flavonoids

Flavonoids are types of phenolic compounds: phytochemicals that appear to possess potent antioxidant, anti-cancer, anti-inflammatory, anti-bacterial, anti-thrombotic and blood vessel-relaxing effects in our bodies. Phenolic compounds are being actively researched, but it seems that they might offer us protection from cancer, stroke, heart disease, circulation problems and the degenerative effects of aging, such as neurological disorders like Alzheimer's disease. Flavonoids have strong antioxidant properties, being much more potent than vitamins C or E, and make vitamin C work more effectively in the body. They are responsible for the red colour of cherries, for example.

Quercetin, found in apples and other fruits, is one of the best-known and most powerful flavonoids, with anti-cancer and anti-inflammatory activities. Eating quercetin-rich foods may reduce the risk of lung cancer by 50 per cent, and it can inhibit the growth of cancer cells, such as those in the colon. Quercetin also helps to lower cholesterol, and in a Finnish study involving almost 3,000 middle-aged men, regular apple eaters had a significantly lower risk of stroke. Apples and onions are excellent sources of quercetin, but it is also present in blackberries, grapes and broad beans.

Kaempferol (found in gooseberries and peas); myricetin (found in strawberries and grapes) and rutin (found in rhubarb and parsley) are other flavonoids that are similar to quercetin.

Anthocyanins and **proanthocyanidins** are another large and powerful group of flavonoid antioxidants, which are responsible for the intense dark colour of certain fruits and vegetables. In one laboratory study, the anthocyanins in blackcurrants were linked to the inhibition of inflammatory mechanisms, suspected to be involved with cancer, heart disease, microbial infections and neurological disorders like Alzheimer's disease. Proanthocyanidins, for example, which are found in many fruits, are twenty times more potent than vitamin C.

Other phenolic compounds

It is only possible to mention briefly some of the many other phenolic compounds that play a part in keeping us healthy. In addition to those listed below, others include apiole, carnosol, carvacrol and rosemarinol.

Condensed tannins, or proanthocyanidins, give red grapes their dark colour and have antioxidant, anti-cancer and other degenerative disease-preventing effects. Resveratrol, for example, protects against heart disease, and shows evidence of anti-carcinogenic activity.

Phenolic acids include gallic, ellagic and salicylic acid, and are mostly found in soft fruit and some herbs. Ellagic acid appears to have strong anti-carcinogenic properties. It is an antioxidant, and is thought to prevent cancer of the prostate, tongue, oesophagus and lungs. Strawberries are an important source of ellagic acid. It is also found in grapes, raspberries and blackberries. Salicylic acid, found in strawberries, blackberries and raspberries, may reduce the risk of heart disease, and can inhibit the development of colon cancer cells. (Aspirin is produced from salicylic acid, which is extracted from the willow tree.)

Genistein, found in legumes, and cumestrol, found in peas, both act as phyto-oestrogens, and may reduce the risk of breast or ovarian cancer.

Capsaicin, a phenolic acid found in chilli peppers, has inflammation-reducing properties.

Lignans such as silymarin, for example, which is found in globe artichokes, may also help to protect the body from heart disease.

Coumarins are thought to prevent nitrosamines (which may cause gastric cancer) from forming in the gut. They also help to prevent blood clotting, and derivatives of di-coumarin are used as anti-coagulant drugs. They are found in strawberries, sweet corn and parsley.

Caffeic acid is thought to increase the production of enzymes that make carcinogens more soluble in water, which may help to rid the body of them. It is found in fruits such as pears, strawberries and cucumbers,

Ferulic acid binds to nitrates in the stomach, and may help to prevent them from being turned into carcinogenic nitrosamines. It is found in fruits such as strawberries, apples and plums.

Chlorogenic acid, and hydroxycinnamic acid, which is found in potatoes, are closely related to ferulic acid.

Other phenolic compounds include apiole, carnosol, carvacrol and rosemarinol.

TOP 20 ANTIOXIDANT- AND PHYTOCHEMICAL-RICH FRUITS AND VEGETABLES

Apples	Carrots	Pumpkins and squashes
Asparagus	Chilli peppers	Spinach
Aubergines	Garlic	Raspberries
Blackberries	Grapes	Strawberries
Blueberries	Kales	Sweet potatoes
Broccoli	Onions	Tomatoes
Brussels sprouts	Plums	

Organo-sulphur compounds

Organo-sulphur compounds and their derivatives are present in the cabbage and onion families. Many studies have shown that the regular consumption of brassicas is linked with a reduced risk of cancer – in particular of the bowel, breasts, lungs, stomach and kidneys. Sulforaphane, for example, which is present in broccoli and Brussels sprouts, has been found to curtail the growth of prostate and breast cancer cells.

Sinigrin is also found in Brussels sprouts and broccoli, and it helps to fight cancer by triggering the death of pre-cancerous cells. It is believed that even the occasional serving of Brussels sprouts could destroy pre-cancerous cells in the colon. Sinigrin is a type of glucosinolate – the compounds that are the cause of the bitter taste and odour of many of the brassicas. Other organo-sulphur compounds and their derivatives in the cabbage family include glucobrassin, indole-3-carbinol and allyl isothiocyanate.

The onion family contains compounds called allyl sulphides. Garlic is a key source of these, although they are also found in onions, leeks, chives and shallots. Allyl sulphides may also help to fight cancers such as stomach cancer. If you crush or chew garlic, the allyl sulphides are turned into allicin, which is thought to help to keep the immune and cardiovascular systems healthy, and may lower blood pressure and cholesterol. It also has anti-microbial properties.

Protease inhibitors

This further group of phytochemicals are found in dried beans, for example, and are thought to suppress the production of enzymes in cancer cells, which may slow the growth of tumours.

Fructo-oligosaccharides

Finally, fructo-oligosaccharides (FOS) – a special type of dietary fibre – are not digested like other food, and help to promote the growth of 'friendly bacteria' in the gut. These beneficial bacteria may also help to regulate cholesterol levels and fight cancer. Jerusalem artichokes contain the greatest amount of FOS, but they are also found in asparagus, leeks and chicory roots.

Getting the most from your produce

The nutritional value of fresh fruits and vegetables begins to fall the moment they are picked. The vitamin B complex, vitamin C, certain minerals and some phytochemicals (such as phenolic compounds) are water-soluble, and leach out of fruit and vegetables if left to soak in water, and during cooking. Green vegetables, when boiled and drained, lose practically all their soluble minerals. Boiling is responsible for three times the vitamin loss of steamed vegetables. Vitamin C is destroyed by water, cooking, heat, light and storage.

Here are some guidelines to help you make the most of your fresh fruit and vegetables:

- Eat a wide variety of fruit and vegetables (see the Top 20 list on page 32) to maximize your vitamin, mineral and phytochemical intake.

■ Eat them as soon as possible after harvesting, and eat raw food regularly.

■ Store them in plastic bags or closed food containers in the fridge, as some vegetables can lose half their vitamins in 24 hours if not refrigerated.

■ Prepare them just before you begin cooking.

■ Avoid storing them in cold water for prolonged periods.

■ Wash carefully or scrub, rather than peel, them, since the majority of nutrients are contained in or directly below the skin.

■ Do not thaw frozen fruits and vegetables before cooking.

■ Boil them for as short a time as possible.

■ Steam, or boil them in as little water as possible (most vegetables have a water content of around 90 per cent, so make use of it).

■ Save and re-use cooking water – in stocks, gravy, stews, soups and casseroles.

■ Stir-fry vegetables using a couple of tablespoons of oil with a high 'smoke point' (e.g. safflower, sunflower, soya and rapeseed oil), leaving your better-quality unrefined, or virgin, oils for salad dressings.

■ Freezing minimizes vitamin and mineral loss.

■ To maximize carotenoid absorption in the body, combine foods that have high levels of carotenes and vitamin E, and cook them with vegetable oils.

■ Crush, or bruise garlic, and allow it to stand for 5–10 minutes to maximize its allicin content. Cooking garlic results in a reduction in some of its beneficial properties so it's best consumed raw.

■ Chew cabbages and other greens thoroughly, to maximize sulforaphane and sinigrin intake.

■ Eat cooked tomatoes (e.g. ketchup and tomato sauces) to increase lycopene intake, because the heating process makes the lycopene more easily assimilated. This applies to tinned tomatoes, too.

PART 2

The gardening year

CHAPTER 3

Winter

This is the quietest time of the year in the garden, as growth slows almost to a standstill. On fine days, winter digging is just the thing – incorporating compost and well-rotted manure into the soil, if it is sufficiently dry. This shouldn't be attempted if the soil is wet or waterlogged, because it will compact it and damage the structure.

The winter months are when bare-rooted trees, vines and soft fruit bushes and canes are planted and pruned. Apples and pears should also be pruned now. It's too early, though, to sow vegetable seeds outdoors, because they won't germinate unless the soil temperature is at least 5°C/41°F, which rarely happens before March. From February onwards, they can be started off under cover – in a glasshouse or polytunnel or, failing that, on a sunny windowsill indoors.

When bad weather makes outdoor work impossible, it's a good time to clean and repair tools, wash pots and seed and module trays, and generally prepare for the coming season. Last year's seeds can be sorted, and badly out-of-date packets thrown away. Now is the time to start a gardening notebook, jotting down notes when you look through seed catalogues as you decide what to grow. Trying something new is often worth the risk! Even if a particular variety didn't do well last year, it's probably worth giving it another go, because a different growing season can make a considerable difference.

Even though outdoor conditions are frequently harsh, there should be plenty to harvest from the garden – winter greens will crop until May, and parsnips and artichokes can be dug up when the soil isn't frozen. Other root crops, too, like carrots and celeriac, can stay in the ground over the winter to be dug up as required, but they need to be safely protected under a covering of straw. Finally, if you have a polytunnel, you shouldn't want for winter salad greens.

DECEMBER Jobs for early winter

Make the most of every opportunity to get out into the garden – digging, planting fruit trees, canes and bushes, and generally tidying up before winter sets in. Clean and oil tools ready for next season.

SOWING AND PLANTING

Vegetables and herbs
- Sow broad beans in pots, cardboard tubes or root trainers.

Fruit
- Plant bare-rooted fruit trees, soft fruit, vines and rhubarb whenever the soil is not frozen or waterlogged.

CULTIVATION

Vegetables and herbs
- Dig the plot on fine days.
- Rake up leaves and add to the leafmould pile (p.105).
- Lift Brussels Witloof chicory roots for forcing (p.142).
- Dig runner bean trenches and fill with kitchen waste (p.123).

Fruit
- Prune all newly planted trees, bushes, canes and vines.
- Winter-prune established apple and pear trees.
- Prune glasshouse vines (p.218).
- Check stakes and inspect tree ties to make sure they are not cutting into the trunk.

PESTS AND DISEASES

Vegetables and herbs

- Set traps for mice, which can unearth broad bean and pea seeds, as necessary.
- Cover brassicas with netting to protect them from pigeons (p.132).
- Check brassicas for cabbage aphids and whiteflies. Remove by hand, or spray with an organic insecticide (p.88).
- Remove and compost any yellowing or dead brassica leaves and stripped stems.

Fruit

- Prune all badly mildewed shoots and cankerous branches (p.203).
- Erect a polythene canopy over peaches and nectarines, to protect them from spores of peach leaf curl disease (p.221).
- Hang up fat to attract aphid-eating insectivorous birds.
- Remove and burn corrugated cardboard that was put on apple trees in July to trap codling moth caterpillars looking for somewhere to pupate (p.202).
- Net wall-trained cherries, gooseberries and other fruits to prevent the buds from being destroyed by bullfinches.
- Fit spiral tree guards to deter rabbits from stripping the bark.
- Spray top and soft fruit and vines with an organic 'winter wash' to kill overwintering aphids and their eggs, scale insects, glasshouse mealybugs and red spider mites.

OTHER JOBS

- Take advantage of the seasonal lull to plan your crop rotation (p.51).
- Look through seed catalogues and place your order.
- Clean out bird boxes in time for next year's occupants.
- Repair damaged rabbit fencing.
- Build a new compost bin (p.49).
- Clean, sharpen and repair tools.
- Repair and paint damaged woodwork in glasshouses, cold frames and other structures.

HARVESTING, PRESERVING AND STORING

- Cover root crops with a protective layer of straw or bracken, if you decide to leave them in the ground (p.249).

VEGETABLES YOU CAN HARVEST NOW

Broccoli	Corn salad	Land cress
Brussels sprouts	Endive	Oriental greens
Cabbages	Hamburg parsley	Parsnips
Cauliflowers	Jerusalem artichokes	Radishes
Celeriac	Kales	Rocket
Celery	Kohl rabi	Spinach
Chicories	Leeks	Swedes
Chinese artichokes	Lettuces	Turnips
Claytonia		

JANUARY Jobs for mid-winter

It's probably too cold to do much in the garden, so relax and plan what you're going to grow. Check packets of seed to make sure they're still in date, and order fresh seed if needed. Pore over seed catalogues and give new varieties a try.

SOWING AND PLANTING

Vegetables

- Sow broad beans in pots under cover, if you missed out in the autumn (p.119).
- Sow summer cauliflowers in a propagator towards the end of the month (p.137).
- Sow tomatoes if you have a heated glasshouse and want an early crop, otherwise delay until March or April (p.190).
- Sow hot chilli peppers in pots, in an airing cupboard or propagator, as they can take a month or longer to germinate (p.170).

Fruit

- Plant bare-rooted fruit trees, soft fruit and vines whenever the soil is not frozen or waterlogged.

VEGETABLES YOU CAN SOW NOW

Broad beans	Peppers
Cauliflowers	Tomatoes

CULTIVATION

Vegetables

- Take advantage of fine days to continue winter digging.
- Work compost and manure into the soil, as appropriate (p.47).
- Add dolomite or ground limestone, if pH tests indicate it is required (p.47).
- Dig runner bean trenches and fill with kitchen waste, if you have not already done so (p.123).
- Dig trenches for celery (p.139).
- 'Chit' seed potatoes in egg boxes to encourage short, stubby sprouts (p.172).
- Lift chicory, and replant in covered pots to produce delicious 'chicons' (p.142).
- Re-plant swedes and cover, as for chicory, to give a supply of blanched salad leaves (p.184).

Fruit

- Prune all newly planted trees, bushes, canes and vines.
- Continue to prune established apple and pear trees.
- Check that stakes are still firm, and inspect tree ties to make sure they are not biting into the trunk.
- Shorten the leaders and laterals on red and white currants and gooseberries; but the few buds that remain will risk bullfinch attack if not netted, so you might prefer to wait until March (p.215), when there will be more buds, so even if the bullfinches attack, some buds will be left to break into growth.
- Cover strawberries with cloches to get an early crop (p.235).

- Place terracotta or other forcers, stuffed with straw, over individual rhubarb clumps to produce forced stems in February/March (p.232).
- Divide rhubarb crowns, if you want to increase the number of plants (p.232).

PESTS AND DISEASES

Vegetables

- Net winter greens, or they are likely to be eaten by pigeons (p.132).
- Check for whitefly and aphids on brassicas, and remove wherever possible (p.133).
- Compost dead Brussels sprout and other brassica leaves, along with stripped stems.

Fruit

- Check that grease bands around fruit trees are still in place and do not have plant debris stuck to them, which can act as a bridge (p.203).
- Pick off and destroy any mummified fruits that remain on the branches (p.91).
- Net wall-trained cherries, gooseberries and other fruits, to prevent the buds from being destroyed by bullfinches.
- Hang up fat elsewhere in the garden, to attract aphid-eating insectivorous birds.
- Fit spiral tree guards, to prevent hungry rabbits from stripping the bark.
- Spray top and soft fruit and vines with an organic 'winter wash' to kill overwintering aphids and their eggs, scale insects, glasshouse mealybugs and red spider mites.

OTHER JOBS

- Take advantage of the quietest month in the garden to prepare for the coming season. Throw away any out-of-date seeds, and send off your seed and potato order, or buy them locally.
- Begin a garden diary/notebook.
- Clean, repair and sharpen tools, and lightly coat with lubricating oil to prevent rust.
- Wash pots, modules and seed trays in a disinfectant such as Citrox.
- Repair or replace torn nets and fleece.

HARVESTING, PRESERVING AND STORING

- Harvest some cabbages, cauliflowers and Brussels sprout stems, if the weather is harsh, and dig up some artichokes, parsnips, celeriac and leeks, and store in a frost-free shed. They can otherwise be left in the ground and dug as needed. (In the bitterly cold winter of 1947, farmers had to use road drills to extract parsnips from frozen ground!)
- Pull pink or red celery (the only sorts that make it through to the New Year).
- Pick winter lettuces, if grown in a cold glasshouse or polytunnel, and the oriental greens that withstand harsh conditions (Chinese mustard, komatsuna, mizuna and mibuna, for example). Also pick (American) land cress, which tastes remarkably like watercress – piquant and peppery, like the oriental salads.
- Check stored vegetables and fruits on a regular basis and remove any that have rotted. Rub any shoots off stored potatoes.
- Rub off the forest of tiny white hairs that often sprout on carrots stored in sand (although these do not cause any harm).

VEGETABLES YOU CAN HARVEST NOW

Broccoli	Chicories	Land cress
Brussels sprouts (late)	Chinese artichokes	Leeks (mid-season)
Cabbages (winter)	Corn salad	Lettuces (winter)
Cauliflowers (winter)	Hamburg parsley	Oriental greens
Celeriac	Jerusalem artichokes	Parsnips
Celery	Kales	Spinach

FEBRUARY Jobs for late winter

You can begin sowing now, but only with protection. Start seeds off on a warm windowsill indoors, or better still, use a propagator. If sowing outdoors, use cloches. Finish off any ground preparation and spread manure and compost.

SOWING AND PLANTING

Vegetables and herbs

- Sow seeds of aubergines, beetroot, cauliflowers, chives, globe artichokes, kohl rabi, leeks and parsley in a propagator if you have one, at around 20–22°C/68–72°F; or start them off on a windowsill or in an airing cupboard.
- Also sow tomato, pepper and cucumber seeds, under the same conditions, but only if you intend growing them in a heated glasshouse.
- Sow asparagus seeds if you wish, but it's easier to plant crowns in April instead (p.117).
- Sow broad beans, carrots, lettuces, peas, radishes and spinach outside under cloches, but bear in mind that most of these can just as well be sown indoors and transplanted later.
- Plant garlic and Jerusalem and Chinese artichokes in dry weather, when it's possible to get onto the soil.
- Plant shallots from mid-February onwards, unless you live in a cold district, in which case wait until next month (p.180).

Fruit

- Plant bare-rooted fruit trees, soft fruit and vines whenever soil conditions permit.

VEGETABLES YOU CAN SOW NOW

Asparagus	Cauliflowers (summer)	Onions
Aubergines	Cucumbers	Peas
Broad beans	Globe artichokes	Peppers
Beetroot	Kohl rabi	Radishes
Brussels sprouts (early)	Leeks (early)	Spinach
Cabbages (summer)	Lettuces	Tomatoes
Carrots		

CULTIVATION

Vegetables and herbs

- Continue winter digging and preparing the ground for planting.
- Spread compost and manure, as required.
- Take advantage of fine weather to weed thoroughly, especially amongst growing crops.
- 'Chit' seed potatoes in egg boxes or trays (p.172).
- Dig in autumn-sown green manures (p.106).
- Apply organic fertilizers to winter brassicas and other overwintered crops (p.48).
- Force chicory, to produce 'chicons' (p.142).
- Thin overwintered Japanese onions (p.162).
- Divide, and re-plant, chives (p.111).
- Force seakale (p.197).

Fruit

- Prune newly planted trees, bushes, canes and vines.
- Continue to prune established apple and pear trees.
- Prune figs (p.213).
- Cut down autumn-fruiting raspberry canes and 'tip' vigorous summer-fruiting raspberry canes (p.228).
- Cover strawberries with cloches for an early crop (p.235).
- Force rhubarb (p.232).
- Cover apricots, nectarines and peach trees with fleece, to protect blossom from frost, and hand-pollinate them if there are few insects about (p.221).
- Hand-weed soft fruit.

PESTS AND DISEASES

Vegetables

- Protect winter greens from pigeons with netting (p.132).
- Check for whitefly and aphids on brassicas (p.133).
- Compost dead Brussels sprout, and other brassica, leaves, along with stripped stems.

Fruit

- Spray top and soft fruit, and vines with an organic 'winter wash' to kill overwintering aphids and their eggs, scale insects, glasshouse mealybugs and red spider mites.
- Lightly fork over the soil, this will expose hibernating pests for hungry birds to eat.
- Inspect the leaves of plums, as soon as they have unfurled, for signs of aphid attack, and either remove affected foliage by hand or use an organic insecticide (p.88).
- Cover fruit trees and bushes with netting, to protect them from bullfinch attack.

OTHER JOBS

- Buy seeds and plants, if you have not already done so. Order 'plug' plants of vegetables that are difficult or time-consuming to raise (p.10).
- Buy new seed and potting composts. Don't use any left over from last year because their nutrient status cannot be relied upon.
- Clean out bird boxes, and put up new ones.
- Make plastic bottle cloches (p.72).
- Fork out the contents of your compost bin, separating finished compost from that which needs to be returned to the bin for further processing (p.47).

HARVESTING, PRESERVING AND STORING

- Harvest the same crops this month as you did last.
- Pick claytonia, sown the previous September and protected through the winter under a cloche, for a welcome supply of fresh salad leaves.
- Use up any stored vegetables, which will deteriorate from now onwards, and remove any that have rotted.
- Lift all parsnips, celeriac and leeks, then heel them in on a spare patch of ground to free up prime land for spring planting.
- Inspect late-keeping apples in store, for signs of rot. Remove if necessary.

VEGETABLES YOU CAN HARVEST NOW

Broccoli	Chinese artichokes	Leeks (mid-season)
Brussels sprouts (late)	Claytonia	Lettuces (winter)
Cabbages (winter)	Corn salad	Oriental greens
Cauliflowers (winter)	Jerusalem artichokes	Parsnips
Celeriac	Kales	Spinach
Chicories	Land cress	

WINTER FEATURE 1 Understanding your soil

All soils are made up of minerals, organic matter, air and water. The mineral particles vary in size from microscopic in clay, to slightly larger but still invisible in silt, and finally to easily visible in sand. To discover where your soil fits in this spectrum, take a fistful of earth and attempt to squeeze it into a ball.

- If it feels gritty and trickles away between your fingers, it's sand. Sandy soils are light and free-draining, warming up quickly in spring. They're easy to work, but low in fertility. You can improve the water-holding ability of sandy soils (and therefore their drought resilience) by adding compost or other organic matter, which acts like a sponge.

- If you can mould it into a shiny, smooth sphere, it's clay. Clays are heavy, and much harder to work, difficult to drain and prone to waterlogging. They become compacted when wet, then turn brick-hard when dry, but by way of compensation, they're usually rich in plant nutrients. Clay soils benefit from compost, which opens up the structure, making them more workable and better drained. Sharp sand or coarse grit has a similar improving effect.

- If it has more of a soapy feel, it's silt. Silty soils behave much like clays.

Most soils, however, are made up of a mixture of particle sizes, and are called loams. If it's a sandy loam, sand predominates; if it's a clay loam, clay predominates; and if it's a medium loam, it has equal amounts of sand and clay.

It's important to know whether your soil is acid or alkaline, by measuring its pH, using either a meter or a kit (sold at most garden centres). A neutral soil has a pH of 7. If the pH is above this level, it's alkaline, if below, it's acid. Vegetables prefer soil that's slightly acid, pH 6.5–7, whereas fruits like it more acid still, pH 6–6.5. Problems can arise when the pH falls below 5, or rises above 7.5, because key nutrients become unavailable to plants, resulting in poor growth and deficiency diseases.

▶

To make soils less acid, ground or dolomite limestone can be added annually, at a rate of 170g/sq. m (6oz/sq. yd), until the pH reaches the desired level. Autumn is the best time to apply lime. Whenever this is done, however, a gap of at least a month should be left before adding compost or manure, because they can react badly to each other. Mushroom compost also tends to be alkaline and will help to increase soil pH, but it should be bought from an organic grower, if possible, to make sure that it doesn't contain harmful pesticide residues. It's much harder to make alkaline soils more acid (those overlying chalk, for example), but adding composted pine needles or sawdust helps to a degree.

The organic matter in the soil is richest in the top-most layer, and is home to billions of bacteria and other microorganisms. They break down dead plant and animal remains, releasing nutrients into the soil that feed plants when they are absorbed by their roots.

Some microorganisms, such as mycorrhizal fungi, supply plants with nutrients directly into their roots, by creating their own extensive secondary rooting system made of fungal threads. They also protect plants from attack by other fungi. 'Nitrogen-fixing' bacteria, on the other hand, live in the pin-head-sized nodules on the roots of peas and beans, where they convert nitrogen in the air into a useable form. Microbial products are now being developed that enhance these natural processes, and several have come onto the market in recent years.

Adding regular amounts of compost, animal manures and other organic matter, to keep the microorganisms in the topsoil well fed, is the most important thing that gardeners can do.

WINTER FEATURE 2 **Making compost**

How do you make compost? Contrary to what many people think, it's not that difficult, if a few simple rules are followed. It's best made in a container, and there are plenty on the market to choose from. Most shop-bought bins are made of plastic, but wooden ones perform better, and it's easy enough to construct one at home, as we show on page 49. It doesn't matter where you site it – sun or shade will do – as long as it's convenient to reach, and in contact with the soil.

Most vegetable and garden waste can be composted, but brassica stems, hedge prunings and any other tough material should be shredded, chopped or mashed first. Couch grass and other pernicious weeds should be laid onto wire racks in the sun to kill them, before being added to the heap, but brassica roots that are infected with clubroot, onions with white rot, or potatoes with blighted foliage all need to go in the dustbin. It's fine to add kitchen waste throughout the growing season (though not fish and meat remains, which attract vermin), but during the winter such material should be put in runner bean trenches and sprinkled liberally with ground limestone (see page 123).

▶

Tough materials need to be mixed with sappy stuff, such as grass clippings. Adding nothing but lawn mowings invariably results in a capped, slimy layer. If there isn't enough stemmy waste around, shredded paper may be used instead. Really tough waste, like straw, must be mixed with animal manure if it is to break down successfully. Dry material should be doused with water, using a hosepipe (with a finger covering the end to create a fine spray), until it is thoroughly moistened – otherwise the microorganisms can't get to work.

A heap that contains a balanced mix of materials, made all at the same time, which is nicely moist, cannot fail to heat up to around 60°C (140°F), and the compost will be ready in less than three months. If the waste is added more gradually, the temperature never rises significantly, and it may take up to a year to produce finished compost. This is fine, but weed seeds won't be destroyed thoroughly. Forking out the contents, re-mixing, and adding fresh material will help to speed things along. The final piece of advice is to cover the bin with a rainproof lid, or, failing that, a piece of old carpet. And, if you don't get perfect results the first time round, you're sure to do better in future.

WINTER FEATURE 3 **Feeding the soil**

Compost is an excellent soil conditioner, but there are other organic materials that perform a similar function. One of the best is well-rotted manure. Wherever possible, it should be bought from an organic farm, where no pesticides are used. In 2008, many gardeners suffered severe plant losses after spreading non-organic manure contaminated with the herbicide aminopyralid. If the bedding material is straw, the manure should be stacked under plastic sheeting for six months, until it has broken down fully. Stable manure made with wood shavings needs at least a year to rot, because if it's dug into the soil too soon, the shavings will continue to decompose, 'robbing' nearby crops of nitrogen. Manure should be spread at a rate of one or two wheelbarrow loads to every 5 sq. m/6 sq. yd. Other sources of bulky organic materials include leafmould, made from fallen leaves (page 105), and green manures (page 106).

Organic gardeners also make use of concentrated sources of nutrients in the form of organic fertilizers. These can be of animal, plant or mineral origin and, like compost, they feed the soil, not the plant. If you look at any packet of fertilizer, it will tell you how much nitrogen (N), phosphorus (P) and potassium or potash (K) it contains. These are the three main nutrients that plants need, and as a rough shorthand, nitrogen promotes the growth of shoots and leaves, phosphorus stimulates root development and potassium is needed for flower and fruit formation.

►

Three of the most commonly used animal-derived fertilizers are hoof and horn, bonemeal, and blood fish and bone. All contain some nitrogen, but hoof and horn has the most, whereas bonemeal is the richest source of phosphorus. Hoof and horn and bonemeal are often used together when planting soft and top fruit, and hoof and horn can provide a boost for winter brassicas. Blood fish and bone contains useful amounts of nitrogen and phosphorus, and it's often used as a general organic fertilizer in the vegetable garden, applied at the rate of 135g per sq. m/4oz per sq. yd. It doesn't contain any potassium, and it's gradually being superseded by pelleted organic chicken manure, which does.

If you prefer not to use fertilizers of animal origin, seaweed-based products are the best alternative. They contain a reasonable amount of potassium, and can be used on tomatoes, gooseberries, peas and beans, and other potash-demanding crops. Seaweed is rich in trace elements, and is sold as a powder or a liquid feed. By far the best source of potassium, however, is a by-product of the sugar beet-processing industry called kali vinasse, usually marketed as 'organic potash'.

Mineral rock dusts make up the third category of organic fertilizers, and they are primarily used to treat specific mineral deficiencies. Ground rock phosphate is added wherever soils are lacking phosphorus, whilst ground limestone and dolomite are used for correcting soils that are too acid. Rock dusts of volcanic origin are a rich source of minerals, and astonishing claims have been made for the increase in productivity they can generate. Gypsum, which is calcium sulphate, can be used alone, or in combination with dolomite limestone, to help make heavy clay soils more workable.

WINTER FEATURE 4 **Making a wooden compost bin**

To make the twin bins shown in the illustration overleaf you will need:

- 18 of 1m/3ft 3in planks, 15cm/6in wide and 2.5cm/1in thick, for the sides (six per side, and another six for the middle section)

- 6 of 1.2m/4ft pressure-treated timber posts, 7.5 × 7.5cm/3 × 3in

- 6 of 2m/6ft 6in planks, 15cm/6in wide and 2.5cm/1in thick, for the rear

- 5 of 85cm/2ft 10in battens, 4cm/1½in wide and 1in thick, to form the channels

- 12 of 1m/3ft 3in planks (cut to fit), for the removable board front

- 2 of 1.15m/3ft 9in planks of wood, 7.5cm/3in wide and 2.5cm/1in thick, with a 5 × 5cm/2 × 2in block on each end, for the ties

▶

1. Nail or screw (decking screws are ideal) six of the side planks to two of the timber posts, leaving no gaps in between. Repeat for the other side and middle sections.

2. Dig six holes, 30cm/1ft deep, where the posts are to go, then drop all three panels into place, and backfill with soil to secure.

3. Attach the rear planks so that from above the construction resembles the letter E.

4. Nail the timber for the channels in place so that the front boards can slide down, trim the removable front planks so that they move easily, then drop them into position.

5. There is a tendency for the side panels to spread outwards when the bins are filled, due to pressure from the compost inside, so place the ties in position to prevent this happening.

6. Finally, paint with an ecologically friendly wood preservative, such as Procol.

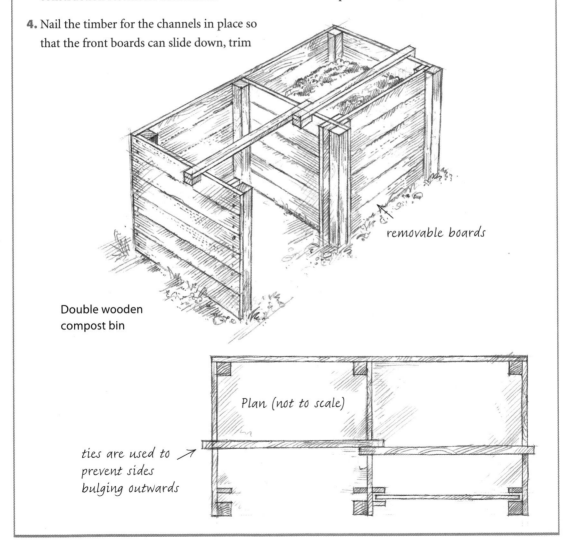

Double wooden compost bin

removable boards

ties are used to prevent sides bulging outwards

Plan (not to scale)

WINTER FEATURE 5 Crop rotation

Crop rotation means growing vegetables that belong to the same botanical family together, and moving them as a group to a different part of the garden every year. This is done to prevent the build-up of soil-borne pests and diseases that occurs if they are grown continuously in the same place, and also because some groups of vegetables are more nutrient-demanding than others. Not all crops need to be rotated, however – only those that are susceptible to serious diseases, like white rot, which affects the onion family; eelworm, which affects the potato tribe; and clubroot, which affects the cabbage family (brassicas).

Main vegetable families

Family	Crops
Onion	Onions, garlic, leeks, shallots
Potato	Potatoes, tomatoes, peppers, aubergines
Cabbage	Broccoli, Brussels sprouts, cabbages, calabrese, cauliflowers, kales, kohl rabi, oriental greens, radishes, rocket, swedes, turnips
Bean	Broad beans, French beans, runner beans, peas
Beet	Beetroot, leaf beet, spinach
Carrot	Carrots, celeriac, celery, Florence fennel, Hamburg parsley, parsnips
Cucumber	Courgettes, cucumbers, marrows, pumpkins, squashes
Others	Lettuces, chicories, cardoon (strictly speaking, it's a perennial, but is grown as an annual), endive, salsify, scorzonera, Jerusalem artichokes, sweet corn
Perennials	Asparagus, globe artichokes, seakale

How does this work in practice? The illustration overleaf shows a traditional four-year rotation. The garden is split into four equal-sized plots, and in year 1, the crops are grown in the positions shown. Onions are frequently included alongside peas and beans. Potatoes and courgettes, which produce dense foliage and share a similar demand for nitrogen, also go nicely together. Brassicas are a large group, so stay together on their own; with beets going with carrots and other roots.

Other vegetables that don't have to be part of the crop rotation can be fitted in anywhere where there is space.

►

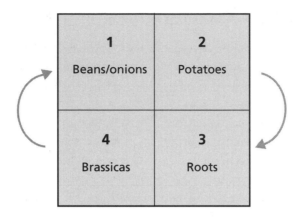

	Plot 1	Plot 2	Plot 3	Plot 4
Year 1	Beans/onions	Potatoes	Roots	Brassicas
Year 2	Brassicas	Beans/onions	Potatoes	Roots
Year 3	Roots	Brassicas	Beans/onions	Potatoes
Year 4	Potatoes	Roots	Brassicas	Beans/onions
Year 5	Same as year 1	Same as year 1	Same as year 1	Same as year 1

In year 2, everything is moved to a different plot. So, for example, the roots on plot 3 move onto land vacated by brassicas (plot 4), which, in turn, move to plot 1. This is repeated annually until everything is back where it started four years later.

Compost and manure should go on the potato and brassica plots, but peas and beans and root crops are less demanding, and they can make do with the residual fertility in the soil.

This is just one example of a crop rotation, but you can easily devise your own, based around your family's preferences and the amounts you intend growing. Crop rotation is much simpler with beds, because you can allocate as many beds as you like to each vegetable family. Nor need rotations last for only four years. The longer you can delay crops from returning to their original plot the better. A rotation of six to eight years is ideal.

Perennial vegetables, rhubarb, herbs and fruit, however, need a permanent home in the garden. Strawberries are the exception – being short-lived, they belong with the vegetables.

Crop rotation in glasshouses and tunnels is trickier, because of the predominance of members of the tomato family, which is why the soil invariably becomes 'tomato sick' after a while. Apart from bringing in fresh soil (or growing tomatoes on grafted rootstocks) there is not a lot you can do, but you should relocate your polytunnel onto fresh ground every four to five years.

WINTER FEATURE 6 **Digging v. no-digging**

Although there's a lot of satisfaction in digging, there's no getting away from the fact that it's hard work, especially if you garden on clay. A workable alternative is a technique called 'no-dig' gardening. The idea is to cultivate the ground as little as possible, to avoid burying the many beneficial microorganisms and creatures that live in the upper layers of the soil. Earthworms, in particular, flourish in undisturbed land, and the tunnels they make, as they travel through the soil, help to aerate and drain it. Weeds are fewer too, because their seeds germinate only when brought to the surface by digging.

Unlike conventional gardening, compost, manure and other organic materials are left on the surface under a 'no-dig' regime, to be incorporated over time by worms and other creatures. It's not possible to avoid disturbing the soil entirely – when you make a seed drill, hoe, or harvest, for example – but it can be kept to a minimum.

No-dig growing of potatoes requires a radically different approach to normal. Each tuber is set into a shallow depression scooped out of the soil surface, surrounded with a shovel-full of well-rotted manure, and covered with a shallow straw mulch. When the first green shoots appear, they are coaxed through the straw. Throughout the season, extra straw and grass clippings are added from time to time, to create a light-excluding mulch, which prevents the developing tubers from turning green. To harvest, the straw is scraped away and the potatoes picked as needed, replacing the mulch each time. The plants will simply carry on growing.

No-dig gardening has some disadvantages, however. The soil must be weed-free before you start – because it will be impossible to eradicate perennial weeds later. And if a pan (compacted soil) develops, it can't be broken up without digging. But these are far outweighed by the advantages, especially on a heavy soil, where a friable surface layer of broken-down mulch is preferable to wrestling with concrete-like clods of clay!

CHAPTER 4

Spring

In March it's usually too cold to sow outdoors, because the ground temperature needs to be at least 7°C/44°F, but sowing is possible under cover, to be ready to plant outside in April. It's also a good idea to prepare seed beds in advance, by warming the soil under polythene sheeting. Early potatoes can be planted out towards the end of the month, and March is the absolute latest time for planting top and soft fruit, and for pruning apples and pears.

April is the busiest month of the year for raising plants, and a lot of time is spent sowing, pricking out, potting on, hardening off and planting out. The weather should be warm enough to sow most crops outdoors, although it's perhaps still preferable to raise them under cover, in seed trays or modules, where you're not at the mercy of the elements.

The months of April and May are traditionally known as the 'hungry gap', and for good reason: most overwintering crops are reaching their end, but new-season fruit and vegetables have yet to arrive in any quantity. A polytunnel can make all the difference at this time of the year, with salads from early spring sowings supplementing what remains of the winter crops

May is another busy month, spent hardening off and transplanting leeks, leafy greens and the many other vegetable seedlings sown earlier in the year. Everything is growing like crazy, including weeds, and hoeing is a major preoccupation. It's important to make sure that plants are kept well watered, especially if the weather turns dry.

MARCH Jobs for early spring

Most seeds can be sown now in modules or pots in a greenhouse or poly-tunnel, or outside under cloches. You've still got time to plant bare-rooted fruit trees, canes and bushes, but don't delay. At the end of the month, plant early potatoes.

SOWING AND PLANTING

Vegetables and herbs

- Use a propagator to sow seeds of asparagus, aubergines, celeriac, celery, cucumbers and peppers.
- Sow tomatoes, if you intend growing them in a cold greenhouse (p.190).
- Sow leafy brassicas, early leeks, lettuces, onions, peas and turnips, under cover.
- Sow broad beans, beetroot, carrots, claytonia, corn salad, Hamburg parsley, kohl rabi, land cress, parsnips, radishes, rocket, spinach and spring onions outdoors, providing cloche protection, if needed.
- Pot up sweet potatoes and put them somewhere warm, to provide 'slips' next month (p.188).
- Harden off sowings you made last month, and plant out when conditions are suitable (p.10).
- Plant onion sets from mid-March, although delay if it is cold because they can bolt (run to seed) (p.162).
- Set shallots – they are much hardier than onion sets (p.180).
- Plant early potatoes towards the end of the month, if the ground has warmed up sufficiently (p.173).
- Plant Jerusalem artichoke tubers (p.153).
- This is your last chance to plant garlic, if the bulbs are to grow to a reasonable size (p.149).
- Plant perennial vegetables, like asparagus and seakale, on a space you have permanently reserved for them.
- Sow a quick-growing green manure crop, like mustard, on land that won't be needed until May or June (p.107).
- Take root cuttings from established comfrey plants, or buy new plants. They'll provide leaves for a liquid feed later in the year (p.69).
- Sow parsley, fennel, chervil and chives outdoors, if it is warm enough.

- Sow dill and sage under cover.
- Sow basil and coriander seeds in a propagator, or in pots on a sunny windowsill.

Fruit

- Plant bare-rooted fruit trees, soft fruit and vines, preferably during the early part of the month.
- It's a good time to plant rhubarb crowns now (p.232).
- Sow alpine strawberry seeds in modules (p.235).
- Sow Cape gooseberry and melon seeds in a propagator.
- Sow seeds of *Limnanthes douglasii* and other flowers amongst fruit, to attract pollinating and predatory insects (p.110).

VEGETABLES YOU CAN SOW NOW

Asparagus	Celeriac	Onions
Aubergines	Celery	Parsnips
Broad beans	Claytonia	Peas
Beetroot	Corn salad	Peppers
Broccoli	Cucumbers	Radishes
Brussels sprouts (early)	Hamburg parsley	Rocket
Cabbages (summer)	Kohl rabi	Spinach
Calabrese	Land cress	Spring onions
Carrots	Leeks (early/mid-season)	Tomatoes
Cauliflowers (summer)	Lettuces	Turnips

VEGETABLES YOU CAN PLANT NOW

Asparagus	Jerusalem artichokes	Seakale (thongs)
Broad beans	Lettuces	Shallots
Chinese artichokes	Onion sets	
Garlic	Potatoes	

CULTIVATION

Vegetables and herbs

- Complete any unfinished digging and weeding.
- Complete preparation of celery trenches (p.139).
- Incorporate manure and compost, as required.
- Dig in overwintered green manures (p.107).
- Give overwintered crops a boost with an organic fertilizer (p.48).
- Divide perennial herbs, like chives, mint, marjoram and thyme (p.111).
- Lightly trim sage (avoid cutting old wood), but prune rosemary hard.
- Take root cuttings of mint and tarragon (p.111).
- Force seakale (p.197).

Fruit

- Finish pruning newly planted and established top and soft fruit – this is your last chance.
- Protect peaches, nectarines, apricots and cherries from frost at night, using fleece or sacking (p.221).
- Prune out any dead, diseased or awkwardly growing fig branches (p.213).
- Hand-pollinate any fruit trees in flower, if there are few insects around (p.221).
- Feed fruit trees, canes and bushes with an organic fertilizer, as required.
- Mulch all newly planted fruit trees, canes and bushes with compost, manure or straw.
- Cover strawberry plants with cloches (p.235).
- Weed around trees and soft fruit.

PESTS AND DISEASES

Vegetables and herbs

- Remove and compost dead brassica leaves.
- Remove and compost stripped Brussels sprout stems, which can host whitefly and cabbage aphids.
- Activate defensive measures against slugs and snails (p.87).

Fruit

- Inspect plums and other top and soft fruit for signs of aphid damage. Remove by hand or use an organic insecticide (p.88).
- Protect fruit bushes and trees against bullfinch attack with netting.
- Remove swollen 'big buds' on blackcurrants to destroy overwintering gall mites (p.208).
- Remove apple and gooseberry foliage affected by powdery mildew by hand, or spray with an organic fungicide (p.203, p.216).

HARVESTING, PRESERVING AND STORING

- Pick Brussels sprouts, kale, purple sprouting broccoli and the first of the spring cauliflowers, if you planted them last summer.
- Pick any remaining winter cabbages.
- Start to pick spring cabbages, initially as thinnings.
- Harvest remaining root crops, like artichokes, parsnips and celeriac, which are all coming to an end.
- Pick spinach, which has remained dormant all winter but begins to put on a spurt now.
- Gather leaves of red and sugar loaf chicories, mizuna and komatsuma, and the last of the mibuna and Chinese mustard, if you have a polytunnel.
- Pick spring onions, grown under cloches.
- Pull scarlet stems of rhubarb. Picked fresh, and stewed with cream, they offer a tantalizing foretaste of fruity delights to come.

VEGETABLES YOU CAN HARVEST NOW

Broccoli	Claytonia	Oriental greens
Brussels sprouts (late)	Corn salad	Parsnips
Cabbages (winter/spring)	Jerusalem artichokes	Seakale
Cauliflowers (spring)	Kales	Spinach
Celeriac	Land cress	Spring onions
Chicories	Leeks (late)	
Chinese artichokes	Lettuces (winter)	

APRIL Jobs for mid-spring

It's non-stop sowing time! Tender crops should be started indoors, but others can be safely sown outside. Seedlings sown during the winter months can also go outside now, after hardening off. Make sure that you have enough pea sticks and supports for runner beans.

SOWING AND PLANTING

Vegetables and herbs

- Sow lettuces, radishes, rocket, spring onions and turnips outside every two to three weeks (sow little and often), to avoid gluts. Don't worry if earlier, speculative, sowings failed to germinate – you can sow again now.
- Start off celeriac, celery, endive, Florence fennel, peppers, sweet corn and tomatoes on a warm windowsill, or in a propagator, because they require heat to germinate successfully. Slips, taken from sweet potatoes, can go into pots now, and they, too, require heat (p.188).
- Sow frost-sensitive crops like French and runner beans, courgettes, cucumbers, pumpkins and squashes in pots or modules indoors, to give them a head start ready for planting out next month.
- Sow everything else on the list outside, either *in situ*, in modules, or in a seed bed for transplanting later (p.67).
- Transplant broad beans, beetroot, leeks, lettuces, onions, leafy greens and any other vegetables sown in late February or March, but don't forget to harden them off first.
- Plant second-early and maincrop potatoes, onion sets, shallots and Chinese artichokes. Plant asparagus crowns – this is your last chance (p.117).
- Transplant tomatoes, sown in March, into unheated glasshouses or poly-tunnels, towards the end of the month (p.190).
- Sow herb seeds under cover this month, and transplant outside in May or June, although most should be fine if sown outside.
- Sow basil and coriander seeds in a propagator, or in pots on a sunny windowsill.
- Plant out hardy herbs, like sage.

Fruit

■ Sow melon seeds in pots under cover, and transplant any from earlier sowings into the greenhouse (p.238).

■ Sow rhubarb seeds outside in a seed bed (p.232).

VEGETABLES YOU CAN SOW NOW

Asparagus	Celtuce	Peas
Broad beans	Claytonia	Peppers
French beans	Corn salad	Pumpkins
Runner beans	Courgettes	Radishes
Beetroot	Cucumbers	Rocket
Leaf beet	Endive	Salsify
Broccoli	Florence fennel	Spinach
Brussels sprouts	Globe artichokes	Spring onions
Cabbages (autumn/winter)	Hamburg parsley	Squashes (winter)
Calabrese	Kales	Sweet corn
Cardoon	Kohl rabi	Sweet potatoes
Carrots (maincrop)	Land cress	Tomatoes
Cauliflowers (summer/autumn)	Leeks (mid-season)	Turnips
Celeriac	Lettuces	
Celery	Parsnips	

VEGETABLES YOU CAN PLANT NOW

Asparagus	Cabbages	Leeks (early)
Broad beans	Cauliflowers	Onion sets
Beetroot	Chinese artichokes	Potatoes
Leaf beet	Globe artichokes	Shallots
Brussels sprouts	Kohl rabi	Tomatoes

CULTIVATION

Vegetables and herbs

- Keep on top of weeds, by hoeing and hand-weeding regularly.
- Erect support structures for runner beans (p.123).
- Check that you have enough pea sticks or netting for peas (p.168).
- Earth up new potatoes (p.173).
- Cover potato foliage with newspapers or fleece, when frost threatens (p.173).
- Take rooted cuttings from globe artichokes (p.150).
- Take softwood cuttings of mint, sage, lavender and lemon balm (p.111).
- Propagate bay and thyme, using layered cuttings (p.112).
- Divide congested herbs, including chives and tarragon (p.111).
- Prune shrubby herbs like bay, thyme and lavender, when there is no risk of frost.

Fruit

- Water newly planted fruit during dry spells.
- Hoe or hand-weed soft fruit carefully
- Feed fruit trees, canes and bushes with an organic fertilizer, as required.
- Tie-in and train vines, pinching out laterals as appropriate (p.218).
- Feed citrus and other container-grown fruit.
- Spray strawberries with a foliar feed every two weeks until ripening (p.70).
- Keep strawberries cloched for an early crop (p.235).
- Stop forcing rhubarb.

PESTS AND DISEASES

Vegetables and herbs

- Dig up any potato 'volunteers' (tubers left in the ground from last year) because they can harbour potato blight.
- Protect crops (especially brassicas) from attack by pigeons (p.132).
- Protect crops with fleece from attack by flea beetles, carrot flies and other troublesome insect pests (p.87).
- Place collars around brassicas to deter cabbage root flies (p.133).
- Inspect crops for aphids and take appropriate action (p.87).
- Activate defensive measures against slugs and snails (p.87).

Fruit

- Check all fruit for signs of aphid attack, and remove by hand, or spray with an organic insecticide.
- Do not be tempted to remove polythene covers from peaches and nectarines, because peach leaf curl can still strike.
- Remove and destroy grease bands from apples, pears, plums and cherries.
- Inspect gooseberries and red and white currants for sawfly damage (p.216).
- Spray mildew-affected gooseberries and blackcurrants with potassium bicarbonate, or remove foliage by hand (p.216).
- Hang up raspberry beetle traps (p.228).
- Remove swollen 'big buds' on blackcurrants, to destroy sheltering gall mites (p.208).

HARVESTING, PRESERVING AND STORING

- Asparagus is the main treat of the month. Picked and eaten within the hour, the difference in taste from shop-bought spears is astounding.

VEGETABLES YOU CAN HARVEST NOW

Asparagus	Claytonia	Oriental greens
Leaf beet	Corn salad	Radishes
Broccoli	Kales	Rocket
Cabbages (winter/spring)	Land cress	Seakale
Cauliflowers (spring)	Leeks (late)	Spinach
Chicories	Lettuces (winter)	Spring onions

MAY Jobs for late spring

Remember to sow salads every two to three weeks to ensure a supply throughout summer. Grow green manures on any unused land. Keep weeds under control by hoeing and hand weeding, and water during dry spells.

SOWING AND PLANTING

Vegetables and herbs

- Sow beetroot, Hamburg parsley, salsify and scorzonera – all relatively trouble-free root crops for winter storage.
- Make successional sowings of summer salads.
- Sow New Zealand spinach (p.182).
- Sow swedes now to avoid powdery mildew, if you live in Scotland or the north of England, but wait until June, or even July, if you live in the south (p.184).
- Buy plug plants if you were unable to sow in time, or experienced germination, or other, problems, to make good the deficiency.
- Sow a green manure, if there is a spare patch of land – don't leave it bare! (p.106).
- Make outdoor *in situ* sowings of frost-sensitive vegetables, like French and runner beans, courgettes, pumpkins and sweet corn, if you didn't sow them under cover last month.
- Sow everything else on the list on page 64 outside, either *in situ*, or in modules or a seed bed for transplanting later.
- Don't plant out tomatoes just yet – it's still a bit too early. Leave them until June, when they can really enjoy the heat of the summer sun (p.190).
- Leave sweet potato plants indoors until June (p.188).
- Sow and transplant most herbs outdoors now, but keep a weather eye open for late frosts. Basil is especially sensitive, and does best in containers indoors, or on a sunny patio, so delay planting outside until June.

Fruit

- Plant out Cape gooseberries under cloches (p.237).
- Plant melon seedlings inside a cold glasshouse or polytunnel, from mid-May onwards (p.238).
- Plant alpine strawberries in a bed outdoors (p.235).

VEGETABLES YOU CAN SOW NOW

French beans	Corn salad	Pumpkins
Runner beans	Courgettes	Purslane (summer)
Beetroot	Endive	Radishes
Leaf beet	Florence fennel	Rocket
Broccoli	Hamburg parsley	Salsify
Brussels sprouts	Kales	Scorzonera
Cabbages (autumn/winter)	Kohl rabi	Spinach
Calabrese	Land cress	Spring onions
Carrots (maincrop)	Leeks (late)	Squashes (winter)
Cauliflowers (autumn)	Lettuces	Swedes
Celtuce	Parsnips	Sweet corn
Chicories	Peas	Turnips

VEGETABLES YOU CAN PLANT NOW

French beans	Cauliflowers	Globe artichokes	Squashes (winter)
Runner beans	Celeriac	Kohl rabi	Sweet corn
Beetroot	Celery	Leeks	Sweet potatoes
Brussels sprouts	Courgettes	Peppers	Tomatoes
Cabbages	Endive	Potatoes	
Calabrese	Florence fennel	Pumpkins	

CULTIVATION

Vegetables and herbs

- Keep that hoe moving constantly, because weeds will be growing like crazy this month.
- Thin seedlings of carrots, lettuces and other direct-sown crops.
- Earth up potatoes and cover them with fleece, if frost threatens (p.173).
- Make sure that crops have sufficient water, especially after transplanting (p.92).
- Stake broad beans, to prevent them from lodging (blowing over) (p.120).

- Erect runner bean supports (p.123).
- Cut comfrey leaves to make a liquid feed (p.69).
- Provide sticks or netting support for peas (p.168).
- Prune shrubby herbs, like bay, thyme and lavender.
- Take softwood cuttings of mint, rosemary, thyme and marjoram (p.111).

Fruit

- Water soft fruit in dry spells. Avoid using tap water (unless soft) on blueberries.
- Keep weeds under control, by mulching and hand-weeding.
- Prune trained forms of cherries, plums, peaches, apricots and nectarines.
- Tie-in and train vines, pinching out laterals as appropriate (p.218).
- Remove all this year's central leader extension, on mature cordon apples and pears (p.202).
- Thin out weak and awkward summer-fruiting raspberry canes (p.228).
- Spray strawberries with a foliar feed every two weeks until ripening (p.235).
- Net strawberries, raspberries and other soft fruit against birds.
- Place straw (or strawberry mats) under strawberries to stop soil-splash (p.235).
- Remove flowers from newly planted strawberries, so all their energies are concentrated on establishing themselves.

PESTS AND DISEASES

Vegetables and herbs

- Activate defensive measures against slugs and snails (p.87).
- Place collars around brassicas, to deter cabbage root flies (p.133).
- Pinch out the tips of broad beans attacked by blackfly (p.120).
- Protect crops (especially brassicas) from pigeons (p.132).
- Protect crops with fleece against flea beetles, carrot flies and other troublesome insect pests (p.87).
- Inspect crops for aphids and take appropriate action.

Fruit

- Check all fruit for signs of aphid attack and take appropriate action.
- Remove polythene covers from peaches and nectarines.

- Inspect gooseberries, and red and white currants, for sawfly damage (pin-prick holes in the lower leaves) (p.216).
- Hang up raspberry beetle traps (p.228).
- Spray mildew-affected gooseberries and blackcurrants with an organic fungicide, or remove foliage by hand (p.216).
- Inspect apples and plums for sawfly larvae, and pick off before they tunnel into fruit.
- Hang up apple codling moth and plum fruit moth traps – one trap for every three to five trees.
- Thin out gooseberries to get larger berries (p.216).

HARVESTING, PRESERVING AND STORING

- Harvest the few winter greens you may still have left. Root crops have long gone, and it will be some time before this year's harvest swings into full production – so you're still in the 'hungry gap'.
- Harvest delicious asparagus and globe artichokes, or tender young carrots and peas.
- Harvest the first pickings of tasty, new-season, baby spinach leaves, whilst golf-ball-sized turnips will be ready by the end of the month.
- Pick early strawberries, for the real treat is in the fruit garden, where they ripen to perfection under cloches. Pick undersized gooseberries, too, thinned to increase the size of the remainder. They are too tart to eat raw, but delicious if stewed.
- Pull sticks of rhubarb, which is now at peak production.

VEGETABLES YOU CAN HARVEST NOW

Asparagus	Cauliflowers	Kohl rabi	Radishes
Leaf beet	Claytonia	Land cress	Rocket
Broccoli	Corn salad	Leeks	Spinach
Cabbages	Globe artichokes	Lettuces	Spring onions
Carrots	Kales	Peas	Turnips

SPRING FEATURE 1 **Seed sowing simplified**

It's well worth taking the time to create the right conditions for sowing, to give seeds the best possible chance of survival. The soil should be weed-free, and, if dug, needs at least three weeks afterwards to settle. It can be trodden down, by shuffling back and forth over the surface, but this runs the risk of damaging the structure of all but sandy soils. The surface should be raked back and forth until any clods have broken down into tiny crumbs, producing a fine, level tilth.

The position of the row is marked out using a line, and a shallow seed drill is created, using the corner of a hoe or a stick. A depth of about 5mm/¼in is about right for most seeds, but peas and beans require 2.5–4cm/1–1½in. Some seeds should be poured into the palm of the hand, and a pinch taken between thumb and forefinger, to be dribbled thinly along the row. They should be lightly covered with soil, by hand or using a rake, and the ends of the row marked with a label. When the seeds have germinated, the seedlings must be thinned, to avoid crowding. Green manures (see page 106) are often sown by scattering the seeds uniformly over the surface (broadcasting), then raking them in.

In some cases it's better to sow 2–3 seeds at set points, corresponding to the final growing positions, and allowing only the strongest seedling to continue to maturity. This is called 'station sowing' and it's used for crops like courgettes and parsnips.

If the ground is exceptionally dry at sowing time, the bottom of the drill should be watered thoroughly, and the seeds pressed into the mud, then covered with dry soil to prevent evaporation.

Vegetables that spend a long time in the ground, like leeks and brassicas, can be sown close together in a separate seed bed, until they are ready to be transplanted to their final positions. Alternatively, they can be grown in pots or modules.

Most seeds can be started off by sowing under cover, in a glasshouse or polytunnel, cold frame or even on a windowsill. Some vegetable seeds require heat to germinate, and for these a propagator or some method of warming the soil is needed (although you can often start seeds off successfully in an airing cupboard). There's a massive choice of receptacles to sow into. Garden

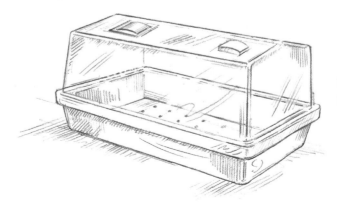

Electric plant propagator

►

centres sell pots, trays and modules, made from plastic or biodegradable materials like fibre or coir. Alternatively, they can be made from yogurt cartons and plastic food containers, punctured with holes for drainage, or even fibre egg cartons. Inner cardboard tubes from toilet rolls make excellent receptacles for beans and other deep-rooted plants, and paper pots can be manufactured at home by wrapping strips of newspaper around a cylindrical wooden former. Also, lengths of rainwater gutter, filled with potting mixture, make excellent temporary homes for peas and salad seedlings, to be slid into position outside when they're ready.

SPRING FEATURE 2 **Container growing**

It's surprising how many crops can be grown in containers. Tomatoes, salads and herbs are the obvious choices, but peaches, figs, beans and potatoes thrive in them too. Only a handful of vegetables are unsuited to life in a pot – those with deep roots, like parsnips, or some of the larger brassicas. Others, like citrus fruits, are rarely grown any other way, here in Britain.

Plastic and terracotta pots, wooden boxes, stone sinks and metal buckets – all can be used as receptacles, let alone the specially designed ones on sale, such as herb or strawberry planters. Almost anything will do, as long as it will hold earth and has sufficient depth: 10cm/4in for seedlings and salads; 20–25cm/8–10in for most vegetables and herbs; from 30cm/12in for newly planted fruit trees, to 45–53cm/18–21in for mature specimens.

All containers need holes for drainage in the base, up to 10mm/½in in diameter, spaced every 7.5–10cm/3–4in apart, and covered with broken terracotta crocks, to prevent blockages. Non-plastic containers should be lined with polythene sheeting, perforated at the base, to stop moisture from evaporating through the sides.

Garden soil is unsuitable for containers, because it becomes compacted by frequent watering, so multipurpose, or specially formulated container growing media are preferred. Fruit trees and bushes need a loam-based (John Innes) growing medium, but this does contain chemical fertilizers. As there are no organic, loam-based media on the market, you may wish to make your own.

Strawberry planter

▶

Plants in containers are cultivated in much the same way as those grown in soil, although they'll have to be watered more frequently during the growing season – once, perhaps twice, daily – with large containers requiring less-frequent watering than smaller ones. Covering the soil with a mulch of compost or stones will cut down evaporation losses. Plants in containers also require a weekly organic liquid feed while they are growing strongly, especially one that is rich in potassium when fruits are swelling (see below).

Vegetable varieties described in seed catalogues and garden centres as 'mini-veg' or 'patio plants', have a bushy or dwarf habit, and are particularly good for container growing. You'll find varietal suggestions under the individual crop descriptions in Part 3. All the herbs mentioned on pages 241–3 can be grown successfully in pots, although dill and fennel should be staked, because they're tall. It's actually very useful to grow invasive herbs like mint in containers, because they can't overrun their neighbours!

Potatoes can be grown in a large tub or stout sack; the tubers planted into a 15cm/6in layer of multipurpose growing medium (three to five tubers will fit into a dustbin-sized tub) and covered with an equal depth of the same stuff. When the foliage appears, more growing medium should be added, leaving just the top few leaves exposed. This should be repeated throughout the season until the tub is full. The potatoes need to be watered regularly, and fed once a week until harvested by emptying the tub.

A great advantage of growing fruit in tubs is that they can be moved under cover during winter. This is essential for citrus fruits, but others benefit as well. Peach trees, for example, avoid diseases like leaf curl. They'll need re-potting in the autumn every couple of years, using fresh growing media. The roots can be teased out at the same time and up to a tenth removed – mostly the thicker ones.

SPRING FEATURE 3 **Liquid feeds**

Although liquid feeds contradict the principle of feeding the soil rather than the plant, they're usually used in situations where soil is lacking –in pots, hanging baskets and grow-bags, for example. Our forefathers made liquid feeds by steeping a sack filled with manure in a rainwater butt, draining off the resulting liquor. Some still do today. Others fill water barrels with young nettle leaves, and extract a similar, nitrogen-rich feed.

A far better feed than this can be made from the leaves of the perennial herb, comfrey. Its roots penetrate deep into the subsoil, searching for minerals, and the leaves are especially rich in potash – they contain twice as much as well-rotted farmyard manure. Half a dozen plants will supply more than enough leaves for all the liquid feed you might need, from three to four cuts each year, with plenty to spare for the compost heap. Comfrey leaves can be soaked in water, but

▶

the smell given off by the rotting leaves is definitely to be avoided! It's far better to crush the fresh leaves under a heavy weight to produce a concentrated extract. Here's how you do it....

The drawing shows an upright length of 15cm-/6in-diameter plastic pipe, capped at the bottom, but with a 5mm/¼in drainage hole drilled in the middle of the base. Stuff leaves in at the top, and compress them with a large bottle of water, lowered into the tube on a length of string. Collect the black liquid that drips out of the bottom into a jar, and dilute it in 10–20 parts of water, to use on tomatoes, onions and other potash-hungry crops.

If you are unable to make liquid feeds yourself, they're available commercially in an organically approved form. Some are made from animal manure, others from rock minerals and plant extracts. Seaweed extracts contain a rich mix of minerals, trace elements and various plant growth stimulants, and when used on plants that are flagging, or not growing as they should, they produce a remarkable restorative effect. It would seem that they can also enhance a plant's ability to fight off pest and disease attack.

Most liquid feeds are applied to the soil at the base of plants, for uptake by the roots, but others, notably seaweed products, can also be sprayed as a foliar feed, to be taken in by the leaves.

Making comfrey liquid feed

SPRING FEATURE 4 **Protected growing**

A glasshouse, cold frame or a few cloches can make a huge difference to the productivity of your garden, by extending the seasons. Some crops can be planted earlier in the spring, and others harvested later in the autumn, than those outside; delicate vegetables, like tomatoes and chilli peppers, which can be a bit of a gamble outdoors, thrive under cover; and problems with pests and diseases are lessened too.

Glasshouses aren't cheap, so it pays to choose wisely. They're manufactured in timber or aluminium, glazed with glass or polycarbonate

▶

plastic (or similar), and can cost anything from a few hundred to thousands of pounds. Freestanding and lean-to mini-greenhouses, suitable for patio use, are much cheaper, being little more than a metal frame covered with polythene. They're designed to grow a few tomato plants, but can be invaluable in the spring for raising plants in seed trays and modules.

A walk-in polytunnel offers many of the benefits of a glasshouse, but at a much cheaper cost, although it's not so attractive looking. It consists of a sheet of polythene stretched tightly over a series of equally spaced, roughly semi-circular, metal hoops, anchored at each side by being buried deep in the ground. It can get very hot in a polytunnel, so it's important to provide adequate ventilation through doors at each end (and side vents, where possible). Exposure to the sun renders the polythene brittle in time, and it'll have to be renewed every four or five years. When this happens, the entire tunnel should be moved onto a new part of the garden to prevent the soil from becoming 'tomato sick'.

Smaller still is a cold frame. In the past, this was a permanent structure, with wooden or brick sides which sloped down from back to front. It would be covered with a hinged, or completely removable, glass-enclosed wooden frame called a 'light'. You may have seen them in stately-home kitchen gardens, where they're often painted white and look very attractive. Nowadays, cold frames are designed to be moved around the garden, and are usually made from aluminium or powder-coated steel, with glass, or clear plastic, walls and lid. They're mostly used for acclimatizing seedlings to life outdoors, but also provide useful additional space for growing cucumbers, or other ground-hugging sensitive crops.

Cloches are invaluable in the garden. Some, like the elegantly shaped bell cloches that the Victorians manufactured in glass, but which are now made of clear plastic, protect individual plants. See illustration overleaf.

Others, called tunnel cloches, are like mini-polytunnels, and protect whole rows or beds. There are many models on the market to choose from. You can also make your own cloches very easily. A large plastic drinks bottle with its

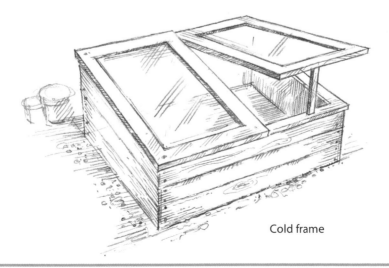

Cold frame

►

bottom cut off makes a perfect mini cloche for newly transplanted seedlings, and has the added benefit of keeping slugs at bay. A couple of opened-out wire coat hangers, bent into a dome shape, pushed into the soil, and covered with a clear polythene bag, will protect young courgettes and pumpkins. And standard polypropylene mains water pipe can be cut into hoop-shaped lengths, which are connected to each other using a length of timber, to form a DIY tunnel cloche.

Here are just a few of the many uses to which cloches can be put:

- Warming up the soil in spring.

- Protecting newly planted seedlings from adverse weather.

- Enabling salad crops to survive the winter.

- Getting an early crop of strawberries.

- Sowing early crops of carrots.

- Growing late-season crops of French and dwarf runner beans.

- Drying garlic and onions.

Bell cloche

Bottle cloche

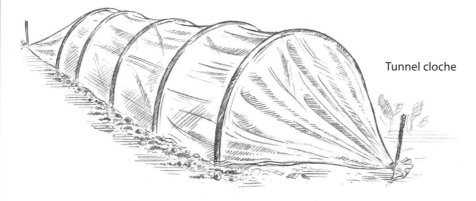

Tunnel cloche

CHAPTER 5

Summer

June arrives, bringing blue skies and sunshine by day, and warm rain at night – that's what every gardener dreams of, anyway! In practice, nature can offer searing drought one year and sullen downpours the next; so be prepared for every eventuality.

At least frosts have been banished, allowing semi-tropical aubergines, peppers, tomatoes and sweet potatoes to be planted outside, in a sunny and sheltered spot. If grown in containers, they must be cared for on a daily basis, so that they never go short of water. They also need high-potash organic liquid feeds on a regular basis.

This is the time of year when pests and diseases reach their peak, so a close eye must be kept on all plants for tell-tale signs of infestations. Barriers, traps, biological controls, and other prevention and control strategies can be put into action. Weeds, too, are a constant worry, threatening to overrun the garden if not kept in check by hoe and hand, but at least they provide the compost heap with plenty of raw material.

Spring-sown crops can be harvested now, bringing the thrill of tasting your first garden peas, summer salads and new potatoes. In the fruit garden, raspberries, strawberries and other soft fruit must be picked on an almost daily basis, if it's not to be wasted.

In the heady warmth of summer, when the garden is full to overflowing, it's easy to forget that, if you don't sow now, you'll have nothing to eat next spring. July marks the latest sowing time for many of the vegetables that will be eaten during the run up to Christmas. By August, the weeds are growing a little slower, sowing is winding down, and the worst of any pest problems are over; which is just as well because, from now on, you're going to be working flat out harvesting and preserving!

JUNE Jobs for early summer

Be prepared for pests: cover crops with fleece and nets, and also use traps and biological controls. Mulch with compost, grass mowings and other organic materials, to suppress weeds and reduce water loss. Thin apples and pear fruitlets after the 'June drop'.

SOWING AND PLANTING

Vegetables and herbs

- Sow lettuces, rocket, kohl rabi and other salad crops every few weeks (although their peak sowing period has passed), to avoid disappointing gaps later.
- Sow Brussels Witloof chicory for forcing – June is the last time you can do this (p.141).
- Sow leaf chicories outdoors (p.141).
- Sow pumpkin and squashes (if you haven't already) to give them sufficient time to fill out and mature (p.176).
- Sow mooli radishes, Chinese cabbages and other oriental greens during the final week of the month, because they often bolt if sown before the summer solstice (21 June).
- Sow late leeks, broccoli and calabrese; plus carrots and beetroot for winter storage.
- Sow swedes now, if you garden south of the Pennines. With a bit of luck, they'll escape powdery mildew (p.184).
- Continue to plant out vegetables sown in earlier months, but make sure that seedlings are properly hardened off.
- Take special care with delicate vegetables, such as aubergines, courgettes, cucumbers, peppers, pumpkins and sweet potatoes, by providing protection during the first week or so.

- Plant out sweet corn in a grid formation to aid pollination – they'll mature a lot quicker if planted through polythene (p.186).
- Plant tomatoes outside, preferably in a sheltered spot (p.190).
- Sow and transplant all herbs outdoors, even basil.

Fruit

- Plant Cape gooseberries outdoors in a sheltered spot (p.237).
- Plant melon seedlings in a cold greenhouse or cold frame (p.238).

VEGETABLES YOU CAN SOW NOW

French beans	Celtuce	Kohl rabi	Purslane (summer)
Runner beans	Chicories	Land cress	Radishes
Beetroot	Corn salad	Leeks (late)	Rocket
Leaf beet	Courgettes	Lettuces	Spring onions
Broccoli	Cucumbers	Oriental greens	Squashes (winter)
Calabrese	Endive	Peas	Swedes
Carrots	Florence fennel	Pumpkins	Turnips

VEGETABLES YOU CAN PLANT NOW

Aubergines	Celeriac	Globe artichokes	Squashes (winter)
Brussels sprouts	Celery	Kales	Sweet corn
Cabbages	Courgettes	Leeks	Sweet potatoes
Calabrese	Cucumbers	Peppers	Tomatoes
Cauliflowers	Florence fennel	Pumpkins	

CULTIVATION

Vegetables and herbs

- Water regularly, especially lettuces, spinach, other leafy vegetables and water-sensitive crops like celeriac.
- Do not water peas until after flowering (p.168).
- Mulch crops with compost and wilted grass clippings, to conserve water.
- Feed plants growing under cover, and in pots, grow-bags and other containers, with comfrey liquid or another organic liquid feed. Use it on other crops such as leeks, celeriac, celery and globe artichokes (p.69).
- Hoe and hand-weed regularly, to keep weeds under control.
- Compost weeds and vegetable waste. Water the heap in dry weather.
- Remove side shoots from indeterminate (cordon) tomatoes (p.190).
- Earth up potatoes (p.173).
- Thin out carrot, beetroot, lettuces and other direct-sown vegetable seedlings.
- June is the best month for taking softwood cuttings from mint, sage, thyme, lemon balm, tarragon, marjoram and rosemary (p.111).
- Pinch out the growing tips of mint, sage, thyme and lovage, to encourage new growth and a bushy habit.
- Propagate rosemary by layering (p.112).
- Put up lacewing chambers and ladybird nests, to provide overwintering accommodation for these helpful predators (p.109).
- Apply light shading to glasshouses, to reduce scorching risk.

Fruit

- Water all fruit, especially in prolonged dry spells, to assist fruiting and prevent splitting. A prolonged soaking is better than more frequent, but briefer, watering (p.92).
- Tie-in blackberries and hybrid berries (p.205).
- Pull up (don't cut) raspberry suckers (p.228).
- Mulch crops with compost, straw and wilted grass clippings, to conserve water.
- Thin fruits of apples and pears (after the 'June drop'), also peaches, plums, apricots and nectarines.
- Remove strawberry runners, or layer them if you want more plants (p.235).

- Feed glasshouse- and container-grown fruit with an organic liquid fertilizer, and any other fruit that appears not to be doing very well (p.69).
- Spray strawberries with a foliar feed every two weeks until ripening (p.69).
- Pinch back new shoots of figs (p.214).
- Train wall-trained cherries, peaches and nectarines.
- Stop laterals on vines and thin out bunches of grapes (p.218).
- Prune fan-trained apricots and plums.
- At the end of the month, remove laterals from gooseberries and red and white currants.
- Support plum and damson branches with timber props, if they're heavy with fruit.

PESTS AND DISEASES

Vegetables and herbs

- Protect peas with fleece against pea moth (p.168).
- Activate defensive measures against slugs and snails (p.87).
- Pick off asparagus beetles from asparagus plants (p.117).
- Place collars around brassicas to deter cabbage root flies (p.133).
- Pinch out the tips of blackfly-infested broad beans (p.120).
- Protect crops (especially brassicas) from pigeons (p.132).
- Protect crops with fleece against flea beetles, carrot flies and other troublesome insect pests (p.87).
- Inspect crops for aphids and take appropriate action.
- Control glasshouse whitefly using the biocontrol *Encarsia formosa* (p.88).

Fruit

- Inspect strawberries for signs of grey mould, and treat accordingly (p.91).
- Check all fruit for signs of aphid attack and take appropriate action.
- Inspect gooseberries and red and white currants for sawfly damage.
- Spray mildew-affected gooseberries and blackcurrants with an organic fungicide, or remove foliage by hand (p.216).
- Hang up apple codling moth and plum fruit moth traps.
- Remove any apple or pear shoots that are badly infected by powdery mildew (p.91).
- Check vines for scale insects and mildew, and treat accordingly (p.218).

HARVESTING, PRESERVING AND STORING

- Start to harvest broad beans, peas, globe artichoke buds and hearts, lots of salads and leafy greens and, best of all, the first new potatoes – all new-season crops that arrive in force this month.
- Say goodbye to asparagus, which needs to recover its strength for next year.
- Pick tomatoes now, if you have a heated glasshouse (and sowed early enough). Most of us will have to wait another month for that pleasure.
- Harvest June-ripening fruits, including strawberries, rhubarb, gooseberries, raspberries, sweet cherries and glasshouse melons. These sound tempting, but it is nothing compared with the treats in store next month!

VEGETABLES YOU CAN HARVEST NOW

Asparagus	Calabrese	Kohl rabi	Rocket
Broad beans	Carrots	Land cress	Spinach
French beans	Cauliflowers	Lettuces	Spring onions
Beetroot	Claytonia	Onions	Tomatoes
Leaf beet	Corn salad	Peas	Turnips
Broccoli	Garlic	Potatoes	
Cabbages	Globe artichokes	Radishes	

JULY Jobs for mid-summer

The garden is in full swing, with fruit and vegetables aplenty. Sow oriental greens and other hardy vegetables to provide fresh greens throughout the winter. Keep on top of your weeds, putting them and other crop waste onto the compost heap.

SOWING AND PLANTING

Vegetables and herbs

- Sow leaf beet, corn salad, claytonia, carrots, radicchio (red chicory) and the oriental greens: mizuna, mibuna, Chinese broccoli and green-in-the-snow. They're hardy and can withstand winter frosts.

- Sow French and dwarf runner beans, though these will require protection from autumn onwards. Sow early, mildew-resistant peas, and you stand a fair chance of eating fresh peas as late as October (p.168).

- Transplant seedlings of leeks, broccoli, Brussels sprouts, cabbages, kales and cauliflowers into their final positions, or buy plug plants, if you didn't get around to sowing them in time.

- Sow rape kales – wonderfully hardy vegetables that will see you safely across the 'hungry gap' next April/May (p.154).

- Sow spring cabbages, swedes and winter radishes, to tide you through the long winter months.

- Fill empty spaces with catch crops of lettuce or summer radish; alternatively, sow a quick-maturing green manure.

- Sow parsley, coriander, chervil and dill, to provide fresh herbs for the coming months.

Fruit

- Plant bare-rooted strawberries this month and you could be eating the fruit next year (p.234).

- Plant pot-grown strawberries, and all other container-grown fruits, at any time.

VEGETABLES YOU CAN SOW NOW

French beans	Claytonia	Peas
Runner beans (dwarf varieties)	Corn salad	Purslane (summer)
Beetroot	Endive	Radishes
Leaf beet	Florence fennel	Rocket
Broccoli	Kales	Spring onions
Cabbages	Kohl rabi	Swedes
Calabrese	Land cress	Turnips
Carrots	Lettuces	
Chicories	Oriental greens	

VEGETABLES YOU CAN PLANT NOW

Broccoli	Cabbages	Chicories	Endive
Brussels sprouts	Cauliflowers	Cucumbers	Kales

CULTIVATION

Vegetables and herbs

- Compost weeds and vegetable waste. Water the heap in dry weather.
- Feed container-grown plants, those under cover, and nutrient-hungry crops, like leeks and marrows, with an organic liquid fertilizer (p.69).
- Mulch crops with compost and wilted grass clippings, to conserve water.
- Pinch out the growing points of runner beans when they reach the top of the canes.
- Hand-pollinate courgettes and marrows, if the weather turns cold and wet (p.144).
- Hoe and hand-weed regularly.
- Earth-up maincrop potatoes (p.173).
- Fold cauliflower leaves over the curds, to protect them from the sun (p.137).
- Water leafy vegetables, and other water-sensitive crops, regularly.
- Tie-in tomato plants and pinch out side shoots (indeterminate types only) (p.190).
- Thin out any carrots, beetroot, lettuces and all other direct-sown vegetable seedlings.
- Take softwood cuttings of lavender and thyme (p.11).
- Trim lavenders, after they've flowered.
- Put up hibernating quarters for ladybirds and lacewings (p.109).
- Apply shading to glasshouses.

Fruit

- Water all fruit, especially in prolonged dry spells.
- Tie-in blackberries and hybrid berries (p.205).
- Prune summer-fruiting raspberries after fruiting, and pull up suckers (p.228).
- Mulch crops with compost, straw and wilted grass clippings, to conserve water.
- Thin apples, pears, peaches, apricots, nectarines and plums.

- Remove and compost strawberry runners and old leaves.
- Feed glasshouse- and container-grown fruit (and any other fruit that appears to be not growing well), with an organic liquid fertilizer (p.69).
- Spray strawberries with a foliar feed every two weeks until ripening (p.69).
- Summer-prune cordon and espalier apples and pears.
- Tie-in laterals on vines, and remove unwanted foliage (p.218).
- Prune laterals of gooseberries and red and white currants, to open up the bushes.
- If they are carrying a full crop, support plums and damsons with timber props.

PESTS AND DISEASES

Vegetables and herbs

- Remove leaves of potatoes and tomatoes at the first signs of blight (p.174).
- Protect peas with fleece against pea moths (p.168).
- Inspect crops for aphids, and take appropriate action.
- Activate defensive measures against slugs and snails (p.87).
- Pick off asparagus beetles from asparagus plants (p.117).
- Place cabbage root fly barriers around brassica plants (p.133).
- Pinch out the tips of blackfly-infested broad beans (p.120).
- Net brassicas against pigeons and cabbage white butterflies.
- Protect crops with fleece against flea beetles (the problem lessens after midsummer), carrot flies and other troublesome insect pests.
- Control glasshouse whiteflies using *Encarsia formosa* (p.88).

Fruit

- Inspect strawberries for signs of grey mould and treat accordingly (p.91).
- Check all fruit for aphid attack and take appropriate action.
- Inspect gooseberries and red and white currants for sawfly damage.
- Spray mildew-affected gooseberries and blackcurrants with an organic fungicide, or remove foliage by hand.
- Take down codling moth and plum fruit moth traps.
- Wrap corrugated cardboard around apple trees, to trap pupating codling moths (p.203).
- Remove any apple or pear shoots that are badly infected by powdery mildew (p.91).

- Check vines for scale insects and mildew, and treat accordingly (p.218).
- Control glasshouse red spider mites, using biological controls (p.89).

HARVESTING, PRESERVING AND STORING

- Make sure you have enough bottles, jars, plastic bags and containers, and everything else you need, to deal with the flow of surplus produce, as you bottle, freeze, juice and jam your way through the summer. During the next few months, with the garden bursting with produce, you're going to be busy!
- Dry herbs, like rosemary, thyme, lemon balm, summer savoury, lavender and tarragon.
- Collect seeds of angelica and caraway.

VEGETABLES YOU CAN HARVEST NOW

Broad beans	Celery	Globe artichokes	Rocket
French beans	Celtuce	Kohl rabi	Shallots
Runner beans	Chicories	Lettuces	Spinach
Beetroot	Claytonia	Land cress	Spring onions
Leaf beet	Corn salad	Onions	Sweet corn
Broccoli	Courgettes	Peas	Tomatoes
Cabbages	Cucumbers	Peppers	Turnips
Calabrese	Endive	Potatoes	
Carrots	Florence fennel	Purslane (summer)	
Cauliflowers	Garlic	Radishes	

FRUIT YOU CAN HARVEST NOW

Apples	Damsons	Peaches
Apricots	Figs	Plums
Black and hybrid berries	Gages	Raspberries
Blackcurrants	Gooseberries	Red and white currants
Blueberries	Melons	Rhubarb
Cherries (sweet)	Nectarines	Strawberries

AUGUST Jobs for late summer

There's still time to sow winter salads, but be quick about it! Pot up herbs to provide winter pickings. Summer-prune espalier, cordon and other trained forms of fruit trees, and soft fruit.

SOWING AND PLANTING

Vegetables and herbs

- Sow a final crop of leafy summer salads, carrots, Florence fennel and kohl rabi, but don't delay beyond the first week to ten days of the month.
- Sow oriental greens now, and they'll provide you with regular pickings of salad leaves throughout winter, if grown in a polytunnel or cold greenhouse (p.164).
- Sow rape kales and spring cabbages for eating next spring (p.154).
- Sow winter-hardy varieties of spinach for cropping in autumn, and again in April and May (p.182).
- Sow Japanese onions now, but timing (which is everything) is dependent on where you live (p.162).
- Sow an early variety of turnip towards the end of the month, to provide a supply of mini-turnips and nutritious green tops next spring (p.194).
- Sow parsley, dill and coriander.
- Pot-up sufficient chives, mint, parsley and marjoram plants for a winter supply of fresh herbs indoors.
- Sow winter-hardy green manures, such as grazing rye or tares, on spare land (p.106).

Fruit

- Plant bare-rooted and pot-grown strawberries (p.234).

VEGETABLES YOU CAN SOW NOW			
Leaf beet	Corn salad	Kohl rabi	Radishes
Cabbages	Endive	Lettuces	Rocket
Carrots	Florence fennel	Onions	Spinach
Claytonia	Kales	Oriental greens	Turnips

VEGETABLES YOU CAN PLANT NOW

Broccoli   Calabrese   Endive

CULTIVATION

Vegetables and herbs

- Feed container-grown and nutrient-hungry plants with an organic liquid fertilizer (p.69).
- Pinch out the growing points of runner beans when they reach the top of the canes.
- Remove any leaves shading fruits of pumpkins and squashes, so that they can ripen.
- Blanch trench celery stems, using corrugated cardboard (p.140).
- Fold cauliflower leaves over the curds, to protect them from the sun (p.137).
- Water leafy vegetables, and other water-sensitive crops, regularly.
- Tie-in tomato plants and pinch out side shoots (indeterminate types only) (p.190).
- Thin carrots, beetroot, lettuces and other direct-sown vegetable seedlings.
- Compost weeds and vegetable waste. Water the heap in dry weather.
- Take softwood cuttings of lavender, thyme, tarragon and rosemary (p.111).

Fruit

- Tie-in blackberries and hybrid berries (p.205).
- Prune summer-fruiting raspberries after fruiting, and pull up suckers (p.228).
- Water all fruit, especially in prolonged dry spells.
- Feed glasshouse- and container-grown fruit (and any other fruit that appears to be not thriving) with an organic liquid fertilizer (p.69).
- Summer-prune cordon and espalier apples and pears.
- Tie-in laterals on vines, and remove unwanted foliage (p.218).
- Prune fan-trained plums, cherries, peaches and nectarines.
- Cut out diseased and awkwardly growing shoots of mature bush plums and cherries.

PESTS AND DISEASES

Vegetables and herbs

- Remove leaves of potatoes and tomatoes, if blight strikes (p.174).
- Activate defensive measures against slugs and snails (p.87).
- Net brassicas against pigeons and cabbage white butterflies.
- Protect crops with fleece against carrot flies and other troublesome insect pests.
- Remove tomatoes affected by blossom end rot, and water more frequently (p.193).
- Control glasshouse whiteflies, using the biocontrol *Encarsia formosa* (p.88).

Fruit

- Check all fruit for aphid attack, and take appropriate action.
- Inspect gooseberries and red and white currants for third-generation sawfly damage.
- Remove any apple or pear shoots that are badly infected by powdery mildew (p.91).
- Check vines for scale insects and mildew, and treat accordingly (p.218).
- Control glasshouse red spider mites, using biological controls (p.89).
- Hang up wasp traps amongst peaches, nectarines, plums and gages.
- Remove and destroy fruits infected with brown rot, on apples, pears and plums (p.91).

HARVESTING, PRESERVING AND STORING

- There is only so much bottling and jam-, jelly- and chutney-making that anyone can do in a day, so if you run out of time, freeze any surplus to be processed when things have quietened down.
- In the meantime, enjoy the pleasure of eating delicious, home-grown fruits and vegetables.

VEGETABLES YOU CAN HARVEST NOW

Aubergines	Claytonia	Peppers
Broad beans	Corn salad	Potatoes
French beans	Courgettes	Pumpkins
Runner beans	Cucumbers	Purslane (summer)
Beetroot	Florence fennel	Radishes
Leaf beet	Garlic	Rocket
Broccoli	Globe artichokes	Shallots
Cabbages	Kohl rabi	Spinach
Calabrese	Leeks	Spring onions
Carrots	Lettuces	Squashes (winter)
Cauliflowers	Land cress	Sweet corn
Celery	Onions	Tomatoes
Celtuce	Oriental greens	Turnips
Chicories	Peas	

FRUIT YOU CAN HARVEST NOW

Apples	Figs	Pears
Apricots	Gages	Plums
Black and hybrid berries	Gooseberries	Raspberries
Blackcurrants	Melons	Redcurrants
Blueberries	Mulberries	Rhubarb
Cherries (acid)	Nectarines	Strawberries (perpetual)
Damsons	Peaches	

SUMMER FEATURE 1 Dealing with vegetable pests and diseases

We briefly described some of the ways in which organic gardeners cope with pests and diseases on pages 14–17. Now we'll examine these in a little more detail.

Barriers

The most widely used pest-control barrier is netting, which is manufactured in sizes ranging from 80mm/3in (for use against pigeons), through 20mm/¾in (for use on fruit cages to keep out birds), to 7mm/¼in (for use against butterflies and moths) and finally down to the extremely fine-meshed fleeces and fabrics that no pests can penetrate. Many gardeners cover crops with fleece, or products like the much tougher Enviromesh, from sowing through to harvest.

All manner of ingenious barriers have been devised to frustrate slugs and snails – most of them abrasive to the creatures' soft underbellies. Traditional barriers include crushed egg shells, gravel, holly leaves and soot, which are scattered around sensitive plants. Newer materials, designed with container-grown plants in mind, include wool pellets, which swell to form a coarse mat when watered, and copper tape, mats and rings, which administer a mild electric shock when slugs and snails come into contact with them. The bottle cloches, mentioned on page 72, also protect seedlings from slug and snail attack, and if pushed a finger's depth into the soil, they will defeat ground-living grubs, such as cutworms, wireworms, chafer bugs and leatherjackets, all of which chew roots and stems.

Traps

An empty yogurt pot filled with beer, if sunk into the soil, so that the rim is only 1cm/½in above the surface, is an irresistible magnet to slugs and snails, which crawl in and then (presumably inebriated!) are incapable of climbing out.

Yellow plastic sticky traps, hung up in glass-houses, attract whiteflies and aphids. They can also be used to monitor whitefly numbers, as an aid to knowing the right time to introduce *Encarsia* biological control.

As for controlling mice and moles, traps are the only realistic way.

DIY slug trap

Hand picking

Many pests deposit their eggs in one place, so on hatching they're all together. If they are caught at this stage, the infestation can be nipped in the bud, before the pests disperse to other parts of the plant. Aphids (e.g. greenflies and blackflies) can be squashed en masse between thumb and

►

forefinger, and caterpillars picked off individually, or whole leaves removed and destroyed. Torchlight expeditions to catch night-feeding slugs and snails can be surprisingly effective. If you don't have any chickens or ducks to feed the slugs and snails to, drown slugs in a bucket of salty water and squash snails underfoot.

Garden hygiene

Many diseases are spread via dead and dying leaves, so ensuring that these are removed to the compost heap, or disposed of in the dustbin, is a top priority. Slugs and snails will make a home underneath mulching matting, rotting timber and other debris (the timber of raised beds is a favourite spot), so clear up any obvious 'hot spots'. It's also worth checking underneath pots for vine weevils, which hide there during the day (and New Zealand flatworms, which devour earthworms, if you live in the wetter areas of the UK).

Pesticides

Only a handful of pesticides are approved for use by organic gardeners, and they're all natural products. Some, like pyrethrum, are derived from plants, and break down quickly in the environment, posing little threat to wildlife. Insecticides, such as rapeseed oil, and those based on fatty acids (insecticidal soaps), block the breathing pores of insects, killing them by suffocation. They can be used against aphids, caterpillars, flea beetles, whiteflies, mealybugs and red spider mites. Slug pellets based on ferric phosphate harm only slugs and snails, unlike conventional slug pellets made from metaldehyde or methiocarb, which can kill any cats and dogs that mistakenly eat them, and wild birds and hedgehogs unfortunate enough to consume any poisoned slugs.

In the past, organic gardeners used fungicides made from sulphur and copper (Bordeaux mixture), but concerns about copper build-up in the soil, after repeated use, led to it being no longer recommended. Potassium bicarbonate has fungicidal properties, and can be used for treating powdery and downy mildew on lettuces, cucumbers and other crops.

Our advice is to only use organically approved pesticides as a last resort, and never spray plants when in flower, to make absolutely sure you don't kill any bees.

SUMMER FEATURE 2 Biological pest control

Instead of using pesticides to control pests, an increasing number of gardeners are turning to 'biocontrols' which make use of each pest's natural enemies. Some, like ladybirds and lacewings, consume a varied diet, and feed on several different species, but most biocontrols are pest-specific and have only one host.

In glasshouses, for example, a tiny parasitic wasp called *Encarsia*, which is no bigger than a pin head, lays its eggs inside whitefly larvae.

►

Upon hatching, they consume the whiteflies from the inside out, eventually emerging as adults to repeat the cycle. A closely related wasp, called *Aphidius*, ensures that aphids suffer a similar fate. Another biocontrol, called *Phytoseiulus*, preys on the red spider mite, which is a serious pest of cucumbers, tomatoes and other glasshouse crops, and an Australian ladybird called *Cryptolaemus* makes short work of waxy-coated mealybugs – the scourge of indoor grape vines.

This may all sound terribly technical, but they're actually very easy to manage and highly effective, as long as conditions are right. Most of these beneficial organisms flourish only when the humidity is at least 60 per cent, and when night-time temperatures don't drop below 16°C/61°F, so they shouldn't be introduced into unheated glasshouses, conservatories or polytunnels before late May or early June. It's a mistake to wait until pest numbers have built up to plague proportions: they should be used when the first adult pests are spotted. Being live creatures, they're available only by mail order from specialist suppliers (see page 305), who send them out as 'seeded' cardboard strips, to hang amongst the plants.

Outdoors, parasitic nematodes are used to combat a wide range of mostly ground-dwelling pests, each type of pest having its own specific parasite. These microscopic creatures burrow inside the pests and release bacteria that initially stop them from feeding, and then kill them. The nematodes reproduce inside their dead hosts and then emerge to seek out new prey. Whilst this is an unpleasant end for the pests, all other living creatures, including ourselves, are unharmed.

Until a few years ago, vine weevils, chafer grubs and leatherjackets were the main species targeted by nematodes. They are marketed under the name of Nemasys and are applied by mixing them with water, and spraying them onto affected land with a watering can or sprayer. Nemaslug followed, aimed at the tiny underground slugs that devastate potatoes. There is also a nematode that will deal with cabbage caterpillars.

In 2010, the manufacturer of Nemasys (Becker Underwood) launched a product called Grow Your Own, containing a mixture of nematode species. It claims to control carrot root flies, cabbage root flies, leatherjackets, cutworms, onion flies, ants, sciarid flies, cabbage caterpillars, gooseberry sawflies, thrips and codling moths. It's too early to say how useful this will turn out to be, but consumer experience with other Nemasys products has shown that they work well, providing the soil is moist and sufficiently warm. The downside is that regular applications are needed – every six weeks in the case of Nemaslug, and fortnightly for Grow Your Own.

New biological controls are coming onto the market all the time, and preparations involving parasitic fungi are in the pipeline, which could revolutionize organic disease control. Watch this space!

SUMMER FEATURE 3 **Weed control**

Getting rid of weeds is a never-ending task, and if they're allowed to grow unchecked, they'll soon overwhelm even the tidiest of plots. Annual weeds, like groundsel, chickweed and fat hen, which grow, seed and die in a single season, are the easiest to control. They should be hoed off while still small, preferably on a sunny day, so that the foliage quickly wilts *in situ*. Larger weeds, and those growing within, rather than between, rows, are best removed manually, using a small hand fork. The important thing with annual weeds is to prevent them from running to seed: a single fat hen plant can produce over 70,000 seedlings!

Perennial weeds have roots that are permanently present in the soil, and present more of a challenge. Some, like docks and dandelions, have long taproots that penetrate deep into the subsoil; others, such as couch grass, ground elder and bindweed, produce tangled mats of mostly shallow, horizontal roots. Hoeing perennial weeds is a recipe for disaster, as you simply slice the roots into fragments, all of which have the potential to grow into new plants. Rotovators can have a similar effect, and should only be used in dry weather in early summer, repeated several weeks later.

Thorough digging is the most effective solution, checking all the time to make sure that every last scrap of root is removed. Digging is best done after heavy rain, when the soil is moistened to a considerable depth, and the roots come out cleanly. Before committing perennial weeds to the compost heap, they need drying to a crisp on wire trays in the sunshine, to ensure that they're dead. Annual weeds can go on straightaway.

Mulching is an alternative, and less energetic, method of controlling weeds, but it may take two or more years to clean land thoroughly. The principle behind mulching is to cover the soil with a light-excluding material, which prevents weeds from producing leaves and shoots, and hence photosynthesising. Newspapers and cardboard make good mulches, especially if disguised with straw or grass clippings, but they need to be replaced more frequently than the various woven polypropylene fabrics sold for controlling weeds. These are better than black polythene sheeting, which damages other soil life by restricting air and water. We used to recommend woollen carpets, but that was before manufacturers began adding pesticides to kill carpet beetle larvae.

Weeds in paths can sometimes be removed mechanically, but are more easily killed with a hand-held, propane-powered flame gun. This works not by incinerating them, but by bursting the cell walls. The plants wilt and die not long afterwards. There's also a weedkiller on the market, based on acetic acid, which has organic approval for paths and spot weeding. We've not tried it, but the manufacturers claim that it will kill perennial weeds, though several treatments may be necessary.

SUMMER FEATURE 4 **Fruit diseases**

Vegetables can be moved around the garden in a crop rotation, to prevent soil-borne diseases from getting out of hand, but this is not possible with fruit. Other control methods have to be used instead.

Hygiene is hugely important. Many diseases, like cankers and diebacks (which cause lesions and girdling of twigs and branches, cracks in the bark, weeping gum, and mummified fruits), can be prevented from spreading by pruning and destroying infected wood and fruits. Powdery mildew is another common fruit disease, easily recognized by the grey-white coating on young leaves and shoots in summer, which become distorted in winter. These sources of infection should be removed as soon as they're spotted, and all dead leaves picked up and composted. This advice also applies to attacks of grey mould, which show as a furry greyish mould on the leaves of top and soft fruit, particularly apples and strawberries. Mummified fruits caused by brown rot, however, which usually starts on fruits as soft dark patches, and eventually causes them to shrivel and die, must go straight into the dustbin.

Scab, on the other hand, is a hugely disfiguring disease of apples and pears, causing brown-black blotches on leaves, and corky scabs on fruits; but the damage is entirely cosmetic and can be simply peeled away. Some varieties are more susceptible than others, but there are plenty of scab-resistant varieties to choose from. Resistant varieties exist, in fact, for all of the previously mentioned diseases, and, when planting fruit, it makes sense to seek them out – we have included examples throughout Part 3.

Most fruit trees, canes, bushes and vines can be attacked by virus diseases, producing assorted symptoms of leaf yellowing, mottling, mosaic patterns and rings. Viruses are usually transmitted in the saliva of aphids, and there's not a lot you can do about them, other than removing affected wood, and occasionally the entire plant. If viruses are suspected, don't propagate from infected stock, and always buy from reputable suppliers who stock virus-free plants.

Other protection/control methods include regular spraying with seaweed foliar feeds, which enhance plants' defence mechanisms; and pruning, which helps to prevent the establishment of fungal diseases, by ensuring air-flow through the open centres of trees and bushes. A protective spray with an organic 'winter wash' will kill aphid adults and eggs, scale insects and other pests.

Regular mulching with compost and other organic matter; periodic feeding with organic fertilizers; and watering (to prevent drought stress) will ensure healthy fruit that is able to withstand disease attack.

SUMMER FEATURE 5 **Watering**

No one can accurately predict how global warming will alter our climate, but the general view appears to be that future summers will be hotter and drier than at present. It remains to be seen how true this turns out to be, but there is little doubt that ever-increasing demand for water, especially in southern England, will result in hosepipe bans and higher charges.

On page 17 we mentioned some of the things that can be done to cut down water consumption, like not using overhead sprinklers, and mulching wherever possible. Water is vital throughout a plant's life, but some stages (when seedlings are transplanted, for example) are more critical than others, and can vary from crop to crop. If they're to grow successfully, salads and other leafy greens need water pretty much all of the time, but if root crops are given the same amount, it can result in excess foliage at the expense of the roots. The optimum time for watering root crops is when the roots or tubers are forming: in the case of potatoes, when the tubers are marble-sized. With 'fruiting' vegetables, like tomatoes, beans and sweet corn, the key watering times are when flowering begins and when the fruits are swelling. However, if you give them too much water, it can lessen the flavour.

If possible, water when the air is cool, early in the morning and in the evening, so that evaporation losses are minimized. Always give the ground a thorough soaking, so that water penetrates deep into the soil – just wetting the surface is useless.

Most garden centres sell irrigation kits that can be connected to mains water, or rainwater butts. Some of these make use of porous pipes that allow water to seep out throughout their length; others are more sophisticated and have on/off valves and nozzles that allow for more accurate water delivery. The obvious use for these is in glasshouses and for containers and hanging baskets, but they can be equally effective in the vegetable garden, and work particularly well with permanent beds, where water can be directed, as and when needed. We have such a system ourselves, which is time-controlled to come on at night.

All gardeners should 'harvest' rainwater, and there are many ingenious collecting devices on the market, in addition to traditional butts. It's surprising how much water can be collected from a small shed or glasshouse. Plants prefer rainwater, which is softer than most tap-water supplies, and it's essential for acid-loving species, such as pot-grown blueberries.

Recycled, or 'grey', water has a place in the garden, but with reservations attached. Waste from dishwashers and washing machines contains caustic detergent residues, which can harm plants, so they should definitely not be used. Soapy bath and shower water is milder, but it's not generally recommended for use on vegetables, because of the risk of taint, unless it's filtered through a tub containing graded layers of sand and gravel. 'Grey' water smells, if left to stand for any length of time, so it should be used immediately and not stored.

CHAPTER 6

Autumn

After all the frenetic activity in the garden throughout the summer, things gradually wind down during the autumn months, as the nights draw in and the temperature cools. This is the time to stock up the larder by bottling, freezing, and making jams, pickles, chutneys and preserves from all the wonderful fruits and vegetables you are harvesting by the bucket load.

There's not too much to do outdoors, but September is not too late to sow seeds of salad crops in a glasshouse or polytunnel, to eat during the winter. As vegetable crops are lifted, leaving empty ground, soil-enhancing green manure plants can take their place. These cover the land with a protective layer of foliage, and play a valuable role in preventing nutrients from being washed from the soil by heavy winter rains.

An early crop of peas and broad beans, to be enjoyed next year, can be sown in October, but only a few varieties stand the winter successfully, so they must be chosen carefully. Garlic and winter-hardy onion sets can also go in now.

All the leaves that have fallen should be raked into piles, and placed in plastic sacks, or an easy-to-construct leafmould container, to break down slowly into an excellent soil conditioner.

Frosts begin to be a problem at this time of the year, usually arriving towards the end of October (unless you're extremely fortunate), putting paid to many sensitive crops.

Autumn is a good time to install a variety of wildlife-friendly features in the garden, such as a pond, or winter hibernation habitats for beneficial creatures like ladybirds and lacewings, frogs and hedgehogs. Organic gardeners rely on these stalwart friends to help keep pests in check.

By November, the ground has cooled considerably, but it's sufficiently warm to enable soft and tree fruit to be planted now. This will give them a significant advantage over those not planted until the spring, because by becoming established, with some good root growth, before the winter sets in, they will be ready to burst into life once the ground starts to heat up. Any warm, dry days remaining can be spent weeding, tidying up and preparing for winter.

SEPTEMBER Jobs for early autumn

You can spend lots of time in the kitchen this month, freezing and bottling, and making jam, chutney and other preserves. Finish pruning stone fruits by the middle of the month. Install hedgehog boxes and other wildlife-friendly overwintering accommodation.

SOWING AND PLANTING

Vegetables and herbs

- Sow Chinese cabbages, pak choi, komatsuma, mizuna, mibuna and other winter salads, in a cold glasshouse, polytunnel or cold frame.
- Sow claytonia, corn salad and land cress. They fare better if protected by cloches, although they're hardy enough to go outdoors.
- Sow turnips, to get a crop of mini-roots and turnip tops in the spring (p.194).
- Plant overwintering onion sets later this month (but be prepared for some losses) (p.162).
- Sow hardy green manures as vegetables are harvested and land cleared, to provide a protective green mantle over the soil during winter (p.106).

Fruit

- Mid-September is the latest time to plant strawberries (p.234).

VEGETABLES YOU CAN SOW NOW

Claytonia   Oriental greens   Spring onions

Corn salad   Radishes   Turnips

Land cress   Rocket

Lettuces   Spinach

CULTIVATION

Vegetables and herbs

- Put boards under pumpkins and squashes, to prevent rotting.
- Stake Brussels sprouts and kales.
- Turn the contents of compost bins, and incorporate bean and tomato haulm (stalks), and other green material, to encourage it to heat up.
- Blanch trench celery stems with newspapers or corrugated cardboard (p.140).
- Blanch cardoons (p.196).
- Collect leaves, and begin a leafmould pile (p.105).
- Trim bay, lavender, marjoram, and other shrubby herbs, before the first frosts arrive.
- Take pots of basil indoors – to a cold glasshouse or windowsill.

Fruit

- Tie-in blackberries and hybrid berries (p.205).
- Complete pruning of all stone fruit by mid-September.
- Prune blackcurrants (p.207).
- Remove immature figs that are gooseberry-sized or larger, leaving only pea-sized embryo fruits (p.213).
- Remove leaves that are shading figs, preventing them from ripening (p.213).
- Tie-in new raspberry canes, and remove any that are weak or in the wrong place (p.228).
- Propagate black and hybrid berries, by fixing the tips of young shoots to the ground with wire hoops. Sever next spring (p.205).

PESTS AND DISEASES

Vegetables and herbs

- Cut down potato haulm (stalks) in the event of blight (p.174).
- Activate defensive measures against slugs and snails (p.87).
- Net brassicas against pigeons and cabbage white butterflies.
- Check courgettes, cucumbers and peas for powdery mildew (p.144).

Fruit

- Inspect gooseberries, and red and white currants, for third-generation sawfly damage.
- Remove any apple or pear shoots that are badly infected with powdery mildew.
- Hang up wasp traps amongst top fruit.
- Remove and destroy all fruits infected with brown rot (p.91).

OTHER JOBS

- Install a hedgehog box at the base of a hedge, as a hibernation home (p.109).
- Pile up logs in a remote part of the garden, to provide winter shelter for frogs and toads (p.109).
- Order bare-rooted fruit trees and bushes from specialist nurseries.

HARVESTING, PRESERVING AND STORING

- Pick globe artichokes and broad beans, which will come to an end this month.
- Pick aubergines, courgettes, French and runner beans, which crop throughout September (unless cut down by frost).
- Listen to weather reports, and if overnight frost threatens, drape fleece over sensitive plants.
- Uproot tomato plants, and hang in a cool glasshouse or conservatory, to ripen the green fruits; or pick and ripen in drawers.
- Pick most of the top and soft fruits that ripened in August, with blackcurrants and gooseberries being notable exceptions.
- Pick autumn-fruiting raspberries, which take over from late summer varieties.

- Pick the first outdoor grapes and Cape gooseberries.
- Bottle, freeze and process!
- Be creative with all those green tomatoes!
- Lift root crops and store in sand, but if time presses, leave them in the ground for another month – they won't come to any harm.

VEGETABLES YOU CAN HARVEST NOW

Aubergines	Cauliflowers	Hamburg parsley	Purslane (summer)
Broad beans	Celeriac	Kohl rabi	Radishes
French beans	Celery	Leeks	Rocket
Runner beans	Chicories	Lettuces	Spinach
Beetroot	Claytonia	Land cress	Spring onions
Leaf beet	Corn salad	Onions	Squashes (winter)
Broccoli	Courgettes	Oriental greens	Sweet corn
Brussels sprouts	Cucumbers	Peas	Sweet potatoes
Cabbages	Endive	Peppers	Tomatoes
Calabrese	Florence fennel	Potatoes	Turnips
Carrots	Globe artichokes	Pumpkins	

FRUIT YOU CAN HARVEST NOW

Apples	Figs	Pears
Apricots	Gages	Plums
Black and hybrid berries	Grapes	Raspberries (autumn fruiting)
Blueberries	Kiwi fruit	Rhubarb
Cape gooseberries	Melons	Strawberries (perpetual)
Cherries (acid)	Nectarines	
Damsons	Peaches	

OCTOBER Jobs for mid-autumn

Sow winter-hardy broad beans and peas, and plant out garlic and over-wintering onion sets. Rake up fallen leaves and pile them up to make leaf-mould. Harvest apples and pears for easting fresh and winter storage.

SOWING AND PLANTING

Vegetables and herbs

- Sow Aquadulce Claudia or Imperial Green Longpod broad beans, and Feltham First, Douce Provence or Pilot peas. Ideally, protect the peas with cloches.
- Plant garlic – the longer it stays in the ground, the bigger the bulbs (p.149).
- Plant onion sets that are bred to withstand winter conditions, like Radar (p.162).
- Sow hardy salad vegetables (see below) - this is absolutely your last opportunity.
- Sow parsley seeds now, if you have a propagator, for a windowsill supply of this vitamin C-rich garnish (p.242).
- Plant spring cabbage plants, spacing them close together – the thinnings will provide you with your first spring greens of the new year (p.132).
- Plant hardy perennial herbs now, while the soil is still relatively warm.

Fruit

- Sow alpine strawberry seeds in a seed tray or modules, in a cold greenhouse, for planting out next May (p.233).

VEGETABLES YOU CAN SOW OR PLANT NOW

Broad beans	Garlic	Peas
Cabbages (spring)	Land cress	Radishes
Claytonia	Lettuces	
Corn salad	Onion (sets)	

CULTIVATION

Vegetables and herbs

- Dig land that will not be cropped over winter.
- Add ground or dolomite lime to land that has become too acid (p.47).
- Earth up stems and/or stake Brussels sprouts and other tall brassica plants.
- Blanch trench celery stems with newspapers or corrugated cardboard (p.140).
- Earth up leeks (p.157).
- Cut down stems of Jerusalem artichokes (p.153).
- Weed recently cleared land.
- Rake up leaves, and add to the leafmould pile (p.105).
- Tidy the herb bed, removing old growth and weeds. Dress with compost or leafmould.
- Cloche parsley, chervil and any other herbs you'll want to pick during winter.
- Divide perennial herbs, such as chives, lemon balm, oregano and sage (p.111).
- Cut down and remove asparagus foliage, and mulch with compost (p.117).

Fruit

- Prepare ground for planting next month.
- Cut down old blackberry and hybrid berry canes and tie-in new growth (p.205).
- Prune blackcurrants (p.207).
- Remove any secondary growth of cordon or espalier apples and pears that has occurred since July.
- Remove gooseberry-sized or larger immature figs, leaving only pea-sized ones behind (p.213).
- Tidy strawberry beds by removing old leaves and runners, then mulch with compost (p.235).
- Complete pruning of summer-fruiting raspberries (p.228).
- Propagate gooseberries and currants, by taking hardwood cuttings (p.207).
- Re-pot any container-grown fruits that have outgrown their pots (pot-bound).

PESTS AND DISEASES

Vegetables and herbs

- Net brassicas against pigeons.
- Check brassicas for cabbage aphids and whiteflies – remove by hand, or spray with an organic insecticide (p.88).
- Remove and compost any yellowing or dead brassica leaves.
- Check courgettes, cucumbers and peas for powdery mildew (p.144).
- Remove and destroy mint leaves affected by rust.

Fruit

- Remove any apple or pear shoots that are badly infected with powdery mildew.
- Hang up wasp traps amongst top fruit.
- Remove and destroy all fruits infected with brown rot (p.91).
- Tie grease bands around the trunks of apple, pear, cherry and plum trees, to trap winter moths (p.203).
- Remove the netting from soft fruit cages, so that birds can eat insect pests hibernating in the soil.

OTHER JOBS

- Order bare-rooted fruit trees and bushes from specialist nurseries.
- Clean out glasshouses, and insulate with bubble wrap.
- Clean, bundle and store bamboo canes and pea and bean sticks for next year.

HARVESTING, PRESERVING AND STORING

- Harvest French and runner beans, courgettes, cucumbers, peppers, sweet corn, sweet potatoes and other tender vegetables, until they are killed by frost.
- Ensure that you take pumpkins, squashes and tomatoes indoors, to ripen in safety.
- Harvest root crops: parsnips, swedes, Jerusalem and Chinese artichokes, salsify and scorzonera.
- Pick the exquisite blanched inner stems and hearts of towering cardoons, which are ready now.

- Begin picking kale – the most nutritious brassica of all.
- Harvest carrots, beetroot, Hamburg parsley, swedes, celeriac, turnips and other root crops, this month or next, if you garden on heavy land. On light soils most can stay in place all winter, and be dug as needed.
- Pick autumn brassicas, such as Brussels sprouts, cabbages, cauliflowers, calabrese and broccoli, which take over from their summer-maturing cousins.
- Pick trench types of celery. They're made of sterner stuff than the self-blanching sort, which is another casualty of the frost, and will carry on cropping until Christmas and beyond.
- Pick the last of the garden peas, which finish this month. With good planning, you'll have been eating them since May, and all good things must come to an end!
- Pick hearting chicories, lettuces, spinach, rocket, summer purslane and oriental greens.
- Pick apples, pears and plums, which remain to be harvested and eaten fresh, or stored and preserved, although peaches, apricots, nectarines, figs and rhubarb have all finished.
- Pick medlars and quinces, which also ripen this month – most of them destined for uniquely aromatic jellies and preserves.

VEGETABLES YOU CAN HARVEST NOW

Aubergines (glasshouse crops)	Brussels sprouts	Celeriac
French beans	Cabbages	Celery
Runner beans (protected)	Calabrese	Chicories
Beetroot	Cardoons	Chinese artichokes
Leaf beet	Carrots	Claytonia
Broccoli	Cauliflowers	Corn salad

▶

Courgettes	Lettuces	Scorzonera
Cucumbers	Oriental greens	Spinach
Endive	Parsnips	Squashes (winter)
Florence fennel	Peas	Swedes
Hamburg parsley	Peppers	Sweet corn
Jerusalem artichokes	Pumpkins	Sweet potatoes
Kales	Purslane (summer)	Tomatoes
Kohl rabi	Radishes	Turnips
Land cress	Rocket	
Leeks	Salsify	

FRUIT YOU CAN HARVEST NOW

Apples	Grapes	Plums
Cape gooseberries	Medlars	Quinces
Damsons	Melons	Raspberries (autumn fruiting)
Gages	Pears	Strawberries (perpetual)

NOVEMBER Jobs for late autumn

Dig runner bean trenches and fill with kitchen waste. Lime land that has become too acid, using ground or dolomite limestone. This is usually the best month to plant bare-rooted fruit trees, canes and bushes.

SOWING AND PLANTING

Vegetables and herbs

- Sow winter-hardy broad beans and peas, if you didn't get round to it in October.
- Plant garlic, onion sets and hardy perennial herbs.

Fruit

- Plant bare-rooted fruit trees, soft fruit and vines, to give them time to become established before winter sets in. If conditions aren't right, heel them in until the weather is more favourable.
- Divide and replant existing rhubarb clumps (p.232).

CULTIVATION

Vegetables and herbs

- Mulch light land with compost or leafmould, to protect the soil from winter rains.
- Add ground or dolomite limestone to land that has become too acid (p.47).
- Dig well-rotted manure into heavy land.
- Weed the garden thoroughly
- Rake up leaves, and add to the leafmould pile (p.105).
- Wrap sacking or bubblewrap around containers, to protect them from frost.
- Dig up Brussels Witloof chicory roots for forcing, to produce chicons (p.142).
- Fold cauliflower leaves, to protect curds from frost (p.137).
- Dig runner bean trenches and fill with kitchen waste (p.123).
- Split mint and chives from parent plants; pot up and bring indoors (p.111).
- Divide and replant perennial herbs.

Fruit

- Prune gooseberries, blackcurrants and red and white currants.
- Begin pruning apples and pears.
- Weed around fruit trees, canes and bushes.
- Prune vines (p.218).
- Propagate grapes, by taking hardwood cuttings (p.207).
- Cover fig tree branches with fleece, to protect embryonic figs (p.213).

PESTS AND DISEASES

Vegetables and herbs

- Mice can unearth broad bean and pea seeds. Set traps, as necessary.
- Net brassicas against pigeons.
- Check brassicas for cabbage aphids and whiteflies. Remove by hand, or spray with an organic insecticide.
- Remove and compost any yellowing or dead brassica leaves.

Fruit

- Rake up dead leaves, and add to the leafmould pile (p.105).
- Prune all badly mildewed shoots and cankerous branches of apples and pears (p.91).
- Remove and destroy all fruits infected with brown rot (p.91).
- Tie grease bands around the trunks of apple, pear, cherry and plum trees, to trap winter moths (p.203).

HARVESTING, PRESERVING AND STORING

- Lift, and store carrots, celeriac, Hamburg parsley and other root crops in sand, if you garden on heavy land. They may be left undug, if you garden on light land, although it's usual to cover them with an insulating layer of straw. (We left carrots completely unprotected throughout the severe winter of 2009/10 as an experiment and they came through unscathed – the last roots being lifted early in April.)
- Leave parsnips and Jerusalem artichokes in the ground all winter.
- Pick brassica plants – cabbages, Brussels sprouts, broccoli, calabrese, cauliflowers, kales and kohl rabi. They provide a plentiful source of nutritionally rich leaves and shoots.
- Pick salad vegetables. Although growth slows dramatically with the advent of colder weather, there should be no shortage, especially if they're grown in a polytunnel or protected by cloches.
- The year's fruit harvest comes to an end this month, apart from a few varieties of late plums and apples, and the odd medlar or two.
- Pick juicy ripe grapes, if you're fortunate enough to grow vines indoors.

VEGETABLES YOU CAN HARVEST NOW

French beans (protected)	Chinese artichokes	Oriental greens
Runner beans (protected)	Claytonia	Parsnips
Leaf beet	Corn salad	Radishes
Broccoli	Endive	Rocket
Brussels sprouts	Hamburg parsley	Salsify
Cabbages	Jerusalem artichokes	Scorzonera
Calabrese	Kales	Spinach
Cauliflowers	Kohl rabi	Swedes
Celeriac	Land cress	Turnips
Celery	Leeks	
Chicories	Lettuces	

AUTUMN FEATURE 1 Making leafmould

Leaves from deciduous trees and shrubs are much tougher than weeds and other garden waste, and take longer to break down, so they shouldn't go on the compost heap. However, they can be collected and turned into leafmould, which is a superb soil conditioner. The simplest way of doing this is to stuff wet leaves into black plastic refuse sacks, tie them at the neck, puncture a dozen or so air holes with a garden fork, and leave them for one to two years. By this time they'll have turned into a dark, friable, crumbly mass, which will improve the structure of your soil no end.

Larger quantities of leaves can be dealt with by piling them into an easy-to-construct enclosure, made by stapling a length of wire netting to four wooden corner posts knocked into the ground. The size and shape of the enclosure is unimportant. An extra two posts will convert it into a two-bay bin (see illustration overleaf) – one for last year's leaves, the other for this year's. Its contents don't heat up like compost, so its function is merely to stop the leaves from blowing around the garden. It should, however, be sited in the shade (under a tree is ideal) to prevent the leaves from drying out.

The process can be speeded up by shredding the leaves, and mixing them with grass clippings. One way of doing this is by running a rotary grass mower over leaves on a lawn, and collecting them up in the grass box. Leafmould should always be made when leaves are wet, so the pile may need to be watered in summer if it shows signs of drying out. Any leaves from deciduous trees and shrubs can be turned into leafmould, but evergreen species, like holly and laurel, tenaciously resist decay and should be kept out.

▶

Leafmould isn't rich in nutrients, but it's an excellent source of humus, ideally suited to improving the water-retaining capacities of sandy soils, and making clays more workable. It can be used as a weed-suppressing mulch around fruit trees and bushes in spring-time, and as a protective covering for bare, light soils in winter.

Before it was superseded by peat, leafmould was used as a major ingredient in seed and potting mixtures, and it's being brought back in this capacity today. You can make your own potting mixture by filling a tub with alternate layers of moist leafmould and comfrey leaves – each about 10cm/4in thick. Use after a few months, when the comfrey leaves have rotted, and the nutrients they contained have been absorbed by the leafmould.

Making leafmould

AUTUMN FEATURE 2 **Green manures**

Green manures are special, non-edible, quick-growing plants that improve soil fertility. Once they're sown, they live for a few weeks, to many months – all the while extracting minerals that might otherwise leach out of bare soils. Then they're deliberately killed, by being cut or dug in; releasing their nutrients back into the soil to be exploited by the next crop. There are different sorts of green manures, and they have different

►

characteristics. Some have deep roots that bring up minerals from the subsoil; some produce masses of weed-suppressing foliage; and others have dense matted roots, which break down to leave a lasting beneficial effect on soil structure. Those that belong to the pea and bean family (legumes) also 'fix' atmospheric nitrogen in the nodules on their roots, which they release into the soil when they are dug in, benefiting crops that follow.

Any spare patch of land that isn't going to be cropped for six weeks or more can be used for growing green manures. In spring and summer, this can be the short gap between the end of one crop and the sowing or planting of the next. In autumn, they're grown after main crops, such as potatoes, have been lifted, and are left to stand through the winter. Sown in August or September, they provide a protective green covering that prevents nutrients from being washed out of the soil by winter rains.

Green manure seeds can be sown in drills, 15–20cm/6-8in apart, or they can be broadcast thinly. If the plants are dug in when they're still young, they'll break down quickly, providing an immediate nitrogen boost. 'No-dig' gardeners tend to leave them until they're older, then cut them at ground level, and either put the foliage on the compost heap or leave it on the surface as a mulch. After incorporating green manures into the soil, the next crop shouldn't be sown for two or three weeks; or even four weeks if grown over winter.

Here are some of the main green manures:

- **Nitrogen fixing**: alfalfa, crimson clover, agricultural lupins, field beans, trefoil, winter tares

- **Extra-fast growing**: mustard, buckwheat, fenugreek, *Phacelia tanacetifolia*

- **Deep rooting**: fodder radish

All green manure seeds can be planted during the spring and summer, but only winter tares, field beans, grazing rye, trefoil, alfalfa and clover live through the winter. Our particular favourite is *Phacelia*, which has a wealth of attractive purple flowers. Although it's killed by hard frosts, it provides masses of dead foliage as a protective cover.

On land that's unlikely to be used for a year or more, perennial red or white clover can be planted as a nitrogen-fixing, weed-suppressing, living mulch. You can either leave it alone or take several cuts for the compost heap.

As well as their soil fertility-enhancing qualities, green manures also benefit wildlife, providing a habitat for predatory ground beetles, and, when in flower, supplying pollen and nectar for bees and beneficial insects. Most green manures will fit anywhere into your crop rotation, but mustard and fodder radish are brassicas, and should be sown only with other members of the cabbage family.

AUTUMN FEATURE 3 **Making the most of your seeds**

All seeds have to meet strict germination criteria, and every packet is stamped with the year in which it was packed. This is frequently accompanied by a 'sell-by' date, which is invariably no more than two years hence, giving the impression that they're not worth sowing after this time. But, as a glance at the table below shows, this isn't necessarily true.

Seed longevity, if stored under optimum conditions

1 year	Chives, mint, parsnips, rhubarb, rosemary
2 years	Leeks, onions, rocket, sweet corn
3 years	Beans (French and runner), carrots, dill, parsley, peas, rocket, sage, salsify, scorzonera
4–5 years	Aubergines, basil, beetroot, leaf beet, brassicas, broad beans, celeriac, celery, fennel, peppers, spinach, thyme
5+ years	Chicories, courgettes, cucumbers, endive, marrows, melons, pumpkins, squashes, swedes, tomatoes, turnips

So how can you maximize the life of your seeds? All seeds begin to deteriorate the moment a packet is opened, and they'll rarely survive in an unopened packet, exposed to the air, for longer than a year. Heat and moisture are the main threats, which is why they should never be stored in a glasshouse. Even a few weeks under such conditions (where a packet has been opened to be re-used for successional sowings, for example) is enough to kill them. This is why later sowings often germinate patchily.

Seeds are best kept in air-tight containers – glass storage jars with rubber seals are ideal – in a cellar, cool shed or, best of all, a fridge. A packet of silica gel dessicant can be popped into the jar, to mop up any excess moisture. When dry, it should be blue in colour, turning pink when moist. A few hours in a warm oven will turn it blue again, and it can be returned to the jar.

If you want to test whether seeds are in good condition, put some kitchen roll (several layers thick is best) on a tray, dampen it, then place the seeds on the surface. Insert the tray into a polythene bag, folding it under the tray to retain the humidity, and put it on a high shelf in a kitchen (or on top of a kitchen unit) where the temperature is warm. If the paper dries out, sprinkle with some extra water. If only a few of them have germinated after a couple of weeks, throw them away. As seed ages, it becomes less vigorous, and although old seed may germinate satisfactorily under optimum conditions, it may well fail to do so if sown outdoors in adverse conditions. Moreover, the resulting seedlings are unlikely to grow as well as they should. To avoid disappointment, always err on the safe side and buy a new packet.

AUTUMN FEATURE 4 **Making gardens wildlife friendly**

Agribusiness has turned the countryside into a battlefield for wildlife, which is why the population numbers of so many creatures, from birds to bumblebees and frogs to fritillaries, have tumbled. We can do our bit to redress the balance by making our gardens welcoming to wildlife, and, at the same time, we can do ourselves a favour, by encouraging species that help to keep vegetable and fruit pests under control. That means providing our garden friends with food, water and somewhere to live.

One of the easiest ways of doing this is to plant a hedge. Native species are best, especially those with edible berries for birds, such as elder, hawthorn, dogwood or sloe. Include a few evergreens, or semi-evergreens, such as holly or wild privet, to provide winter cover. Hedges shouldn't be cut before mid-summer, to give any nestlings the chance to flee; nor should they be trimmed in winter, until the birds have devoured all the fruits.

But it's not just the birds that benefit. Numerous insects live in the long grass and leaf litter that naturally accumulate at the base of hedges, including ferocious-looking predatory ground beetles, which are avid consumers of slugs and their eggs, cutworms, caterpillars and other ground-dwelling 'nasties'. This is also the place to conceal a hedgehog box in the autumn, to provide overwintering quarters for these attractive, slug- and snail-snacking mammals. They are easily made from untreated timber, and should be large enough to fit a fat hedgehog, with an entrance tunnel to prevent cats or foxes from pestering the hibernating inhabitants – or they can be bought from a wildlife supplies specialist. Alternatively, a loose collection of logs can be piled up, leaving sufficient space for a hedgehog to squeeze inside. So don't be over-zealous in tidying up!

Most beneficial, predatory and parasitic insects also spend the winter in hibernation, concealing themselves in convenient nooks and crannies. A length of rolled-up corrugated cardboard, stuffed into a bottle cloche and held in place with a wire across the bottom, makes an excellent home for overwintering lacewings, when it's hung from the branches of a bushy

Hedgehog
hibernation
house

►

shrub or tree in early September. Bespoke 'houses' for ladybirds and lacewings are also readily available.

During the summer, the best way of acquiring your own snatch-squad of voracious aphid-eaters, including hoverfly larvae, lacewings (adults and larvae) and others, is to grow plants that have readily accessible pollen and nectar on which the adult insects can feed. Annual convolvulus (*Convolvulus tricolor*), poached egg plant (*Limnanthes douglasii*), yarrow (*Achillea millefolium*), corn marigold (*Chrysanthemum segetum*), and the green manure *Phacelia tanacetifolia* are all excellent attractant plants.

Every garden should also have a pond. It doesn't have to be a major construction: as long as it's tablecloth-sized, or larger, it will provide a valuable wildlife drinking station. Pre-cast fibre-glass pools come in all shapes and sizes; and flexible liners, preferably made of butyl rubber for longevity, can be moulded to fit almost any space. Wildlife-friendly ponds should have shallow margins for easy access by frogs and other amphibians, and, contrary to popular opinion, do not have to be especially deep in the middle. A mixture of oxygenating and floating plants will help to keep the water clear, but beware of introducing invasive species like duckweed (*Lemna minuta*) or parrot's feather (*Myriophyllum aquaticum*).

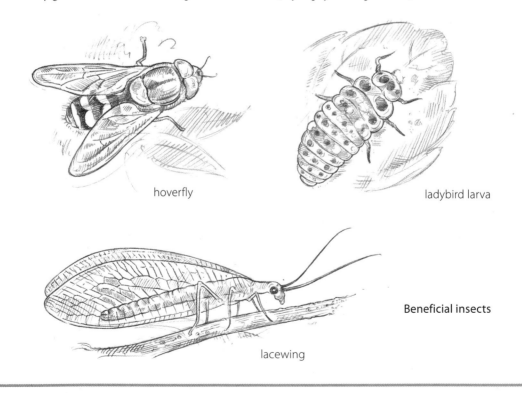

hoverfly

ladybird larva

Beneficial insects

lacewing

AUTUMN FEATURE 5 **Propagating herbs**

Annual herbs (such as basil, dill and coriander), and biennial herbs, which flower only in their second year (like parsley), are always grown from seed. Perennial herbs can also be raised from seed, but it's much easier and faster to propagate them 'vegetatively', by taking cuttings from the shoots, or roots, of the parent plant. Some can also be split by hand, in a process called division, and they can also be 'layered'. Cuttings taken from spring to mid-summer, when the shoots are young and tender, are called 'softwood'; those taken from mid-summer to mid-autumn, when the shoots have hardened at the base, are called 'semi-ripe'. The technique, with minor variations, is the same for both, and can be used to propagate many other perennial plants.

Softwood cuttings

Use for propagating marjoram, rosemary, sage, tarragon and thyme. Select a young shoot, cut it just above a leaf joint, approximately 7.5–10cm/3–4in from the tip, and place it in a plastic bag to prevent wilting. Fill a pot with a low-nutrient growing medium suitable for raising cuttings, made from 50 per cent coarse sand, or perlite (volcanic mineral granules), and 50 per cent coir, and press down firmly. Snip the cutting just below a leaf joint with a knife, and strip away all the lower and intermediate leaves. Make a hole in the compost with a pencil, and insert the cutting up to its leaves.

Several cuttings can go into a pot, so long as their leaves don't touch. Cuttings root fastest when they're supplied with bottom heat, so transfer to a propagator, if you have one.

Alternatively, cover them with a polythene bag, held in place with a DIY wire frame. Place in the shade and spray with water (to ensure high humidity) each morning for a week. After three to four weeks, when the cuttings have rooted, harden them off and plant out.

Semi-ripe cuttings

Use for propagating rosemary and lavender. Change the mixture to make it more free-draining, by mixing equal amounts of coir, coarse sand and bark. Otherwise treat as for softwood cuttings, but without the basal heat/polythene bag. Water once a week, or if the rooting medium appears to be dry. Leave in a cold frame or glasshouse over winter, and harden off in the spring.

Root cuttings

Use for propagating mint and tarragon. In spring or autumn, cut sections of root into 5cm/2in lengths, and plant vertically into a pot filled with well-watered cutting medium (use the same mix as for softwood cuttings), so that the tops are flush with the surface. Cover with a thin layer of compost, topped off with 10mm/½in perlite. Water when the shoots appear two to three weeks later. Harden off and pot on.

Division

Use for propagating chives, fennel, marjoram, mint and thyme. This is the simplest method of all. Lift the parent plant, and tease it apart into individual rooted plants/clumps, using your hands or a fork. Pot up or plant out. Periodic

►

division is essential to prevent overcrowding, even if you don't necessarily want to increase the number of plants.

Layering

Use for bay, rosemary and sage. In spring or early summer, lower a vigorous young shoot into a V-shaped slit, 7.5–10cm/3–4in deep, in the ground. Nick the underside of the shoot where the roots are to form, and hold it in place using a wire peg, with the growing tip poking up vertically, just above the soil. Backfill with soil, firm and water well. In the autumn, detach the new plant from the parent plant, and move into a permanent position or a plant pot.

PART 3

A crop-by-crop guide

How to use this section

Part 2 told you what needs to be done when. Now this section tells you how to go about doing it. Vegetables and fruit are arranged in alphabetical order, and the information deals with sowing or planting through to harvest, and all the stages in between, plus their dietary value is provided. Most of this is straightforward, but the following notes explain our choice of varieties and how to interpret the nutritional data.

Varieties

Our selections are based, in the main, on varieties we know and trust, with an emphasis on flavour. This is obviously subjective, but there it is. If we have missed out your favourites, please forgive us. All the varieties were commercially available, from one or more of the suppliers on pages 304–5, at the time of writing, but it is inevitable that some will eventually disappear from catalogues. This is unlikely to happen with heritage varieties, however, most of which date back a hundred years or more. The ones we have chosen have survived because they have outstanding qualities, flavour being top of the list, which was a far more important consideration in the days before supermarket standardization and breeding for appearance and yield.

Nutritional value

In the majority of cases, we have used figures taken from McCance and Widdowson's *The Composition of Foods* (see page 303), which is compiled by the UK Foods Standards Agency (FSA). These refer to food in its raw, or uncooked, state. Most fruit and vegetables contain a wide spread of nutrients, but many occur in relatively small amounts, so we have included only those minerals and vitamins that are present at levels greater than a tenth of the FSA's current adult recommended daily allowances (RDA), as follows:

*** = 100g/4oz contains more than half of the RDA. If greater than the RDA, the number of multiples by which it is exceeded is also given.

** = 100g/4oz contains between a quarter and a half of the RDA.

* = 100g/4oz contains between a tenth and a quarter of the RDA.

So, to give an example, the listing for asparagus of

Vitamins: folate, K***; C, E**; B1*

means that it contains more than half the RDA of folate and vitamin K, a quarter to a half the RDA of vitamins C and E, and a tenth to a quarter the RDA of Vitamin B1.

We have used the standard energy unit of kcals per 100g/4oz for the calorific value of each crop, and have also included the Glycaemic Index, expressed as high (HGI), medium (MGI) or low (LGI), for those readers who are diabetic or who are following a GI weight-reduction diet.

As you will have seen in Part 1, research into the valuable role that phytochemicals play in preventing and fighting potentially life-threatening diseases is complex and fast-moving and is still in its infancy. This means that the information we have presented represents a snapshot of what is currently known, and is not meant to be exhaustive. Rich sources of particular phytochemicals are indicated by bold type.

Recommended daily allowances (RDAs) of vitamins and minerals

Vitamin	RDA	Mineral	RDA
A	700µg*	Calcium	700mg
B1	1mg	Copper	1.2mg
B2	1.6mg	Iron	14.8mg
B3	17mg	Magnesium	300mg
B5	6mg	Manganese	2mg
B6	1.4mg	Phosphorus	550mg
C	40mg	Potassium	3,500mg
E	4mg	Selenium	75µg
K	75µg	Zinc	9.5mg
Folate	200µg		

1µg is one thousandth of 1mg

CHAPTER 7

Vegetables

Now comes the technical bit, but don't be put off, because the crop-by-crop details are very easy to follow. Although the ultimate goal is the luscious taste of your freshly picked, oh-so-sweet tomatoes, or buttery, melt-in-the-mouth potatoes, if you make the most of each step along the way, you'll find that growing your own vegetables is a reward in its own right. So enjoy!

ASPARAGUS

If you have the space and the patience, asparagus is an easy-to-grow perennial crop. It can live for up to twenty years, providing delicious spears from April to June. Ground preparation is everything.

Planning and preparation

Because asparagus takes so long to crop, most people start off with one-year-old crowns. Plants are either male or female, and can be green, white or purple, although most are green with a purple tip. Males are generally thinner and more plentiful. Female plants produce spears that are thicker, but they also have berries, which can self-seed and be troublesome to weed. Most modern varieties are all-male hybrids. Maximize your cropping by choosing a mixture of early and late types. Some varieties are suitable for November planting – check with your supplier.

Asparagus prefers light, well-drained soil with a pH of 6.5–7.5. Choose a sunny spot where the 1.5m/5ft foliage will be protected from strong winds. Dig the soil thoroughly down to 60cm/2ft and work in some compost or manure.

The important point is to ensure that the land is completely clear of couch grass, bindweed or any other perennial weeds. For clay soils, add grit or grow on raised beds.

Sowing and planting

In March or April, dig a trench 20–25cm/8–10in deep and 30cm/12in wide, and plant the octopus-like roots on a raised mound, 7.5cm/3in high, running along the centre of the trench. Backfill, so that plants are covered with 5cm/2in of soil. Space them 30–40cm/12–16in apart, in rows 1m/3ft 3in apart; or, if growing on beds, 30cm/1ft each way.

Alternatively, sow seeds in pots or modules in a propagator, or on a windowsill, in February or March. Maintain at a temperature of 13–16°C/55–61°F until plants are 15cm/6in tall, then plant outside. Delay transplanting if the weather is cold and wet. You can also sow outdoors in a seed bed from late March onwards, in rows 30cm/12in apart, thinning to 15cm/6in between plants. In either case, plant out the following year as crowns.

Cultivation

Gradually fill in the trench as the plants grow, always leaving about 10cm/4in of stem showing, so that the beds are level by October. Water well in the first year and keep weeded: hand-weed rather than hoe to avoid damaging the roots. When the ferns turn yellow, in October/November, cut them down close to the ground and mulch with compost or leafmould. In subsequent years, if you prefer longer or whitened spears, ridge up the rows. Mulch with organic matter in the autumn, and feed with an organic fertilizer in the spring.

Pests and diseases

Pests

Asparagus beetles: Adults are 1cm/½in long, with a reddish body and yellow/black wings. They, and their dirty-grey 'hump-backed' larvae, feed on the foliage, attacking between June and October. Pick them off, or spray with an organic insecticide.
Slugs, snails and cutworms: Will also damage asparagus (see page 87).

Diseases

Violet root rot: Plants turn yellow prematurely and begin to die. Waterlogging is often to blame. Lift and burn any affected roots, and plant replacement roots in a new bed elsewhere.
Rust: Remove affected leaves.

Harvesting and storing

Cut spears using a serrated knife just below the soil surface, from mid-April to mid-June. However, don't harvest until the second year after planting (and then for only four weeks), and cut for only six weeks in year three. Eat as soon as possible after picking, preferably within the hour. Otherwise keep in the fridge for no more than a few days – not upright in water as is often recommended. Asparagus can be frozen, or bottled in brine (see Part 4).

Nutritional value

Vitamins: folate, K***; C, E**; B1*
Minerals: manganese*
Phytochemicals: flavonoids, carotenoids, saponins (green varieties contain more than white). Also contains a rich source of fructo-oligosaccharides. 25kcal, LGI

AUBERGINES

Usually glossy purple in colour, this tender crop belonging to the potato family is only really successful when grown under cover. When it was first introduced to the UK, the fruits were smaller, white and ovoid, hence its alternative name: eggplant.

Planning and preparation

Will grow in any sunny, well-drained, reasonably fertile soil with a pH of around 6.5.

Sowing and planting

Sow from mid-February onwards in a propagator, or on a windowsill in a warm room, never letting the temperature drop below 21°C/70°F. When the plants are 5cm/2in tall, prick out into 10cm/4in pots and maintain at 16–18°C/61–65°F. Transplant into the ground when 10–15cm/4–6in tall (preferably in a greenhouse or polytunnel), but don't plant outside until all risk of frost has passed: usually late May at the earliest. Alternatively, transplant into individual 20cm/8in pots, or grow-bags – three plants per bag. Space plants 45cm/18in each way; dwarf varieties 35–40cm/14–16in.

Cultivation

Restrict outdoor plants to five fruits per plant (indoor plants up to a dozen, although some varieties, which produce mini-aubergines, will yield more). Pinch out the growing tips when plants are 25cm/10in tall, and restrict fruits to one per lateral (three per lateral if plants are under cover). Remove all unwanted flowers and side shoots, as for tomatoes (see page 190). Stop laterals three leaves after the last fruit. Once the fruits have set, aubergines must be kept well watered and fed with a high-potash liquid feed every two weeks.

Pests and diseases

As a member of the Solanaceae plant family, aubergines share the same pests and diseases as tomatoes (see page 192).

Harvesting and storing

Pick from August onwards, once the fruits have reached maturity, using scissors. Plants will continue cropping until September outdoors, and a month later indoors. Aubergines will keep in a fridge for a couple of weeks and can be frozen (see Part 4).

Nutritional value

Vitamins: E**
Phytochemicals: phenolic acids, phytosterols. They also contain caffeic acid and nasain, which gives purple varieties their skin colour. Aubergines are rated among the top five vegetables with antioxidant properties.
15kcal, LGI

VARIETIES

Early: Moneymaker F1
Dwarf: Orlando F1, Bambino
Heritage: Black Beauty, Long Purple, Rosa Bianca (pink and white fruits)

BROAD BEANS

Broad, or fava, beans are one of the easiest crops to grow, producing good crops of tasty beans from June onwards.

Planning and preparation

Broad bean varieties are usually described as being either 'longpod', which have 8–10 kidney-shaped seeds per pod, or 'Windsor', which have 4–7 round seeds per pod. Seeds are generally white or green.

They prefer a sunny spot, and a well-drained soil with a pH of 6–7. Apply compost during the winter months before sowing. If soil is low in potash, lightly fork in kali vinasse (organic potash) fertilizer in the spring at 50–100g per sq. m/2–4 oz per sq. yd. Ten plants should produce around 2.5kg/5½lb of beans.

Sowing and planting

You can sow certain varieties outside in October/November, but seeds will occasionally rot during a cold wet winter, especially if grown on heavy soils. Alternatively, sow under cover in pots, deep modules or cardboard toilet rolls between December and February to give the plants a head start in the spring. Otherwise, sow outdoors under cloches in February, or in the open from March to April. Once the temperature rises above 15°C/59°F, the plants slow down considerably, so later sowings are inadvisable.

Space plants equidistantly 23cm/9in

apart if growing on beds. Traditionally, broad beans were grown as double rows about 23cm/9in apart with 15cm/6in between each plant and 75cm/30in between pairs of rows. Sow seeds 5cm/2in deep using a dibber; sow a few extra at the end of the row to fill in any gaps.

Cultivation

Keep well watered, especially when the pods are swelling. Broad beans are prone to being blown over in strong winds, so erect a barrier around them using 1m/3ft canes and three parallel rows of string. To encourage pod formation (and to discourage blackfly – see below), pinch out the top 7.5cm/3in of the growing tips when the plants are around 1m/3ft 3in tall. When plants have finished cropping, dig them up and compost them, roots and all. Only a small amount of nitrogen remains in the tiny white root nodules (it all goes into the bean seeds), so none is available for the succeeding crop.

Pests and diseases

Pests

Black bean aphids (blackfly): These jet-black aphids feed on the growing tips and leaves in spring. Remove affected foliage and leave any aphids that are sparsely populating other leaves for ladybirds and other garden predators.
Mice: Will unearth plants to get to the beans. Set traps.
Pea and bean weevils: Attack young plants, producing scalloped notches on leaf edges. Don't worry, as most plants will recover, but if infestations are high, cover with fleece after sowing. Doesn't affect winter-sown crops.
Slugs and snails: Are very partial to young plants.

Diseases

Chocolate spot: Round dark brown spots on leaves, stems and pods, later turning black and coalescing. Worse on soils that are low in potash. There is no cure, but plants rarely die and it is perfectly safe to eat the crop.
Broad bean rust: rust-coloured pustules develop underneath foliage. Remove and compost affected leaves.

Harvesting and storing

Pick when pods are 5–7.5cm/2–3in long, to eat whole. Otherwise wait for pods to fatten until beans show through, then shell. Autumn-sown beans will begin cropping in early June, spring-sown three weeks later, continuing until September. You can freeze broad beans: the green-seeded varieties freeze better than the white (see Part 4).

Nutritional value

Vitamins: B5 ***; B3, C, E, K, folate*. Contains between one and two times the RDA for vitamin B5 (pantothenic acid)
Minerals: copper, phosphorus**; iron, magnesium, manganese, zinc*
Phytochemicals: beta-carotene, genistein and quercetin

Broad beans contain almost as much protein as soya beans, and far more than French or runner beans. Dietary lectins in protein improve the ability of cells to fight cancer. Broad beans are also high in fibre, rich in lecithin (a nutrient that helps to lower cholesterol), and low in fat.

81kcal, HGI

VARIETIES

Longpod: Aquadulce Claudia, Bunyard's Exhibition, Express, Imperial Green Longpod

Windsor: Green Windsor, Jubilee Hysor, The Sutton (dwarf variety, grows 30cm/12in high).
Other: Stereo (eat as mange tout), Red Epicure (red seeds, turn yellow on cooking)
Autumn sown: Aquadulce Claudia, Super Aquadulce, The Sutton
Heritage: Crimson flowered. Many of the varieties above date back to Victorian times.

FRENCH BEANS

Also called kidney beans, this is an easy-to-grow, frost-susceptible crop, that has dwarf or climbing (pole) types. Beans are usually eaten fresh and whole as 'haricots verts', and can be flat or cylindrical (pencil-shaped) – the ubiquitous 'Kenyan green bean'. Shelled beans for drying from flat varieties are variously called haricot, butter or lima beans. Navy beans, which we all know as 'baked beans' when covered with tomato sauce, are also harvested dried, but do not grow well in the UK – pea beans are probably the nearest equivalent.

Planning and preparation

French beans like a light soil and a sunny, sheltered position. They don't do well on heavy clays. Dig in compost during the winter, and aim for a pH of 6.5–7.5. Ten plants should produce around 10kg/22lb of beans (climbing): expect under half this amount with dwarf varieties.

Sowing and planting

Sow outdoors from early May, but only if the soil temperature is more than 12°C/54°F – anything less and the seeds will not germinate successfully and are likely to rot. It's safer to sow under cover from mid-April onwards in cardboard tubes, root trainers or 7.5cm/3in pots, and transplant when you can be confident that the last frosts are over. Sow every three weeks, or as preferred, until early July.

Sow seeds 4–5cm/1½–2in deep, spaced 23cm/9in apart each way for dwarf types – commercial growers pack them in even closer at 30–40 plants per sq. m/4 plants per sq. ft. Grow climbing varieties up canes or other support systems, with 10–13cm/4–5in between plants.

Always sow spares, as germination is often patchy.

Cultivation

Water well, once the flowers have set, unless it is exceptionally dry, in which case earlier watering will be needed too. Mulch between plants with grass clippings or comfrey leaves (which also supply potash) to suppress weeds and reduce water loss. Because French bean plants invariably self-pollinate before the flowers open, you're unlikely to experience setting problems, unlike runner beans, and so consequently home-saved seed is at little risk from cross-pollination.

Pests and diseases

Pests

Slugs and snails: Attack young seedlings.
Black bean aphids (blackfly): These black aphids feed on the foliage. Remove badly affected leaves or spray with an organic insecticide.
Bean seed flies: Attack seeds and seedlings from April to September. Cover plants with fleece immediately after sowing.
Mice: Will unearth plants to get to the beans. Set traps.
Bean seed weevils: Eggs are laid on seeds and the larvae tunnel into them.

See 'Harvesting' for control.

Diseases

Although French beans can be attacked by several diseases (which usually appear as dark blotches on pods foliage), they are fortunately not that common. There are no cures, so either ignore the problem if minor, or remove seriously affected plants

Harvesting and storing

Pick beans around sixty days from sowing: pods should snap when bent. It's important to pick regularly – preferably every two to three days – during the five- to seven-week harvesting period. Beans are ready from the end of June through to late October (or November if protected). Leave some plants unpicked for the pods to dry until brittle, to provide next year's seed or if eating as haricots. If not completely dry by the end of the season, lift the plants and hang them somewhere cool, dry and airy until the pods split open. Store the beans in a jar, but freeze first for two days to kill any bean seed weevils and their eggs. French beans freeze well (see Part 4).

Nutritional value

Vitamins: K***; C, folate**
Minerals: manganese*
Phytochemicals: lutein and zeaxanthin
24kcal, LGI

VARIETIES

Dwarf: Royalty (purple), Slenderette, Tendergreen
Climbing: Blauhilde (purple), Goldfield (yellow), Hunter
Disease-resistant: Concador, Delinel – both dwarf
Dried as haricots: Borlotto Lingua di Fuoco (red/yellow mottled),

Canadian Wonder. Drying beans need a long season – sow early.
Unusual: Pea bean (climber with cream and brown round seeds)
Heritage (dwarf): The Prince,

Canadian Wonder, Triomphe de Farcy
Heritage (climbing): Blue Lake, Lazy Housewife, Cherokee Trail of Tears
Note: purple varieties turn green when cooked

RUNNER BEANS

Tender perennial, but usually treated as an annual – one of the most popular crops. Modern varieties are usually stringless, and whilst almost all require support, some will grow happily in containers on a patio.

Planning and preparation

Runner beans require a light and fertile, moisture-retentive, slightly acid soil (pH 6.5), in a sunny, and preferably sheltered, position. In November, dig two parallel trenches 60cm/24in apart between centres, each 25cm/10in wide and a spade's depth. Line with newspapers and gradually fill with kitchen waste. Dust with ground limestone and cover with a layer of soil to deter rats. Over the next few months the soil will sink, and it's into this depression that you sow the seeds. Yields are as for climbing French beans.

Sowing and planting

Runner beans will grow 2.4–3m/8–10ft tall and so require a support system. Our preferred method is to take opposing pairs of 2.4m-/8ft-long bamboo canes at 30cm/12in intervals and push them firmly into the middle of each trench. Join each pair with string 15cm/6in from the top, and into this V-shaped notch that runs along the row, attach a horizontal cane, which further binds each pair of canes together. Attach a horizontal cane to each side of this structure, approx 15cm/6in above the soil, then tie a length of twine midway vertically between each pair of canes for the beans to clamber up, stretched taut between the top and bottom canes (see illustration overleaf). We don't advise wigwams, as plants can get too congested at the top.

Sow seeds 5cm/2in deep, positioning them every 15cm/6in to coincide with the positions of canes/string. Delay sow-ing until May, when the soil temperature is at least 12°C/54°F. Alternatively, sow under cover in April (see French beans) and transplant in late May. Sow dwarf varieties 30cm apart each way, or in 9cm/1 litre pots – you can get a late crop by sowing in July, but then covering with cloches in October to beat the frost.

Runner beans grow best with their roots in association with soil-living

Runner bean cane supports

string in between each pair of canes

Rhizobia bacteria, which fix nitrogen (see page 47). You can buy specific soil inoculants (though they can be difficult to source), but alternatively take a shovel-full of soil from ground where runners were grown the previous year and lightly fork it in before sowing. This should be as effective.

Cultivation

Runner beans must be agitated by foraging bees, or by wind, but flowers may fail to set in hot summers – especially when night-time temperatures climb above 14°C/57°F. There's not a lot you can do about this – according to the RHS, syringing the flowers with water is unhelpful. Water plants regularly in dry weather anyway and keep well weeded.

Pests and diseases

Runner beans suffer from the same pests and diseases as French beans (see page 122). In cases of heavy slug infestations, delay sowing until June, to give plants the opportunity to grow away from the problem. Birds can also be a nuisance by pecking and destroying flowers, thereby disrupting pollination.

Harvesting and storing

Runner beans are ready for picking after 12–14 weeks, usually in July, when the pods are 15–20cm/6–8in long. Harvest every couple of days without fail – if any pods are allowed to ripen, so that the beans start to bulge inside the pods, the plant will cease production. Most plants finish cropping in September, but can carry on until November if given frost protection. Fresh young beans freeze well (see Part 4) – but do not freeze tough old ones!

Runner beans are perennial plants, so you can lift and store the fleshy tubers (which are poisonous, by the way), keeping them moist, until you plant them out the following May. Most people, however, grow them from seed each year.

Nutritional value

Vitamins: C, K, folate**

Minerals: manganese*

Phytochemicals: lignans (they normalise oestrogen activity)

22kcal, LGI

Dwarf: Hestia, Pickwick, Hammond's Dwarf Scarlet (all grow around 40cm/16in tall)

Attractive flowers: Painted Lady (red/white), Sunset (pink/orange), Celebration (pink)

Drying: Czar – can be eaten fresh, or dried as butter beans (see page 252)

Heritage: Scarlet Emperor, Czar, Painted Lady

VARIETIES

Climbing: Enorma, Red Flame, Lady Di, Yard Long, White Emergo

BEETROOT

Most beetroot are red and globe-shaped, but they can also be cylindrical. Colours also include white, yellow and pink. They're easy to grow, and are rarely troubled by pests or diseases.

Planning and preparation

Beetroot prefer an open sunny site, and soil that is reasonably fertile – light rather than heavy – with pH 6.5–7.5. Like carrots, they are likely to fork on freshly manured ground. Choose round varieties for early sowing, eating fresh and for growing as 'mini beets', and cylindrical sorts for higher yields and storing. Ten plants should produce around 1.4kg/3lb of globe-shaped roots, or 2.5kg/5½lb of cylindrical beets.

Sowing and planting

If you want a really early crop, sow in a propagator at 20°C/68°F in mid-February, and grow on under cover until you can plant out in early April. Alternatively, sow indoors in modules in early March and transplant outside when 5cm/2in tall. There's no point in sowing in the open until the soil temperature reaches 7°C/44°F, which is usually around late March in most districts. You can help things along by warming the soil under polythene for a couple of weeks prior to sowing – a sheet of black polythene laid underneath a clear sheet works best. Young plants may run to seed (bolt) in cold weather, so for early crops choose non-bolting types. If you want beets for winter storage, don't sow before the end of May, otherwise they will become too big and tough.

Most beetroot seeds are actually a cluster of four or five seeds fused together, technically known as 'multigerm'. Sow two clusters at a time, 2.5cm/1in deep. When they have germinated, remove all but the most vigorous seedling. Some varieties are 'monogerm', consisting of a single seed, which avoids the need for thinning.

Spacing seeds is a moveable feast, and it depends on how big you eventually want your beetroot to be. 'Baby' beet can be grown as close as 2.5–5cm/1–2in apart, but for tennis ball-sized roots, it is usual to sow or transplant at 5cm/2in intervals, thinning to 10cm/4in when about half this size. Rows should be about 23cm/9in apart. If you're growing beetroot for storing, space a little wider at 10cm/4in between plants and 30cm/12in between rows. Another way of growing is 'multisown', in which four seedlings are allowed to grow in each module and then planted out in a 30cm/12in grid formation. Experiment until you find what works best for you.

Cultivation

Keep well weeded and mulch with compost. In hot, dry weather, water weekly to prevent plants from going woody, or splitting.

Pests and diseases

Beetroot are remarkably trouble-free and, apart from the odd attack by aphids, you're unlikely to encounter any problems.

Harvesting and storing

June is usually the earliest time you can start picking beetroot, though the leaves of earlier thinnings are fine in salads, and you can continue harvesting until October. Cutting the tops off will cause the roots to 'bleed' when cooked: twist off instead. Beet can be stored in sand, paper sacks, clamped or left in the ground. They can also be frozen, bottled or turned into pickles and chutney (see Part 4).

Nutritional value

Vitamins: folate***; C*. Beet greens are rich in vitamins A, C, E and K.
Minerals: manganese**; potassium*
Phytochemicals: phytosterols, rich in betalains

Beetroot juice has been shown to lower blood pressure – its high nitrate content is thought to be responsible.
36kcal, MGI

VARIETIES

Bolt-resistant: Boltardy, Red Ace F1, Moneta (monogerm)
Coloured: Burpee's Golden (yellow), Albina Vereduna (white), Chioggia (concentric pink and white rings)
Mini beets: Monaco, Pronto, Solo F1
Other good globe types: Detroit Globe, Wodan F1,
Cylindrical (ideal for storing): Cylindra, Forono
Heritage: Cheltenham Green Top, Bulls Blood (grown for its spectacular purple leaves), Egyptian Turnip Rooted

LEAF BEET

Leaf beet is a member of the beetroot family and is also closely related to spinach, but much easier to grow. There are two sorts – chard (also called seakale beet) and perpetual spinach (also known as spinach beet). A row of colourful chard can make a striking display in the garden.

Planning and preparation

It will grow in poorer soil than spinach. Expect to harvest around 2.7kg/6lb of fresh leaves from ten plants.

Sowing and planting

Although you can sow early under cover in March in modules, there is a risk of bolting if the spinach is planted out into cold soil, so it's safest to delay sowing until April or even May. Space the multigerm seeds 13–15cm/5–6in apart, in rows 38cm/15in apart, selecting only the most vigorous seedlings to grow on. When about 10cm/4in tall, remove alternate plants to give a final spacing of 25–30cm/10–12in. Alternatively, sow seeds in a grid formation, spacing them 25cm/10in apart in each direction (within the row and between each row). Repeat sowings every four weeks to provide continuous crops throughout the summer. A final sowing in late July/early August will give pickings well into the autumn and the following spring.

Cultivation

Keep well weeded and watered. Mulch with compost. The plants look dead during the winter, but unless the weather is exceptionally severe, they will put on a rapid spurt of growth in April/May before running to seed. White chards are hardier than coloured varieties; spinach beet is hardiest of all.

Pests and diseases

Slugs: May nibble young seedlings.

Harvesting and storing

Leaf beet can be harvested from June to November and again in April/May. Young leaves are ready to pick for salads after eight weeks, or for cooking after twelve. You can eat the fleshy stems and the leaves of chard. Always pick the outer leaves first, leaving those in the centre to continue developing. Leaves will keep in the fridge in a plastic bag for a couple of days. You can also freeze them (see Part 4).

Nutritional value

Vitamins: A, C, K***; E**. Contains eleven times the RDA for vitamin K.
Minerals: magnesium**; potassium, iron, copper, manganese*
Phytochemicals: flavonoids, beta-carotene, lutein and zeaxanthin
22kcal, LGI

see varieties overleaf

VARIETIES

Chard: Swiss chard, Bright Yellow, Rhubarb, Lucullus, Bright Lights
Spinach beet: Perpetual spinach, Erbette (suitable for 'cut and come again' crops)

BROCCOLI (SPROUTING) and CALABRESE

Broccoli comes in two forms – heading and sprouting. Heading broccoli, or calabrese, is the sort universally sold in supermarkets in this country, but most gardeners tend to grow the purple sprouting sort, which is much less commonly seen in shops. Both are relatively easy to grow, and with careful planning you could be eating fresh broccoli all year round.

Planning and preparation

All members of the cabbage (brassica) family have similar requirements. Soil should be fertile, as most brassicas are in the ground for a long time (some varieties of broccoli take 50 weeks to reach harvest), and should have been manured/composted a couple of months before sowing. They also benefit from following on from a green manure (see page 106). If the soil is on the acid side, apply ground or dolomite lime-stone the previous autumn: this will also reduce the risk of clubroot disease. Finally, choose an open, sunny spot and ensure that the soil is firm and has not been freshly dug so it will provide a good anchorage for the tall plants. Calabrese is less demanding than sprouting broccoli and will succeed on poorer soils. Ten plants should produce around 7kg/15lb of spears.

Sowing and planting

For early crops of calabrese, sow in modules in March under cover, and plant out under fleece. Sow outside in late March or April, as soon as the soil temperature has reached 5°C/41°F, spacing plants around 35cm/14in each way and the seeds 2cm/¾in deep. Sow three seeds at each position and thin out to the strongest, as calabrese does not like root disturbance. Continue to sow, as required, until July.

Sprouting broccoli germinates at higher soil temperatures than calabrese (7°C/44°F) so delay sowing until mid-April, or sow under cover in March. Sow in modules or in a seed bed (in rows 15cm/6in apart). When plants are 5cm/2in tall, transfer from modules into 9cm/3in pots, and thin seed bed-grown plants to 7.5cm/3in apart. Transplant into final positions in July, when plants are around 10cm/4in tall, in rows 75cm/30in apart and with 60cm/24in between plants. Bury the stem up to the first leaf joint to encourage additional rooting.

Cultivation

Keep well watered in dry weather (especially calabrese, which will run to seed). If the plants appear to be growing slowly – for example, over-wintered crops in early spring – apply a general organic fertilizer. Calabrese grows to only around 60cm/24in tall and is self-supporting, but you will need to stake sprouting broccoli, which grows another 30cm/12in tall.

Pests and diseases

See cabbages (page 132).

Harvesting and storing

Calabrese matures much more quickly than sprouting broccoli and is chiefly harvested from July to November, once the central head is well formed. Plants will go on to produce another couple of smaller side shoots after the main head has been cut.

Sprouting broccoli usually begins cropping in February and continues until May, although there are fast-maturing varieties that will produce spears in the summer and autumn. Break off the flowering shoots, before the buds have opened, when they are around 15cm/6in long. Pick on a regular basis, to encourage continuous production of spears over the six- to eight-week harvest period. You can freeze calabrese and broccoli, but why bother when it's in season for so long?

Nutritional value

Vitamins: C, K***; E, folate**; A, B1, B6*
Minerals: potassium, phosphorus, iron, manganese*
Phytochemicals: It is a rich source of phytochemicals, including lignans, indoles, carotenoids and flavonoids. It is an excellent source of sulforaphane and sinigrin.

Broccoli also contains a useful amount of dietary fibre.
33kcal, LGI

VARIETIES

Broccoli
Winter maturing: Rudolph, Red Arrow
Late winter/spring maturing: Cardinal, Claret F1
Summer/autumn maturing: Bordeaux F1, Summer Purple, Santee F1
Heritage: Early Purple Sprouting, Late Purple Sprouting, Early White Sprouting

Calabrese
Standard: Belstar F1, Fiesta F1, Chevalier F1, Samson F1 (downy mildew-resistant)
Italian broccoli: Romanesco (has spectacular yellow/green pyramid-shaped heads)
Perennial: Nine star Perennial (produces up to ten small creamy heads each year)

BRUSSELS SPROUTS

Brussels sprouts are not just for Christmas Day! You can enjoy them from August through to March. A firm soil is essential if sprouts are to be firm and tight. Modern hybrid varieties, which crop heavily and uniformly, mean that we have more-or-less seen the end of traditional, open-pollinated varieties.

Planning and preparation

See broccoli, but do not attempt to dig the soil in the spring – just rake it level and hoe off any weeds. Brussels sprouts are more tolerant of alkaline soils, and will grow in pH 6.5–8. Ten plants should produce around 9kg/20lb of sprouts.

Sowing and planting

If you want to eat sprouts in September, sow under cover in late February/early March into seed trays or modules that are at least 5cm/2in deep. Plant out from mid-April to mid-May, as for broccoli.

Outdoor sowings in a seedbed can begin in late March/early April, as soon as the soil has warmed to at least 7°C/44°F, and can continue until the end of May. Transplant seedlings into their final positions when they are about 10cm/4in high.

Early-cropping cultivars, which usually grow around 35cm/14in tall, may be spaced as close as 45cm/18in between rows and plants. Later-maturing varieties reach 75cm/30in tall and require a wider spacing of 60–75cm/24–30in each way.

When transplanting Brussels sprout plants, bury the stems up to the first leaves to encourage new roots. This will also discourage cabbage root flies. Use a dibber to keep disturbance to a minimum, and press the soil firmly around the plants.

Cultivation

Water transplants well, until the plants have established, but then leave them to fend for themselves, unless it becomes exceptionally dry. In mid-summer, apply an organic fertilizer such as pelleted chicken manure. You will need to stake Brussels sprouts to stop them from blowing over (lodging). Use a 1.2m/4ft bamboo cane and tie plants close to the ground and at the top.

Take advantage of the wide spacing between plants during the summer months (before they have grown tall) by growing a 'catch crop' (see page 13) of salad leaves or spring onions.

To prevent diseases, remove and compost yellowing and dead leaves from autumn onwards.

Pests and diseases

See cabbages (page 132). Aphids will overwinter on spent Brussels sprout stumps, so lift and chop/crush or shred before putting on the compost heap.

Harvesting and storing

Begin picking from the base (the bottom-most buttons are often of poor quality and should be discarded) and work your way upwards. Entire stems may be lifted and their roots placed in a bowl of water to provide up to a month's supply. You can eat 'blown' sprouts, those that run to flower, and the cluster of leaves at the tip of the plant (which are delicious). Sprouts also freeze well (see Part 4).

Nutritional value

Vitamins: C, K, folate***; B6**; B5, E*. Contains twice the RDA for vitamin K and three times the RDA for vitamin C.
Minerals: potassium, phosphorus, manganese*
Phytochemicals: indoles, dithiolthiones, isothiocyanates, carotenoids, flavonoids, coumestrol and sinigrin

Brussels sprouts also contain a useful amount of dietary fibre.
42kcal, LGI

VARIETIES

Early (September to December): Brilliant F1, Nautic F1, Nelson F1
Mid (November to January): Igor F1, Noisette, Trafalgar F1
Late (December to March): Wellington F1
Red buttons: Rubine, Falstaff
Heritage: Bedford Fillbasket, Early Half Tall

CABBAGES

Cabbages crop all year round and are relatively easy to grow, as long as you protect them from caterpillars and pigeons.

Planning and preparation

Like other brassicas, cabbages are nutrient-demanding crops that require a rich, firm soil with a pH of at least 6.8 (see broccoli). For planning purposes, work on a yield of around 4kg/9lb from ten spring cabbages; 7kg/15lb from ten summer or autumn cabbages; and 11kg/25lb from ten winter cabbages and Savoys. Choose a Savoy if you are looking for a cabbage that will stand through a really tough winter.

Sowing and planting

Summer cabbages: Start seeds off in February in a propagator set to 13°C/55°F or on a windowsill, and grow on in a cold greenhouse or polytunnel. Sow seeds 2cm/¾in deep, in seed trays or modules. If heat isn't used, delay sowing until March (but still under cover). Plant outside when plants are 10cm/4in tall, in April or May.

When the soil temperature reaches 7°C/44°F, cabbage seeds can be sown safely outdoors, but they are best started off under cover. Space plants 45cm/18in each way; mini varieties can go closer.

Autumn cabbages: Sow in modules/ seed trays or in a seed bed (spacing 15 × 7.5cm/6 × 3in) in April/May, and plant out at 50cm/20in intervals each way in June.

Winter cabbages and Savoys: Sow in April/May in modules/seed trays or in a seed bed, and plant out at 50cm/20in intervals each way from June through till August.

Spring (greens) cabbages: Sow in July/August in modules/seed trays or in a seed bed, and plant out in rows 30cm/12in apart with 10cm/4in between the plants, in September and October. Thin the following spring to 30cm/12in between plants – you can eat the thinnings.

Cultivation

The most important thing about growing cabbages is protection from pest and disease attack (see below). To minimize the risk of clubroot disease, do not grow cabbages on land where other brassicas have been grown during the previous three years.

In dry weather, cabbages benefit from a good soaking, at least once a week. If growth is sluggish, use an organic fertilizer, but beware of overfeeding cabbages that grow through the winter – soft, sappy leaves are more susceptible to frost damage. Earth up stems, especially on light soils, to provide better anchorage.

Pests and diseases

When you look at all the problems that can beset cabbages, and other members of the brassica family, it makes you wonder if it's worth bothering to grow them at all! Some pests, like pigeons, cabbage caterpillars and clubroot, can wipe out an entire crop. Don't be downhearted, however. They can all be overcome with a little bit of forethought and effort.

Pests

Pigeons: They love feasting on brassicas at all stages of development, from tiny seedlings to mature crops. Bird scarers may be helpful but are unlikely to put off determined birds. Netting is the only really effective answer.

Cabbage caterpillars: Three species attack brassicas: the large white butterfly, which lays oval yellow eggs (in clusters of ten to twenty on the underside of leaves) that hatch out into gold and dark green hairy caterpillars; the small white butterfly, whose pale green larvae hatch from eggs laid singly; and the mottled brown cabbage moth, which produces a dull grey caterpillar. Caterpillars of all species are active from May to October – the butterfly larvae feeding by day, the moth larvae by night.

Inspect plants regularly, turning over leaves to search for eggs, which can be destroyed by hand, and caterpillars, which can be picked off. Commercial growers use a biological control (see page 88) called *Bacillus thuringiensis*, but unfortunately it's not available to gardeners. However, there is another effective parasite called *Steinernema carpocapsae*, which you can spray onto brassicas in July; or you can use an organically approved insecticide like pyrethrum. In our own garden we grow all our brassicas in 1m-/3ft 3in-tall by 1.2m-/4ft-wide wooden cages, covered with small-mesh 'butterfly' netting, which fit over the beds. These have the added advantage of protecting against birds too.

Cabbage root flies: Lay their eggs in the soil at the base of brassica plants from May to October. The tiny white grubs tunnel into the roots, causing the plants to cease growing and collapse. You can buy brassica 'collars' to place around newly transplanted cabbages, but we make our own, cutting out 10cm/4in squares of carpet underlay with a single scissor cut from the middle of one side to the centre so it will fit snugly around the stem.

Mealy cabbage aphids: Dense clusters of waxy grey/mauve insects, which cause the leaves to pucker and growth to be stunted. They occur from May to November, but worsen from August onwards. Inspect plants regularly, and either tear off the affected parts of the leaves, rubbing the insects with your fingers, or spray with an organically approved insecticide. Cover very young seedlings with fleece.

Cabbage whiteflies: Small, white, delta-shaped insects that take to the air when leaves are tapped. The damage is done by their larvae, which live underneath the leaves as dark oval 'scales'. They feed on plant sap, and secrete a sugary substance that is colonized by black moulds. Whiteflies can usually be ignored, unless infestations are severe, but adults and larvae can be killed by insecticidal soap. You can also 'hoover' them up with a battery-powered vacuum cleaner. This works best early in the morning when the adults are still sluggish! Sponge the mould off carefully with soapy water.

Slugs and snails: They will attack brassicas at all stages, making unsightly holes in the leaves (see page 87).

Flea beetles: These 2mm-/$\frac{1}{12}$in-long black insects jump up in alarm when

Protect brassica crops from pests, using 'collars' and net-covered cages

disturbed (hence the name). They make tiny pits and 'shot holes' in seedlings (radishes and rocket can be badly affected, too) and their larvae feed on the roots. They are most active from mid-April to the end of May, but damage can also be severe in June and July – especially in hot and dry weather. Fleece is the best preventative, applied immediately after sowing.

Diseases

Clubroot: This is a devastating fungal disease that lives in the soil, causing the roots to distort into knobbly arthritic-looking lumps, preventing the plant from feeding. Crop rotation is the best insurance – once you have the disease, the fungal spores can survive for twenty years! There's no cure, but resistant varieties have been developed. If your soil has the disease, grow brassicas in 15cm/6in pots before transplanting, and earth up stems to encourage secondary rooting. The fungus also dislikes alkaline conditions, so add lime before planting to raise the pH to 7.5. Make sure that you burn all affected roots, or throw into the dustbin; but you can compost the leaves and stems. Turnip gall weevil, which also affects cabbages, produces similar symptoms. If the root is hollow, or there is a grub inside, you can breathe a sigh of relief, because gall weevils are not really a problem.

Other diseases: Brassicas also can suffer from virus diseases (for which there is no cure), mildews, and various other fungal diseases – but these are rarely serious.

Harvesting and storing

Cut cabbages close to the ground with a sharp knife. If you inscribe a cross in the stump, it will throw up new and softer growths you can harvest weeks later. Cabbages will keep for 16 weeks, hung up in nets in a cold, but frost-free shed at 0°C/32°F. (They last for only half this time if shed temperatures are 4–10°C/39–50°F.) You can freeze cabbage leaves, and preserve them as pickles or in brine as sauerkraut (see Part 4), but fresh is best!

Nutritional value

Vitamins: C, K***; A, folate**; B1*. Contains three times the RDA for vitamin K.
Minerals: manganese*
Phytochemicals: zeaxanthin, alpha-carotene, flavonoids, dithiolthiones, indoles, sulforaphane, sinigrin, indole-3-carbinol

Cabbages are a good source of fibre. They also contain significant amounts of the amino-acid glutamine, which has anti-inflammatory properties.
26kcal, LGI

VARIETIES

Spring (March to June): Durham Early, Wintergreen, Spring Hero F1
Summer (June to September): Derby Day, Golden Acre, Hispi F1
Autumn (October to December): Autumn Queen F1, Stonehead
Winter (October to March): Tundra F1, Holland Late Winter
Savoy: Savoy King F1, Tarvoy F1

Red (summer and autumn): Redcap F1, Red Jewel F1

Mini-cabbages: Minicole F1 (summer), Pixie (spring)

Clubroot-resistant: Kilaxy F1, Kilaton F1 – both autumn cropping

Heritage: Greyhound (summer), Christmas Drumhead (winter), January King (winter), April (spring), Flower of Spring (spring), Ormskirk (Savoy), Red Drumhead (red)

CARROTS

Carrots are slow to germinate, fussy about soil conditions and prone to a destructive pest, but the scent and taste of freshly dug carrots makes growing them well worth the effort – and they're good for you! They come in a variety of shapes – long and tapered, cylindrical (stump-rooted) and round – and in colours varying from the traditional orange through red, yellow, purple and even white.

Planning and preparation

Carrots grow best on light, stone-free soils, pH 6.5–7.5, that haven't been recently manured (which encourages them to fork). They will, however, grow on heavy soils if you choose a round, or stump-rooted, variety. In all cases, carefully rake the soil to produce a fine seed bed. Ten plants should produce around 2kg/4.5lb from maincrop varieties, or 0.8kg/1¾lb from earlies.

Sowing and planting

Sow outside in late February under cloches, provided that the soil temperature has reached 7°C/44°F, for very early crops. Carrots dislike being transplanted (the delicate tap root easily becomes damaged), but it's possible to grow round varieties in modules. Take out a shallow drill no more than 2cm/¾in deep and sow the tiny seeds as thinly as possible, covering with leafmould if you have it, then wait four to six weeks for them to germinate. Sowing can continue at intervals throughout the spring (when germination times more than halve), with those destined for winter storage going in around May. A final sowing in August will provide fresh carrots for pulling in November.

Space rows 15cm/6in apart and progressively thin plants to a final spacing of 2.5–5cm/1–2in for earlies, and up to 7.5cm/3in for maincrop varieties.

Cultivation

Once they are up and away, keep them weed free, well watered and safe from the ravages of carrot fly.

Pests and diseases

Pests

Carrot flies: These are the major pest of carrots. Adult flies lay their eggs in the soil in May, and their larvae feed on the fine root hairs at first, later tunnelling into the mature roots (usually near the base). A second generation of eggs is laid in August/September. Covering the crop with fleece throughout its life is the only guaranteed way of avoiding the problem. If you sow in early June and harvest before late August, you should miss attack, and there are several varieties that are partially resistant. In our experience, companion planting with onions is a waste of time.

Carrot-willow aphids: These pale green aphids overwinter on willows and migrate to carrots from late May to early July to feed on foliage. Seedlings wilt and become stunted, and may become infected by viruses. Protect with fleece, or spray with an organic insecticide.

Slugs, snails and cutworms: See page 87.

Diseases

Carrots suffer from several fungal diseases, such as violet root rot, and viruses for which there are no cures. When plants are heavily watered after a prolonged dry spell, splitting occurs. Forking (fanging) can be caused by stones, or by soil that is too rich in nitrogen.

Harvesting and storing

Begin harvesting in May and continue until November. Early crops can be pulled from the ground by hand; maincrops need to be gently eased out with a fork. You can store carrots in sand or a clamp (cut off the foliage around 5mm/1/4in above the crown), or leave them in the ground and cover with at least 15mm/6in of straw in December. Don't store damaged roots (they'll rot), but you can chop the undamaged parts into batons and freeze them (see Part 4).

Nutritional value

Vitamins: A***; B1, B6, C, E, K*. Contains three times the RDA of beta-carotene (a vitamin A precursor). **Phytochemicals:** alpha and beta-carotene, flavonoids, coumarin, lycopene, terpenes

Useful source of fibre. Deep-orange carrot varieties contain the most beta-carotene; white varieties have none. 35kcal, LGI

VARIETIES

Earlies: Early Nantes, Adelaide F1
Maincrop: Autumn King, Bangor F1
Carrot fly-resistant: Resistafly F1 and Flyaway F1 (partially resistant)
High carotene: Healthmaster F1, Sugarsnax F1
Unusual coloured: Purple Haze F1, Rainbow F1, Yellowstone, Red Elephant
Heritage: Chantenay Red Cored (early), Amsterdam Forcing (early), Long Red Surrey, James Scarlet Intermediate, White Belgian

CAULIFLOWERS

Cauliflowers are a year-round crop, but they are the hardest of all the brassicas to grow. They take up a lot of space in the garden, and are at risk from several formidable pests and diseases, but they are well worth the effort. In small gardens you can grow them best as 'mini veg'.

Planning and preparation

Like other brassicas, cauliflowers need a firm and fertile soil (see Brussels sprouts). Ten plants should produce about 3kg/7½lb of summer types and 14kg/30lb of autumn/winter varieties.

Sowing and planting

Summer cauliflowers: Sow in modules in a propagator set to 22°C/72°F in late January/early February and plant out in April when the young plants are 7.5cm/3in tall. Plant them in a grid formation, spacing them 53cm/21in apart in each direction (within the row and between each row), or plant them in rows 60cm/24in wide, with 45cm/18in between plants.

During March, you can also sow under cover in modules, and outside in April in a seedbed (space seeds 7.5cm/3in apart in rows 15cm/6in apart) as soon as the soil temperature has reached 7°C/44°F. Transplant to final positions after about six weeks.

Autumn cauliflowers: Sow in modules or a seed bed from mid-April to mid-May and transplant in late June, spacing plants 69cm/27in apart each way.

Winter/spring cauliflowers: Sow in modules in late May and transplant a month later at 75cm/30in each way.

Mini cauliflowers: As for summer and autumn types, but space transplants 13cm/5in apart each way.

Cultivation

Cauliflowers require regular weekly watering – early summer cauliflowers are extremely sensitive in this respect – otherwise growth will be checked and they can run to seed. Keep well weeded. The leaves of most modern varieties fold over naturally to protect the curds, but with older sorts you may have to tie up the leaves if severe frosts are forecast. In summer, bend over the outer leaves to shade the curd from harsh sunlight.

Pests and diseases

As for cabbages.

Harvesting and storing

Summer cauliflowers mature from June to September, autumn types from September to November, and winter/spring types from December to May. Harvest once the heads have matured but before the individual curds (which are the flower heads) have begun to open. You can bottle or freeze individual florets, or lift and store entire plants, hanging them by their roots from the roof of a frost-free shed (see Part 4).

Nutritional value

Vitamins: C***; K, folate**; B1, B5, B6*
Minerals: potassium, phosphorus, manganese*
Phytochemicals: sulforaphane, indole-3-carbinol, flavonoids, terpenes. Purple cauliflowers contain anthocyanin, which gives them their purple colour.

Cauliflowers are high in fibre and low in fat.
34kcal, LGI

CELERIAC

Celeriac is widely grown in mainland Europe, and it is gradually becoming more popular here. It tastes like, and is closely related to, celery. Although you can eat the strongly flavoured leaves as seasoning, it's grown for its root-like, celery-flavoured, swollen stem base.

Planning and preparation

If celeriac is to do well, the soil must be fertile and moisture-retentive with pH 6.5–7.5. A sunny site is preferred but it will tolerate semi-shade. Add compost or well-rotted manure prior to planting. Ten plants should produce around 5kg/11lb of celeriac.

Sowing and planting

If you have a propagator, sow early in March in a seed tray or modules at 16°C/61°F. When the plants are 1cm/½in tall, transfer them to 4cm/1½in modules, or equivalent-sized pots, indoors. Alternatively, wait until April and sow into pots on a windowsill (the kitchen is ideal, where the air is usually more moist). Celeriac is slow to germinate: typically taking anything from two to three weeks. It's also very sensitive to cold, so if you sow too early, plants are likely to bolt. Harden off in a cold frame when the plants are about 7.5cm/3in tall, and plant out in May, with the bulbous base just brushing the soil. Space plants 35cm/14in each way, or 30cm/12in apart in 45cm/18in wide rows.

Cultivation

Celeriac requires regular watering – twice a week in dry weather. Any interruption and growth will be checked. Apply an organic fertilizer immediately after transplanting, and boost with an occasional liquid feed. Remove any yellowed leaves, and side shoots as they appear, from August onwards. At the same time, earth up around the stems if your taste runs to blanched roots.

Pests and diseases

Celeriac shares the same pests and diseases as celery (see page 140), but is generally trouble-free.

Harvesting and storing

Lift, using a fork, when around 10–13cm/4–5in in diameter, usually from September onwards. If you leave them to get bigger, they can become tough. On light soils they can remain in the ground, under a blanket of bracken, straw or heavy fleece, and dug as required until March. On heavier soils it's best to lift them in November, then trim away the foliage and store in sand. Celeriac can also be frozen, as slices or batons (see Part 4).

Nutritional value

Vitamins: K***; B6, C*
Phytochemicals: coumarins
High in fibre.
42kcal, LGI

VARIETIES

Brilliant, Monarch, Prinz (resistant to bolting)
Heritage: Giant Prague

CELERY

Celery is a real test of a gardener's skill, because it is one of the most difficult and time-consuming of crops. Blanching improves the flavour and makes the stems less stringy and crisper. Self-blanching types are easier to grow than traditionally blanched 'trench' celery, but they lack the taste and texture. If you'd like to eat fresh celery from July to January, you have to grow both.

Planning and preparation

Moist, rich soils are essential (celery grows wild in coastal marshland). For trench celery, dig a trench 38cm/15in wide and 30cm/12in deep during the autumn or winter, no later than March. Loosen the base with a fork and add a layer of manure or compost, well-trodden down. Top up with earth to within 7.5cm/3in of the soil surface.

Space trenches 1m/3ft 3in apart. For self-blanching celery, there's no need to dig a trench, but you'll need to incorporate compost or manure into soils prior to planting. Ten plants of either type should provide around 4kg/9lb.

Sowing and planting

Sow in a propagator from mid-March to early April, in a seed tray or modules at

16°C/61°F. Seeds germinate best if left uncovered. Prick out into modules when plants have five leaves and keep under cover, ensuring that the temperature never drops below 10°C/50°F for more than 12 hours. Harden off, and plant out in late May, spacing trench varieties every 30cm/12in, and self-blanching types 23cm/9in each way.

To short-circuit this process, buy celery plants ready for planting in May.

Cultivation

Plants must never be allowed to dry out. Water daily in hot weather and feed with liquid manure once a week. Cover with fleece immediately after planting.
Trench varieties: In early August, when the plants are around 30cm/12in tall, wrap a collar of corrugated cardboard or newspaper loosely around the stems (so that the green tips peep over the top)

and tie with string. Repeat with another collar three or so weeks later to cover the new growth, and a final one after a similar interval. In our view, this method is an improvement on the traditional approach of progressively earthing up the stems, because it avoids soil getting into the hearts.
Self-blanching varieties: These rely on the leaves and close spacing to effect the blanching process. Place straw around the perimeter of the celery bed to blanch the outer plants.

Pests and diseases

Pests
Slugs and snails: These love celery! For control methods see page 87.
Celery flies: Also called celery leaf miners on account of the tunnels the larvae make in the leaves. Ideally, cover crops with fleece after planting. Remove and destroy any blotched and blistered leaves.
Carrot flies: Damage is rarely severe (see page 136).

Diseases
Celery leaf spot: Small brown spots appear on leaves and stems. Apart from removing affected foliage, there is nothing more you can do.
Celery crown rot: Symptoms include stunted growth, yellow foliage. No cure.

Blanch celery using corrugated cardboard

Harvesting and storing

Begin harvesting self-blanching varieties in July, and continue until the first frosts. Trench celery takes over in October, and can be picked until Christmas (white varieties) or January (pink/red sorts). It will not survive hard, or prolonged, frosts. Under such circumstances, protect with a layer of bracken or straw. You can lift celery and store it in moist sand, a cool cellar, or heeled in inside a cold frame. Celery will keep for a couple of weeks in a fridge, and can be frozen or incorporated into pickles and relishes (see Part 4).

Nutritional value

Vitamins: C*
Phytochemicals: apigenin, coumarin, limonene, 3-n-butylphthalide (which gives celery its distinctive odour) and coumarins
7kcal, LGI

VARIETIES

Self-blanching: Daybreak F1, Lathom Self Blanching, Victoria F1, Green Utah
Heritage (trench): Giant Red, Giant White, Solid Pink, Solid White
Heritage (self-blanching): Giant Pascal, Golden Self Blanching

CHICORIES and ENDIVE

Chicories and endive are closely related members of the dandelion family, with slightly bitter-tasting leaves. There are three types of chicories – radicchio or red, sugar loaf (like a large cos lettuce) and Brussels Witloof, which is forced, producing blanched buds (chicons) in winter. Endive comes in two sorts – curly leaved or frisée, and the more hardy broad-leaved Batavian (escarole) types.

Planning and preparation

Like dandelions, chicories are not fussy about where they grow; most reasonably fertile soils (pH 5.5–7.5), in sun or partial shade, will do. Endives are slightly more demanding, and grow best in a well-composted soil. The roots of forcing types of chicory resemble slender parsnips, and grow 30cm/12in long; so they need a deep soil. If you wish to grow winter crops, you'll need a cool greenhouse, polytunnel or cloche. Ten plants should produce around 1.4kg/3lb of chicons. A large sugar loaf chicory can weigh 2kg/4½lb.

Sowing and planting

Chicories

Sow forcing chicories 10mm/½in deep in modules, from May to early June – minimum soil temperature 10°C/50°F.

When transplanting, space plants 23cm/9in apart in 35cm-/14in-wide rows. To avoid bolting, sow non-forcing chicories from mid-June to July in modules and plant out at the same spacing.

Endive

Endive requires a much higher temperature to germinate: 20°C/68°F. Sow in modules from April/May (under cover) to August and plant out at 30cm/12in intervals each way. Alternatively, station-sow three to four seeds at 30cm/12in intervals and thin to the strongest.

You can sow endive and chicories outside these periods, especially as a 'cut and come again' seedling crop, but the plants will need protection with cloches or equivalent. Endive will bolt in prolonged cold weather, if the temperature drops to below 5°C/41°F for more than three weeks.

Cultivation

Water until the plants are well established; after that they can usually fend for themselves.

Pests and diseases

Slugs are attracted to young seedlings (one good reason for growing them in modules) but otherwise both crops are pretty much pest- and disease-free. Chicories are prone to basal rots, for which there are no cures.

Harvesting and storing

Chicories

You can eat chicons (blanched buds) from December to April. Dig up roots with a fork in November. Trim away any side shoots and cut the foliage back to 2.5cm/1in and the main root to 20cm/8in – so they will fit into forcing pots. Store in moist sand until required. Then pack four to five roots into a 23cm/9in pot, filled with dampened soil or spent potting medium, so that it lightly covers the crowns. Place an inverted pot of the same size over it (plugging the drainage hole with a cork, or similar, to exclude light), and put somewhere warm (a greenhouse or spare bedroom?) at a temperature of 10–16°C/50–61°F. After about three weeks, cut the chicons when 15cm/6in high, just above the base, and

Forcing chicory roots

eat fresh, or store in a fridge for about a week. The plants will produce an inferior second crop, but it's not really worth it, so put the spent roots on the compost heap. You can harvest unforced chicories from August to December (March/April under glass). Radicchio hearts will keep in cardboard boxes, kept moist, in a cool shed for several weeks. Sugar-loaf types will store for two months in the shed, too.

Endive

Endive can also be blanched to produce sweeter leaves. Tie leaves of escarole types loosely together, or cover with a large plant pot, for ten days (three weeks in winter); alternatively, you can buy pottery endive blanchers. Frisées are less bitter and do not usually require blanching. Harvest from September to December (or virtually all year round if you have protection).

Nutritional value

Vitamins: B1, K*
Phytochemicals: chicory root contains fructo-oligosaccharides
11kcal, LGI

VARIETIES

Chicories
Forcing: Witloof, Lightning
Radicchio: Palla Rossa, Castelfranco, Rosso Treviso (can be forced)
Sugar loaf: Milano, Sugar Loaf, Jupiter F1
Other: Misticanza (mixture), Magdeburg (dried, ground roots make a coffee substitute)

Endive
Broad-leaved (escarole type): Batavian, Blonde Full Heart, Cornet de Bordeaux
Curled (frisée type): Moss Curled, Pancalieri

Most seed catalogues list only a few varieties. Seeds of Italy (Franchi) sell a much greater range.

COURGETTES and MARROWS

A courgette (zucchini) is merely an immature marrow; which is, in turn, a type of summer squash – a member of the cucurbit family. Courgettes are easy to grow, and are usually cylindrical, though they can also be spherical, in shades of green or yellow. Plump, disc-shaped summer squashes with scalloped edges are called custard marrows or 'patty pans'. Yellow, bulbous marrows with a warty skin and a hooked neck are termed 'crookneck squashes'.

Planning and preparation

All cucurbits require a well-composted soil, pH 5.5–6.8, in full sun, to do well.

A word of caution, however: if the soil is too rich, plants will produce foliage at the expense of crop, so do not over-manure.

One plant should produce around 15–20 courgettes, or five to six marrows weighing at least 1.5kg/3lb each.

Sowing and planting

Cucurbits are frost-sensitive, so early sowings outdoors are inadvisable – June is soon enough in most places, when the soil has warmed to at least 13°C/55°F. You can start them off under cover, sowing two seeds in a 7.5cm/3in pot in late April, and thinning to the strongest, for planting out at the end of May or early June, when all risk of frost has passed.

Sow seeds about 2.5cm/1in deep. Ignore advice saying that seeds must be set edge upwards: it makes no difference to germination how they're placed. Harden off carefully, and transplant when the plant has made two true leaves and the third is just beginning, spacing them at least 90cm/3ft each way or 1.2–1.8m/4–6ft for trailing sorts. If you're sowing outdoors, place three seeds at each station, cover with a bottle cloche (see page 72), and thin to the strongest.

Cultivation

It's worthwhile protecting new trans-plants with fleece, or a cloche, for a week or so until they're established. Keep them weeded and well watered. Once the plants have started flowering, give them a boost with a liquid seaweed fertilizer if they seem to be lacking vigour. Pollination is rarely a problem, except in the dullest and wettest of years when there are only a few insects on the wing. If flowers do fail to set, however, remove a male flower and dust it into the open centre of a female flower (females have a small swelling behind the flower).

As the fruits develop, mulch with straw, or similar, to protect them from soil splashing onto the skins. Alternatively, lay a black plastic or other weed-suppressing membrane prior to transplanting and grow through this.

Pests and diseases

Cucurbits are largely problem-free. Slugs are partial to young seedlings (another reason to use bottle cloches), and glasshouse red spider and whitefly (see tomatoes) can be a nuisance. Powdery mildew (see page 88) is almost inevitable from August onwards, especially in hot spells, as the leaves turn chalky grey, but if the plants are well watered, they'll carry on fruiting. Cucumber mosaic virus produces mottling of the leaves and stunted growth. There's no cure – dig up and burn infected plants.

Harvesting and storing

Cut courgettes from July to October, when they're 10–15cm/4–6in long. It's important to pick every day or so – leaving just a couple of fruits to develop into marrows will cause the plant to cease production. They'll keep in the fridge for a couple of weeks and can be frozen.

Leave marrows on the vine until mature – around 38–45cm/15–18in long – but cut before the first frosts arrive. They should sound hollow when tapped. Place in the sun, underside uppermost, so that the skins can harden. Stored at a temperature of 7–10°C/44–50°F in a well-ventilated shed, they should last a couple of months.

Nutritional value

Vitamins: C***; folate**; A, B1, B6*
Minerals: potassium*
18kcal, LGI

CUCUMBERS

The long, smooth, straight fruits on sale in the shops will have been raised indoors and are quite tricky to grow. These 'frame' cucumbers differ from outdoor, or 'ridge', sorts, which tend to be chunkier and have prickly skins, but are a lot easier to cultivate. Growing only the modern, all-female varieties avoids the 'bitterness' that can occur with traditional glasshouse cucumber varieties that are pollinated by mistake. There are 'mini' varieties, which are only 10–20cm/4–8in long: just right for small households. Gherkins, which are short, ridge cucumbers that are picked young, are especially bred for pickling.

Planning and preparation

Outdoor cucumbers require a well-composted, fertile soil (pH 5–5.8), preferably in a sheltered and sunny position, although they will tolerate a little shade. Plant next to a fence, wall or some other structure they can clamber over. It's worth creating a special planting hole – 30cm/12in square and deep – filled with compost or rotted manure, mixed with sieved soil. If grown under cover, use 25cm/10in pots, grow-bags (two plants per bag), or plant directly into the soil, prepared as for outdoor growing. You'll also need to rig up a method of support, such as a cane secured at the roof, or strings tied to wires attached to the glasshouse struts. One glasshouse plant should produce at least 10–20 full-size cucumbers and over 30 mini cucumbers; outdoors, expect 5–10 fruits or 15 or so minis.

Sowing and planting

Cucumber seeds germinate within two to three days, but need a minimum germination temperature of 20°C/68°F, so it's best to start them off in a propagator. The roots dislike disturbance, so sow individually in modules, or sow two seeds to a 7.5cm/3in pot and thin to the strongest. Do this in late February or early March, for planting in May, if you have a heated greenhouse. If you're growing in a polytunnel, unheated glasshouse or cold frame, leave it until late April. In either case, transplant when the plants have made two true leaves and the third is just beginning; spacing them 45cm/18in apart. You may need to supply additional heat at night, until you can be sure that temperatures won't fall below 16°C/61°F.

Wait until late May or June before attempting to sow outdoors. (Alternatively, you could sow in modules in late April, harden off, and plant out in early June.) Place three seeds in the centre of each planting hole, in a triangular pattern, 7.5cm/3in apart and 1cm/½in deep, spacing each hole 60cm/24in apart, and remove all but the strongest.

Cultivation

Modern glasshouse varieties are bred to produce female flowers on the main stem, producing seedless fruits without pollination. This has done away with the chore of eliminating the male flowers, because fertilized fruits can become bitter. Train the main shoot upwards, tying it to a cane or string until it has reached the roof and is around 2.1m/7ft long, then pinch it out. Remove all lateral shoots.

With heritage varieties, the fruits are produced on side growths, which must be stopped two leaves beyond the first female flower (flowers with a swelling behind them). Fruit-producing secondary shoots may sprout from these side growths, and they must also be pinched out two leaves after a flower, or removed altogether if no flower develops.

Water daily, and feed at least fortnightly with a general-purpose, organic liquid fertilizer. In summer, lightly whitewash the glass to provide some shade.

By contrast, most outdoor varieties produce both male and female flowers and must be fertilized if they're to fruit. Happily, pollinated outdoor cucumbers do not become bitter. You may need to give nature a helping hand (see courgettes). Pinch out the growing tip after the first seven leaves, to encourage bushy growth. Remove any side shoots at the seventh leaf, if they haven't produced female flowers. Keep well watered, feed as necessary, and mulch with straw to protect the fruits from soil splash.

Pests and diseases

Cucumbers are subject to the same pests as other members of the cucurbit family (see courgettes). Indoor varieties can suffer from red spider mites, whiteflies and aphids (see tomatoes). Daily damping down of the inside of the glasshouse is one of the best ways of controlling spider mites. The chief diseases are powdery mildew and cucumber mosaic virus (CMV), but resistant varieties are available – see right.

Harvesting and storing

Cucumbers fruit from July to October and, like all cucurbits, they need to be cut regularly to encourage growth. Cucumbers will keep for several weeks in the fridge, especially if wrapped in cling film, but do not freeze well. They're traditionally preserved in vinegar as pickles and relishes. Pickle gherkins when they're about 5cm/2in long, or half that size as 'cornichons' (see Part 4).

Nutritional value

Vitamins: K**
Phytochemicals: caffeic acid, chlorogenic acid and protease inhibitors

VARIETIES

Glasshouse
All Female: Diana F1, Flamingo F1
Powdery mildew-resistant: Swing F1, Carmen F1, Silor F1 (also CMV-resistant)
All Female Mini: Cucino F1, Melon F1, Rocky F1
Heritage: Conqueror, Telegraph Improved

Outdoors
Standard: Burpless Tasty Green F1, La Diva F1, Masterpiece
Resistant: Marketmore (CMV), La Diva F1 (powdery mildew)
Heritage: Boothby's Blonde, Crystal Lemon (lemon-shaped), King of the Ridge
Gherkin: Adam F1, National Pickling, Diamant F1

FLORENCE FENNEL

Grown for its aniseed-flavoured, swollen stem base, Florence fennel, or finocchio, is not an easy vegetable to grow, because of its tendency to bolt if growth is checked in any way. Like its herb relative, you can also eat the green feathery leaves.

Planning and preparation

To do well, the crop needs a sunny spot and a light, well-drained yet moisture retentive soil, pH 5.5–7.5. It doesn't thrive on clay soils. Ten plants should produce 5–10kg/11–22lb of bulbs.

Sowing and planting

Florence fennel can't tolerate root disturbance – it'll bolt – so start the seeds off in modules or biodegradable pots, not seed trays. They need a soil temperature of at least 15°C/59°F to germinate, so sow under cover from April to May (transplanting outdoors in May or June), and outdoors from May to July (two or three seeds per station, thinning to the strongest). Sow every couple of weeks to ensure a succession, ending in early August for a late crop. When sowing before mid-June, always choose a bolt-resistant variety, but it's safest to sow from mid-summer onwards.

Sow seeds 1cm/½in deep in a grid formation, spacing them 30cm/12in apart in each direction (within the row and between each row).

Cultivation

Florence fennel must be kept weed free and well watered, otherwise it'll bolt. Mulch with compost or grass clippings to aid water conservation. Protect early and late sowings with fleece – any cold snap and they will bolt. It's usual practice to earth up the bulbs when they've begun to swell, in order to blanch them, but this isn't essential.

Pests and diseases

Apart from the risk of bolting, and slug attack, in the early stages, Florence fennel is pretty much problem-free.

Harvesting and storing

Pick the crop from June to October, either lifting with a fork or cutting the bulb just below its base – the root will throw up a few salad leaves. Can be frozen (see Part 4).

Nutritional value

Vitamins: C, folate*
Minerals: potassium*
Phytochemicals: beta-carotene, flavonoids and other phenolic compounds
12kcal, LGI

VARIETIES

Standard: Romanesco, Rondo F1, Montebianco
Bolt-resistant: Finale, Victoria F1

GARLIC

For a crop that epitomizes Mediterranean sunshine, garlic is astonishingly hardy and will stand through the hardest winters. Bulbs vary in colour, from ivory-white to shades of pink and purple, and in strength, from mild to eye-wateringly fierce. They are categorized according to whether they produce a stiff, flowering stalk (hardnecks) or pliable, plaitable leaves (softnecks). Hardneck garlic is called rocambole, or serpent garlic, in the US, on account of its sinuous edible flowering stem called a 'scape', which can be harvested before the bulbils form. Elephant garlic is not garlic at all: it's a type of leek, producing enormous bulbs, with a mild garlic-like flavour.

Planning and preparation

Garlic grows best on light, fertile soils, pH 6–7.5, in a sunny spot. Improve soil conditions by adding compost (but not manure). The crop also benefits from the addition of an organic potash fertilizer, like sugar beet extract (kali vinasse), which also provides some protection against leek rust. Garlic isn't grown from seed, but from individual cloves. Although you can grow garlic from shop-bought bulbs, sold for eating, they're unreliable, having been produced in much warmer climates than ours. One bulb will provide around eight to twelve cloves for planting.

Sowing and planting

The longer the time in the ground, the bigger the bulbs, so it's preferable to plant garlic in the autumn, during October and November. Carefully break up bulbs into their constituent cloves, and plant them with the corky, flat base downwards in a dibbered hole up to 10cm/4in deep. The rule is, the lighter the soil, the deeper the planting – with a minimum soil covering of 2.5cm/1in. On really heavy soils, grow in pots or large modules, overwinter in a cold frame and plant out in March/April. Space plants 10–15cm/4–6in apart, in rows 23–30cm/9–12in wide. If you miss the autumn planting slot, you can sow in February or March – some varieties are more successful from spring sowings than others. Elephant garlic bulbs can be 10cm/4in across and require bigger, 30 × 30cm/12 × 12in, spacing.

Cultivation

Garlic plants pretty much take care of themselves, apart from an occasional weeding. Several weeks before lifting, cut back the flowering stem of hardnecks to provide a helping of 'scapes', and to boost bulb size.

Pests and diseases

Like other members of the *Allium* genus, garlic can be attacked by leek rust (see leeks) and onion white rot (see onions) but otherwise it's mainly trouble-free.

Harvesting and storing

When the foliage turns yellow and dies down, usually from June to August, bulbs are ready to be lifted. Gently prise them from the ground, using a fork, and place them on wire racks on the ground (or under cover in wet weather) to dry for a week or so. Store in a cool, dry shed: lying on trays, plaited (softnecks) or tied in bunches (hardnecks – leaving around 7.5cm/3in of stem). Do not store anywhere warm and humid (e.g. the kitchen), otherwise they'll start to sprout. Hardneck garlic is reckoned to have the better flavour, but rarely keeps beyond Christmas; softnecks store until the following spring. Keep aside some bulbs for replanting – they can adapt to the conditions in your garden.

Nutritional value

Vitamins: B6, C**; B1*
Minerals: phosphorus**; potassium, iron, zinc, manganese*

Phytochemicals: quercetin, thiosulphanates, limonene, coumaric acid, allicin, saponins, organosulphides, fructo-oligosaccharides.

Garlic possesses strong anti-bacterial properties, is mildly anti-hypertensive and helps to prevent blood clotting. It also appears to offer protection from some forms of cancer.
98kcal, LGI

VARIETIES

Hardneck: Early Wight, Moldovan Wight, Illico
Softneck: Germidour, Solent Wight, Albigensian Wight
Suitable for spring planting: Picardy Wight, Cristo

The Garlic Farm on the Isle of Wight sells a good range of varieties (see Resources, p.304).

GLOBE ARTICHOKES

Growing to over 1.2m/4ft tall, and with a spread of 1m/3ft 3in, this is a vegetable for those with plenty of space. The edible flower buds are so delicious and nutritious, however, that it's worth making space for a couple of plants.

Planning and preparation

Globe artichokes are greedy feeders, requiring a sunny, sheltered spot and well-manured and well-drained soil, pH 6.5–7. They don't like heavy soils. Their decorative foliage and striking mauve thistle-like flowers make them a good candidate for the rear of a herbaceous border. A single plant will produce one head in the first year, around six in year two, and a dozen in years three and four.

Sowing and planting

If growing from seed, sow indoors in February, making sure that the soil temperature is at least 18°C/65°F. Harden off, and plant out in May. Alternatively, sow outside in a seed bed in early April and transplant into final positions, at 1m/3ft 3in intervals each way, in late May. The quality of plants from seeds can be extremely variable, however, which is why most people buy plant 'offsets' taken from rooted suckers in April.

Cultivation

Apply a heavy dressing of manure each spring; mulch to keep plants weed-free, and water generously during dry spells. During the summer, feed with a liquid fertilizer every few weeks. In November, cut down the stems and protect the crowns by covering them with bracken, leafmould, straw or bark chips. Remove the following April.

Productivity will start to decline after four years, at which point propagate from the parent plants by taking offsets in April. Slice downwards with a spade into the crown, taking a chunk with several shoots and roots attached, and replant in fresh soil.

Pests and diseases

Blackflies will sometimes attack, but they rarely cause appreciable damage. Slugs and snails can be a problem, attacking young shoots (see page 87). Dark spots on developing buds indicate the presence of petal blight. The flowers will eventually rot, so remove and destroy.

Harvesting and storing

Pick the heads to eat when they're still tight. In May and June they'll be small enough to be cooked and eaten whole, but by July they'll be full-sized and tough, so only the fleshy base of the bracts and the 'heart' itself, concealed beneath the hairy 'choke' are edible. Eat only the central 'king' head in the first year. In later years, smaller, egg-sized, heads develop on side stems. The last picking is usually in September, but you can also freeze the heads (see Part 4).

Nutritional value

Vitamins: C, folate**; K*
Minerals: potassium, phosphorus, magnesium, copper, manganese*
Phytochemicals: silymarin, cynarin, lignans, caffeic acid, ferulic acid

High in fibre and low in fat
53kcal, LGI

VARIETIES

Green: Imperial Star
Purple: Concerto F1, Romanesco, Violetta di Chioggia
Heritage: Green Globe, Gros vert de Laon

HAMBURG PARSLEY

This easy-to-grow, versatile vegetable is commonplace in Germany and Eastern Europe, but is something of a rarity here. This is a pity, because its parsnip-shaped root, which has a nutty taste with a hint of celery, can be eaten raw or cooked, and its leaves are like flat-leaved parsley.

Planning and preparation

Hamburg parsley will tolerate a degree of shade, and it prefers a light, stone-free, well-drained soil (pH 6.5–7). Prepare the ground by digging in compost or well-rotted manure during the winter before sowing. Ten plants should produce around 2kg/4.5lb of roots.

Sowing and planting

Hamburg parsley germinates when soils have warmed to 7°C/44°F, from March to May. Station-sow seeds 1cm/½in deep every 23cm/9in, in rows 30cm/12in wide, or sow seeds in a grid formation, spacing them 25cm/10in apart in each direction (within the row and between each row). Thin to the strongest.

Alternatively, start them off individually in root trainers and transplant when the tops have made 5cm/2in of growth. If space is at a premium, grow them in 25cm/10in pots (three seeds per pot), because the roots rarely grow longer than 20cm/8in. Like other members of the carrot/parsley family, germination is slow.

Cultivation

Weed as necessary, and water if dry; otherwise the crop looks after itself.

Pests and diseases

Hamburg parsley isn't troubled by pests, but can be affected by the fungus that causes parsnip canker (see page 167), for which no resistant varieties have been bred, as yet.

Harvesting and storing

The crop is ready for lifting from September to January. Prise roots gently from the ground with a fork, as you would parsnips, taking care not to pierce them. Like parsnips, Hamburg parsley

tolerates harsh winter weather and can remain in the ground throughout. Some say that the flavour improves after a hard frost. If it looks as though the land is likely to be frozen for a long period (making lifting impossible), don't leave in the ground, but store in moist sand in a shed. Snip off the leaves while the plant is growing, to provide an alternative to flat-leaved parsley.

Nutritional value

Vitamins: A, C, K, folate***; E*. Contains 21 times the RDA for vitamin K.
Minerals: calcium, potassium, iron, phosphorus, copper, zinc*
Phytochemicals: beta-carotene, lutein, zeaxanthin
10kcal LGI

VARIETIES

Most seed catalogues offer a single, unnamed variety. Berliner is the only other we have come across.

JERUSALEM and CHINESE ARTICHOKES

This 3m/10ft tall member of the sunflower family produces a knobbly, edible root, with a delicate, ginger-like, nutty taste. Unfortunately, it has a well-deserved reputation for causing flatulence, which is perhaps why it's not that popular. Chinese artichokes are similar, but much smaller, and belong to a different botanical family so do not give rise to the same antisocial problems.

Planning and preparation

Jerusalem artichokes are not fussy about soil conditions (pH 6–7.5) as long as

they don't become waterlogged, and can (indeed should) be grown in the same place every year. Dig in manure the year before planting and add compost annually. Ten plants should produce around 18kg/40lb of tubers.

Sowing and planting

Both Jerusalem and Chinese artichokes are grown from tubers, not seeds. Plant Jerusalem artichokes 13–15cm/5–6in deep in March (February if conditions permit), 45cm/18in apart, in 75cm-/30in-wide rows. Space Chinese artichokes 35cm/14in each way, but plant them only 10cm/4in deep, in April. They are also suitable for container growing.

Cultivation

Jerusalem artichokes are at risk from being blown over, so earth up the stem to a height of around 15cm/6in and surround the bed with a stake and string barrier (see broad beans, p.120) using 1.8m/6ft canes. Water in dry weather. Remove the flowers, and cut back the stems to 1.5m/5ft in July/August to aid tuber formation. Cut back again to 15cm/6in above the ground in October.

Chinese artichokes never grow more than 75cm/30in tall so do not need staking, but the flowers should also be removed.

Pests and diseases

Slugs and snails cause occasional damage, and lettuce root aphids can cause wilting, but the crop is usually problem-free.

Harvesting and storing

Lift tubers with a fork from October to March. They can stay in the ground throughout the winter (protect Chinese artichokes with fleece or straw), so lift only when needed. In either case, dig the land thoroughly after the crop has been harvested – the tiniest fragment will re-grow the following year.

Chinese artichoke tubers are only 5cm/2in long and are extraordinarily difficult to clean because they are so knobbly. Treat the task as meditation! If stored in a fridge, they will quickly shrivel.

Nutritional value

(Jerusalem artichokes)
Vitamins: B1, C*
Minerals: potassium, phosphorus, copper*
Phytochemicals: flavonoids, inulin. Jerusalem artichokes have greater levels of fructo-oligosaccharides, a type of dietary fibre, than any other cultivated plant.
76kcal, MGI

VARIETIES

Most seed catalogues offer an unnamed variety, or the smooth-skinned heritage variety, Fuseau, which is easier to peel. Gerrard is a round, red-skinned variety. There are no varietal forms of Chinese artichokes. Dwarf Sunray has a good reputation for flavour, but is rarely found nowadays.

KALES

Of all the leaf brassicas, kales are the least demanding to grow, and the hardiest. There are lots to choose from: Scotch kales, also called borecole, which have plain or tightly curled leaves, in shades of green and purple, and the later-cropping rape kales, which, confusingly, also have curly or plain leaves. In recent years, cavolo nero (Black Tuscan kale), with its dramatic, dark green blistered leaves, has become something of a wunderkind vegetable for fashionable foodies.

Planning and preparation

Similar to broccoli (see page 128). In really cold districts, grow rape kales – they'll survive anything winter can throw at them. Ten plants should produce around 9kg/20lb of leaves.

Sowing and planting

Although you can sow in February (minimum soil germination temperature 7°C/44°F for a summer crop), kale is usually eaten during winter. Sow all but the rape kales in April/May in modules, or in a seed bed, 2cm/¾in deep (see broccoli), and transplant to final positions in June/July. Space most varieties 45cm/18in each way, but taller sorts need extra room and should be given 60cm/24in between plants. Cavolo nero can go in 35cm/14in each way.

Rape kales crop late into the winter during the proverbial 'hungry gap' in April and May, when there is little else to eat, and so should be sown later, at the end of July or early August, 45cm/18in each way, in their final positions. Sow three seeds at each station and thin to the strongest.

Cultivation

Apart from keeping plants weed-free and watered, kales do not need much looking after. In exposed conditions, stake tall varieties to protect them from blowing over. Remove and compost lower leaves throughout the growing period, as they progressively yellow and die. In early spring, feed with an organic liquid fertilizer to give the plants a bit of a fillip for their final spurt.

Pests and diseases

Kales are not immune from all the troubles that beset members of the brassica family (see cabbages for details), but they somehow seem to suffer less. For example, pigeons only attack kales in our garden when there's nothing else to eat. Pests also appear to dislike varieties with purple-red leaves. Even so, the only way to avoid sleepless nights is to net everything!

Harvesting and storing

With a suitable mix of varieties, you can be eating kale from October to May. Start from the bottom of the plant and work your way up, discarding any leaves that are old or tough-looking, although they should be fine if you cut out the midrib. Pick a few leaves from each plant to allow it to re-grow. Cease picking when flower buds form. Red-leaved kales turn green on cooking. Kale freezes well (see Part 4).

Nutritional value

Vitamins: A, C, K, folate***; E**; B6*. Kale contains three times the RDA for vitamin C and eight times the RDA for vitamin K.

Minerals: manganese**; calcium, potassium, magnesium, iron, phosphorus*. Calcium in kale is absorbed more easily than calcium from milk.

Phytochemicals: beta-carotene, **lutein**, zeaxanthin, flavonols, quercetin, sulforaphane and other organosulphur compounds, coumarins, terpenes. Kales have the highest overall antioxidant ability of all the leafy green vegetables. 33kcal, LGI

VARIETIES

Curly-leaved (green): Dwarf Green Curled, Darkibor F1, Westland Winter

Curly-leaved (red): Redbor F1, Red Curled

Plain-leaved: Red Winter, Pentland Brig (also produces spears)

Rape kale: Asparagus, Hungry Gap, Red Russian

Cavolo nero: Nero di Toscana

Heritage: Cottager's, Ragged Jack, Thousand Headed

Novelty: Jersey Tree (grows to 3m/10ft and can be carved into a walking stick!)

KOHL RABI

An increasingly popular vegetable in the brassica family, with a swollen stem base the size and shape of a billiard ball, and a nutty, cabbage/turnip flavour.

Planning and preparation

Kohl rabi will grow reasonably well on poorer land than most brassicas, and whilst they will tolerate heavier ground, their preference is for light, fertile, moisture-retentive soils with pH 6–7.5. Purple-skinned varieties are hardier than white-skinned types, so choose them if sowing after mid-summer. Ten plants should produce around 1.6kg/3½lb of 'roots'.

Sowing and planting

Begin sowing in February/March in a propagator, at a seed depth of 1cm/½in. Plant out in April/May at a spacing of 25cm/10in each way, or 15cm/6in apart in 30cm-/12in-wide rows. Sowing can begin outdoors in March, providing the soil temperature is at least 10°C/50°F (anything less and the crop will bolt). Plants may be reared in modules and planted out, or else station-sown *in situ* and thinned to the strongest. Use bolt-resistant varieties for early sowings. Repeat sowing every fortnight until August.

Cultivation

Kohl rabi become tough and woody if checked, so mulch with compost and keep the soil weeded and well watered. This will also reduce the risk of splitting.

Pests and diseases

Slugs and flea beetles can be a problem for seedlings, and pigeons will attack at all stages, so it's best to cover with fleece. Other brassica problems, like clubroot, are rarely any trouble, because the crop is only in the ground for around ten weeks.

Harvesting and storing

Pick when around 5–7.5cm/2–3in diameter – billiard-ball to tennis-ball size – from May to December. Lift the entire plant and trim off the leaves with a knife. Roots can be stored in damp sand, frozen, or wrapped tightly in cling film and kept in a fridge for a week.

Nutritional value

Vitamins: C***; B6, E*
Minerals: potassium*
Phytochemicals: beta-carotene, flavonoids, dithiolthiones, isothiocyanates, flavonoids, coumarins, terpenes

VARIETIES
....

White: Olivia F1, White Delicacy
Purple: Azur Star, Purple Delicacy
Bolt- and split-resistant: Noriko, Superschmelz (grows to football size, 8kg/18lb, without becoming woody)
Heritage: Green Vienna, Purple Vienna

LEEKS

Leeks occupy the ground for a long time, but they are relatively easy to grow. You could be eating leeks from August to May if you choose suitable varieties. Summer- and autumn-maturing sorts are slimmer, and have a longer shank, than winter-harvested leeks. If you're short of space, grow them in a container.

Planning and preparation

Leeks grow best in a sunny spot, in fertile, moisture-retentive soils (pH 6.5–7.5) that have been composted or manured the previous autumn. Ten plants should produce around 2.5kg/5½lb of leeks.

Sowing and planting

Early: Sow in February/March in modules, either on a windowsill or in a propagator, at a depth of 1–2cm/½–¾in. Transplant after hardening off in April or early May, when the leeks are pencil-thin and about 20cm/8in tall. Early leeks

do well when multi-sown in modules (four seeds per module) and not thinned; plant out 23cm/9in each way.
Mid-season: Sow indoors in March/April, or outside if it's warm enough (leeks need a minimum soil temperature of 7°C/44°F to germinate) in modules, root trainers or a seed bed – spacing seeds 2.5cm/1in apart in 15cm-/6in-wide rows. Transplant in June, allowing 15cm/6in between plants, in rows 30cm/12in apart. Alternatively, sow seeds in a grid formation, spacing them 23cm/9in apart in each direction (within the row and between each row).
Late: Sow outdoors in modules, root trainers or a seed bed in May/June and transplant to their final positions in July, spacing as for mid-season leeks.

When transplanting, use a dibber to make a hole at least 15cm/6in deep (this is needed to whiten the stem) and drop the leek seedling into it. There is no need to trim the leaves and roots, as sometimes advised. Do not backfill with soil, but water in well.

Cultivation

Water regularly until the plants are well established, and continue if the weather is dry. Leeks benefit from occasional feeds with comfrey liquid (see page 69), and, as a bonus, the extra potassium this provides also helps to protect them against a fungal disease called leek rust. The hole will eventually fill in, but if you wish to extend the length of blanched stem, either earth up or slip a cardboard tube (toilet or kitchen roll) over the stem. If the leek is too big for the tube to fit over, cut it lengthways and secure with string.

Pests and diseases

As a member of the onion family, leeks are susceptible to onion pests and diseases like onion fly and white rot (see onions). They also suffer from slug and cutworm attack.

Pests

Leek moths: These are becoming more of a problem. Originally confined to southern England, they have now made their way into Midland counties (a consequence of global warming?). The moth lays her eggs in May/June, and the pale green caterpillars burrow into the leaves (and eventually the stem) like a leaf miner, emerging to pupate in 'net-like' pupae attached to the foliage. These emerge as a second generation, to attack from August to October. Squash any larvae and pupae you find, or grow permanently under fleece.

Diseases

Leek rust: This is a fungal disease that covers the leaves in tiny, bright orange spore-bearing pustules. Although this reduces plant vigour, and looks unsightly, it's rarely fatal. It's worse in heavily fertilized, nitrogen-rich soils, or those lacking potassium. There are no cures, but resistant varieties are starting to appear.

Harvesting and storing

Leeks stand well at any time of the year, so lift as required. Begin harvesting early varieties in August, and move onto mid-season types in November. Late leeks, like Bandit, will crop until early May. In the event of freezing weather, lift and trim off the roots and top growth, and store in trays in a cool shed, where they'll keep for several weeks. Alternatively, lift and place at an angle (heeled in) with the roots lightly covered in a shallow trench. You can freeze leeks (see Part 4).

Nutritional value
Vitamins: B1, B6, C, folate**; E, K*
Minerals: manganese*
Phytochemicals: allylic sulphides, flavonol, fructo-oligosaccharides
22kcal, LGI

VARIETIES
Early (August to November): King Richard, Jolant, Roxton F1
Mid (November to February): Autumn Mammoth, Hannibal, Porvite
Late (February to May): Bandit, St Victor (blue leaves), Toledo
Rust-resistant: Flextan F1, Pandora, Sultan F1
Heritage: Monstruosa de Carentan (early), The Lyon (mid), Musselburgh (late)
Suitable for containers: King Richard, Tornado, Zermatt

LETTUCES and other SALAD LEAVES

Lettuces will crop for twelve months, but are chiefly grown during the spring and summer. There are various hearted sorts: 'butterheads', which have soft, rounded leaves; 'cos/romaines', which are taller and more upright; 'crispheads', which are crunchy, and described in shops as 'icebergs'; or 'loose-leaved', which are often grown as cut-and-come-again crops.

There is a bewildering choice of lettuces, in assorted leaf shapes, which vary in colour from pale green through to deep bronze. Other, lesser-known leafy vegetables, like lamb's lettuce, land cress, miner's lettuce and sorrel, add even more variety to a wide choice of winter salads.

Planning and preparation
Lettuces are more than nine-tenths water, and need lots of it while growing. Add plenty of compost if your soil is not sufficiently water-retentive. Salad leaves thrive in a sunny position (though they prefer it to be lightly shaded in mid-summer) in a neutral soil (pH 6–7). When deciding when, and how much, to sow, aim for 'little and often', sowing short rows every few weeks during the main growing season to avoid gluts. Lettuces and salad leaves grow well on patios and in window boxes.

Sowing and planting
Late spring, summer and autumn lettuces: Lettuce seeds will not

germinate until the soil temperature is at least 5°C/41°F, so start them off in a propagator on a low setting, or on a windowsill, in modules (lettuces dislike being transplanted, so try not to use seed trays) in late February/early March. Aim for two seeds per module and thin to the strongest, lightly covering the seeds, so they are less than 5mm/¼in deep. Plant outside in March or April after hardening off, covering with a cloche or fleece for the first few weeks. Sow every two to three weeks from April onwards. Although these later sowings can go direct into the soil to be thinned later, young lettuce seedlings are so attractive to slugs and other ground-dwelling pests that we prefer to use modules to reduce the chances of them being attacked.

Final sowings in July are at risk from poor germination – problems occur when temperatures exceed 25°C/77°F – though we have rarely experienced any difficulties ourselves. Sowing late in the day, and placing the module trays in the shade, should overcome the problem. Ideally, protect autumn-grown crops with a cloche or fleece.

Spacing depends on which type of lettuce is being grown. As a general rule, plant crispheads and cos sorts every 35cm/14in; butterheads every 25cm/10in; leaf lettuces every 25cm/10in; and mini varieties (containers and window boxes) every 15cm/6in. If growing in rows, space them every 30cm/12in.

Winter lettuces under cover: Sow outside in modules from August to October and transplant from September to November into a polytunnel, cold greenhouse or cold frame.

Early spring lettuces grown outdoors: Choose winter-hardy varieties and sow in August/September directly into the soil, thinning to 7.5cm/3in in November. You may need to cover with fleece during exceptionally cold weather. Thin again to 15–20cm/6–8in in March.

Cultivation

Keep well weeded and do not allow the soil to become too dry. Lettuces can run to seed (bolt) if not watered adequately, if their roots are disturbed during transplanting, or if they are not picked when mature.

Pests and diseases

Pests

The biggest threat to young salads comes from slugs, snails, cutworms and leatherjackets (for control methods, see page 87). Birds may also attack young seedlings. If lettuces suddenly wilt and die (usually in late summer), they have probably been attacked by lettuce root aphids, which are greyish-white and can be found on the roots. Lift and destroy. Yellow-green leaf aphids are less of a problem – remove affected leaves, wash off, or spray with a soap-based insecticide.

Diseases

Lettuces can suffer from downy mildew and botrytis (grey mould), but these are mostly a problem with crops grown early or late in the season, or under cover in winter. Resistant varieties exist.

Harvesting and storing

Harvest hearted types as soon as they have headed up. Cos lettuces will stand for longer than butterheads or crispheads without bolting. Pull plants from the ground and trim away the roots. With loose-leaf lettuces, tear (do not cut) several leaves from the outside, leaving new growth to sprout from the middle. To maximize 'shelf-life' once they have been picked, harvest lettuces early in the morning when they're still cool. Wrap in polythene/cling film and immediately place in a fridge, where they should keep for up to two weeks. Do not freeze.

Nutritional value

Vitamins: K***; A, folate**; B1, E, C*. The outer green leaves may contain fifty times as much of beta-carotene, the precursor to vitamin A, as the inner white ones. Contains 1½ times the RDA for vitamin K.

Phytochemicals: beta carotene, lutein, zeaxanthin, phenolic acids, flavonoids, **quercetin.** The deeper the colour of the lettuce, the more phytochemicals it contains; for example, Lollo Rosso contains ten times more quercetin, than 'white' lettuces.

14kcal, LGI

VARIETIES

Butterhead (B): Buttercrunch, Marvel of Four Seasons (red), Sylvesta (mildew-resistant)
Crisphead (Cr): Bedford, Saladin
Cos (C): Little Gem, Nymans (red), Tantan (mildew- and root aphid-resistant)
Loose-leaf (L): Lollo Rosso, Salad Bowl (red and green), Oakleaf
Winter growing: Arctic King (B), Lattughino (L), Winter Density (C), Valdor (B)
Mini: Little Gem (C), Mini Green Improved (Cr), Tom Thumb (B)
Heritage: All The Year Round (B), Lobjoits Green Cos (C), Webb's Wonderful (Cr)

Other salad plants

Try the following, more unusual, salad leaves as an alternative to winter lettuces. They are quick-growing, so can be used for inter-cropping, or as catch crops, and most will be ready for eating at other times of the year too. None is fussy about soil conditions, and some tolerate shade. For best results, keep them well watered. You can broadcast the seeds (if growing as a 'cut-and-come-again' crop), sow *in situ* or plant out from modules, spacing plants 15–20cm/6–8in each way. Over-wintering salad leaves are hardy enough to stand outdoors without protection, but all benefit from some cover in a cold greenhouse or polytunnel or under cloches. Most readily self-seed, providing a plentiful crop of seedlings to be either kept or hoed away, according to preference.

Claytonia

Also called miner's lettuce or winter purslane. Sow in March/April for summer use, in July/August for autumn cropping and September/October for eating from February through till May. Cover with a cloche during the winter.

Corn salad

Also called Lamb's Lettuce. Sow from March to August for a summer/autumn crop, or September/October to crop from December to May. Large-leaved (English) types differ from the hardier, more rosette-shaped leaves of the French (Louviers) sorts.

Land cress

Also called American Land Cress, with a hot taste, like watercress. Sow from March to July for summer use, and September/October for picking from November to March. Prefers damp shade. Member of the brassica family. Half a dozen plants should be enough for most families' needs.

Red-ribbed dandelion

This is not a dandelion, but a member of the chicory family. Sow from spring to autumn for autumn/winter picking.

Sorrel

A short-lived perennial plant (three to four years) with a tangy, citrus flavour. Sow from April to June in modules, for planting out 30cm/12in each way. Begins cropping in March and extends through to November. Remove flowering stems as they appear from May onwards. There are various sorts: buckler-leaved sorrel has small, rounded leaves and is used in salads; broad-leaved sorrel has larger, spinach-like leaves and can be cooked; whilst blood-veined sorrel has dark green leaves with red veins. Remove dead leaves in winter – they will re-sprout in February. Contains high levels of oxalic acid – so eat sparingly! Also note that the plants can be invasive!

Summer purslane

Sow from May to July for eating from July to October. Can also be cooked.

ONIONS

Most people nowadays grow onions from small immature bulbs, or 'sets', for convenience. Modern varieties, and heat treatment of sets, have largely overcome problems of bolting, as well as reducing the risk of onion fly and mildew. On the downside, sets are more expensive and there are fewer varieties. Spring-grown onions (not to be confused with spring onions, see page 180) are harvested from July to October. Onions grown in the autumn are ready for eating from late May onwards. Most onions are round (globe-shaped), but the autumn-grown Japanese onions are flatter, and are often described as semi-globe.

Planning and preparation

Prepare the ground the previous winter by digging in compost or manure; if acid, raise the soil pH to 6–7 using dolomite limestone several weeks prior to sowing or planting. Tread the land firmly, and rake to give a fine tilth. Sets are much less fussy than seed, which require a higher level of fertility, and benefit from an application of general organic fertilizer prior to sowing. Ten plants should produce around 1.25kg/2¾lb of medium-sized onions, but specimens bred for exhibition can easily weigh 2kg/4½lb each.

Sowing and planting

Growing from sets

Plant sets from mid-March to mid-April (if it's too cold, there's a risk of bolting), burying the sets so that the tips are just beneath the soil surface. Discard any that are soft or puny, and trim away straggly brown top growth to prevent birds from tugging the bulbs out of the soil. In really bad weather, plant in pots and transplant later. Space rows 23cm/9in apart with 10–15cm/4–6in between plants – the wider the spacing, the bigger the onion.

Plant overwintering sets from mid-September to early November.

Growing from seed

Boxing Day is the traditional sowing date for show onions, but February/March is soon enough otherwise. Sow in trays or modules under cover in gentle heat, 10–15°C/50–59°F, harden off, and plant out when around 10cm/4in tall. Like leeks, onions respond well to being multi-sown – six seeds per module. If sowing outdoors, wait until mid-March, when the soil has warmed and is dry. (Although seeds will germinate when soil temperatures reach 5°C/41°F, there's a risk of bolting if the weather turns cold.) Either sow sparingly in rows that are 23cm/9in apart, and thin to 10cm/4in in May or June, or station-sow at the same spacings and thin to the strongest. Space multi-sown modules 25cm/10in each way.

Sowing Japanese varieties at the right time in the autumn is critical to success. Work done at Wellesbourne (home of what was the National Vegetable Research Station) during the 1970s established that gardeners in Scotland should sow during the first week of August, those in northern England a week later, the Midlands and East Anglia during the third week, and the rest of England and Wales during the final week of the month. If sown too early, they can bolt, and if too late, they won't have enough time to make sufficient growth to survive the winter. Sow in 23cm-/9in-wide rows with 2.5cm/1in between seeds, and thin to 5cm/2in in the spring.

Cultivation

Keep well weeded, especially in the early stages. Onions also benefit from a liquid seaweed feed, applied several times during the spring.

Pests and diseases

Pests

Onion flies: Their maggots feed on roots, stems and bulbs from May onwards, causing them to wilt and die. Remove affected plants, so that the pest is unable to pupate in the soil. Protect with fine mesh netting, as for carrot fly (see page 136). Sets are usually unaffected.

Onion thrips: Symptom is mottled foliage, which is worse in hot weather. Spray with an organic insecticide.

Birds: They will occasionally yank out newly planted sets. Carefully dig up and replant.

Diseases

Onion neck rot: Onions rot in store, with a greyish fluffy mould developing in their necks. Store bulbs properly and buy sets from a reputable supplier.

Onion white rot: This is one of the most serious fungal diseases – spores can survive for up to 15 years in the soil – and one of the reasons why crop rotation is so important. Leaves turn yellow prematurely, roots rot and plants fall over. In advanced cases, the white fungus with tiny black spots can be spotted at ground level. There is no cure. Lift carefully and remove infected plants and soil, then dispose in a dustbin.

Onion downy mildew: Another devastating fungal disease that can kill plants. Leaves turn brown/purple and shrivel, and onions rot in store. It is worse in cool, wet seasons. There is no cure, but resistant varieties have been developed. Control as for onion white rot.

Harvesting and storing

Lift onions when the foliage has turned brown and flopped. Do not bend stems over. Gently prise the bulbs up, using a fork, and leave to dry on wire racks outside for up to two weeks, until the skins rustle. If the weather is wet, dry them on a bench indoors. Overwintered onions, harvested in June/July, will keep for around three months. Maincrop varieties mature from July to September, and can be stored in nets or plaited on string until the following April. Check periodically to prevent spreading of infection from any rotting bulbs. Onions may be frozen (sliced or finely chopped) or used in pickles, chutneys and relishes (see Part 4).

Nutritional value

Vitamins: B1, B6, C*

Phytochemicals: quercetin, kaempferol, thiosulphanates, organosulphides, fructo-oligosaccharides. Red onions contain the most quercetin, yellow onions contain less and white ones none.

36kcal, LGI

VARIETIES

Seeds

Yellow/brown: Ailsa Craig, Hystar F1, Marco F1

Red: Long Red Florence (torpedo-shaped), Mammoth Red, Red Baron

Autumn sowing: Hikeeper F1, Keepwell F1, Senshyu Yellow

Heritage: Bedfordshire Champion,

▶

Giant Zittau, Rousham Park Hero,
Up To Date
Pickling onions: Paris Silverskin,
Purplette

Sets
Spring planting: Centurion F1, Red
Baron, Santero F1 (downy mildew-
resistant)

Autumn planting: Electric (red),
Radar, Senshyu
Downy mildew-resistant: Santero

Thompson & Morgan stock a good
range of onion sets. W. Robinson &
Son Ltd specialize in seeds of
mammoth varieties for exhibition.

ORIENTAL GREENS

Chinese cabbages, pak choi and most of the other Asian leaf crops come into
their own from late summer through to the end of autumn. All are fast-
growing members of the brassica family, providing young leaves for salads or
larger ones for stir-fries. They are excellent plants for intercropping and
catch cropping. New types and varieties are being introduced all the time –
here are some of the more widely available.

CHINESE CABBAGES

Some varieties look like a cos lettuce, but
shapes vary. The leaves are all tightly
packed, with a white base and green
tops. Chinese cabbages are ready for
picking within eight weeks of sowing.

Planning and preparation

Like all oriental greens, Chinese cabbages
are shallow rooting and need humus-
rich, moisture-retentive soils. Dig in
plenty of compost, and add ground
limestone, if necessary, to raise the soil
pH to 6.5–7. Will tolerate slight shade.

Sowing and planting

Station-sow two or three seeds, from
June to September, 1cm/½in deep in a
grid formation, spacing them 35cm/14in
apart in each direction (within the row
and between each row), thinning to the
strongest. Alternatively, grow in modules
and transplant to avoid pests. If you
sow any earlier, plants will invariably
bolt, unless a specifically bolt-resistant
variety is chosen. As a general rule,
most oriental brassicas will run to seed
if sown before 21 June; ideally, wait
another week or so. After the end of
August, module sowings can be
transferred to a cold greenhouse or
polytunnel to provide small salad leaves,
or leaves for stir-fries, over winter.

Cultivation

Make sure that they never go short of
water and are kept weed-free. Rotate
crops as for other brassicas.

Pests and diseases

Chinese cabbages and other Asian vegetables suffer from the same pests as cabbages (see page 132). Slugs and flea beetles can be a serious problem for young seedlings, which is why modules should be used whenever possible. Growing under fine mesh netting will solve most of the problems.

Harvesting and storing

Begin picking young leaves from four weeks, and mature heads in another four to six weeks. The main harvesting period is from August until the end of November. Chinese cabbages will keep in a fridge for several weeks.

Nutritional value

Vitamins: A, C***; K, folate**; B6*
Minerals: calcium*
Phytochemicals: carotenoids, sulforaphane, dithiolthiones, isothiocyanates and indoles
13kcal, LGI

VARIETIES

Wong Bok, Green Rocket F1, Nikko (bolt-resistant)

PAK CHOI

Also known as bok choy. Its scientific name is *Brassica rapa* var. *chinensis*, and it is closely related to Chinese cabbage (*Brassica rapa* var. *pekinensis*), though with a looser head. Grow at the same time and in the same way, and harvest within six weeks. Vary the spacing according to the eventual size of plants required, from 15cm/6in each way for young leaves, through to 45cm/18in for mature heads.

CHINESE BROCCOLI

Has edible flowering shoots like sprouting broccoli. Sow in July/August *in situ*, or in modules and transplant when 5–7.5cm/2–3in tall. Space 35cm/14in each way. Harvest from September to November, or later if the final sowing is transplanted under cover.

GREEN-IN-THE-SNOW

A type of oriental mustard. Sow in July/August for cropping through to spring. Benefits from being grown in a cold greenhouse, but will survive the winter outdoors. Space 30cm/12in each way. Protect with fleece.

KOMATSUNA

Also known as mustard spinach. Less prone to bolting than other oriental leaves, so may be sown from April onwards. However, it's safest to sow from June to August, for cropping until February. Protected September sowings will provide a supply of leaves until well into the spring. Vary the spacing according to the eventual size of plants required, from 13cm/5in each way for young leaves, through to 40cm/16in for mature heads.

MIZUNA

The leaves resemble rocket, but with more sharply defined serrated leaves, and a peppery, mustard flavour. Sow from June to August outside, and in September for transplanting under cover. Space plants 35cm/14in each way or less (see komatsuna) if only small leaves are needed. With careful planning, it's possible to eat mizuna all year round.

MIBUNA

This is the same species as mizuna and has a similar flavour, but with smooth-edged leaves. It's not quite so hardy, and more susceptible to running to seed. Cultivate as for mizuna.

PARSNIPS

Slow-germinating, but easy-to-grow, reliable root crop.

Planning and preparation

Parsnips prefer a light soil, pH 6.5–8, that was manured or composted for the previous crop. If you have a heavy soil, grow shorter-rooted varieties like Avonresister. Rake well and prepare a fine tilth. If sowing early, warm the soil under polythene (see beetroot). Ten plants should produce around 2kg/4½lb of roots.

Sowing and planting

Parsnips germinate when soil temperatures reach 7°C/44°F, but resist the urge to sow during a warm spell in February (as many books advise), because there is a risk that the seeds will die during a subsequent cold, wet phase. Parsnip seed, which must never be more than one year old, is notoriously slow to germinate, typically taking at least three weeks before shoots appear. If there's still no sign of life after four weeks, sow again. Station-sow from late March until May, spacing seeds 1cm/½in deep, three at each station, every 15cm/6in in rows 20cm/8in apart. If bigger roots are required, adjust the spacing to 30cm-/12in-wide rows. Radishes may be used as a catch crop, sown between stations to mark the rows. Thin to the strongest plant when the parsnip seedlings are about 2cm/¾in tall. Growing in modules and transplanting is possible, but runs the risk of damaging the taproot.

Cultivation

Hoe regularly and water only in a prolonged dry spell – the long roots will search out moisture. Otherwise, parsnips take care of themselves.

Pests and diseases

Parsnips can be affected by carrot fly (see carrots), although not usually seriously. If you grow them adjacent to carrots, however, there's a risk that maggots will migrate to the over-wintering parsnip roots, thereby acting as a 'bridge' between this and next year's carrot crop. Plan your crop rotation so the two crops avoid each other. Parsnips can also be attacked by celery fly, whose maggots mine into the leaves. Squash the maggots or remove leaves.

Canker is the most serious disease, caused by a fungus that causes the skin to turn chestnut brown or black, especially at the shoulder. It's worse in acid soils, and when parsnips are sown early. Fortunately, there are many resistant varieties.

Harvesting and storing

Lift roots from October until early March, as and when required. Use a fork to lever them from the soil, taking care not to spear them. Store as for carrots, or 'heel in' as for leeks, to get round the problem of extracting roots from frozen ground. The flavour of parsnips improves after a frost, as the starch is transformed into sugars. Can be frozen (see Part 4).

Nutritional value

Vitamins: C, E, folate**; B1*. Parsnips contain more vitamin C than potatoes and other roots.
Minerals: potassium, phosphorus, manganese*
Phytochemicals: coumarin, quercetin, phytosterol

Parsnips are one of the best sources of dietary fibre.
64kcal, HGI

VARIETIES

General: Cobham Improved Marrow, Countess F1, Javelin F1
Good canker resistance: Avonresister, Gladiator F1, Panache F1
Heritage: Hollow Crown, Tender and True, The Student

PEAS

Nothing beats the taste of peas picked fresh from the garden. Delicious, but difficult! Mice, mildew and maggots are just some of the problems you may have to face, but persevere – it's worth it.

Planning and preparation

Peas crop for five months, from the end of May until October, but early and late harvests can be tricky. There are two sorts of 'shelling' peas – round-seeded and marrowfat. Round-seeded are hardier, but produce smaller yields. Sow these first.

Marrowfats are sweeter and more tasty, and their seeds are wrinkled when dry. Follow with them, beginning with early varieties (which take 11–12 weeks from sowing to harvest), then second

earlies, and finally maincrop varieties, which need up to 14 weeks to mature. Peas vary in height from 30cm/12in, to the more usual 60–75cm/24–30in, although they can exceed 2m/6ft 6in.

As well as 'shelling' peas, there are 'mangetout' types (French for 'eat all'), which are flat-podded, and 'sugarsnaps' which are also eaten whole when plump and swollen with peas. Petit pois are specific varieties, not regular sorts picked young.

Peas require fertile, well-drained soils, pH 6–6.8, that have been manured or composted the previous autumn. Like other legumes, peas co-exist with nitrogen-producing bacteria, so don't require additional nitrogen. Crop yields depend on the type and variety – but a harvest of 3.5kg/7½lb of shelled peas from a 3m/10ft row is satisfactory.

Sowing and planting

Peas picked from late May to June: Sow round-seeded varieties outside (or in a polytunnel or cold greenhouse) in October/November and protect these with cloches over winter. Alternatively, sow under cloches in February/early March. Peas don't grow well if it's cold and wet (they require a minimum soil temperature of 7°C/44°F to germinate) and are at risk from attack by fungal organisms, so it's safest to make early spring sowings in modules, then harden off and transplant when 10cm/4in tall. You might also try sowing in lengths of builder's guttering, gently sliding the contents into a shallow trench when the plants are 5–7.5cm/2–3in tall.

Peas picked from June to early September: Start with round-seeded or early wrinkle-seeded varieties, sown during the latter part of March. Follow up with second earlies in the first two weeks of April, and then maincrops until the end of May. In colder districts, you may need to protect earlier sowings with cloches.

Peas picked during September and October: Choose an early wrinkle-seeded variety, preferably one with mildew resistance, for a final sowing from mid-June to mid-July.

Take out a shallow drill, a spade's width, and sow seeds 4–5cm/1½–2in deep in a triple row. Space them like the dots on a number 5 domino, with 5cm/2in between seeds (or 7.5cm/3in for tall varieties). Decrease the sowing distance for winter sowings to 2.5cm/1in to compensate for losses. Rake soil over the seeds and immediately protect from bird attack with wire guards, cotton thread criss-crossed from canes over the row, or small twigs placed on the surface. Set traps for mice, which can be a problem, especially in winter.

If additional rows are being grown, space them according to the eventual height of the variety – usually from 60cm/2ft to 1.2m/4ft.

Cultivation

Water in early stages until the plants are well established. Do not water again until after flowering, otherwise you'll get foliage at the expense of pods. When the plants are 7.5–10cm/3–4in tall, erect something for them to clamber up, on each side of the rows. Traditionally, 'pea sticks' cut from hazel or birch have been used, and, with the revival in coppicing, it's worth looking out for your nearest supplier. Tall peas require something more robust, like plastic netting or wires secured to stout stakes.

Pests and diseases

Pests

Pea moths: These attack from June to mid-August, when females lay their eggs on the foliage, which hatch to become tiny white maggots that burrow into the developing pods. The first time you know about it is when you shell the peas. Early and late sowings avoid the problem, or you could cover with fleece from early June onwards. Hang a pheromone trap amongst the peas – this contains a scent lure that attracts male moths to a sticky end, so any eggs that are laid are unfertilized. The caterpillars complete their life cycle underground as pupae during the winter, so lightly fork over the land and give the birds a treat!

Thrips: These tiny black insects are better known as 'thunderflies'. They reduce yields, feeding on pods and foliage, producing a mottled, silvery and scarred appearance. There is not a lot you can do, other than spray with an organic insecticide.

Pea and bean weevils: They eat the leaves of young seedlings, producing a characteristic scalloped notch. Plants invariably recover, but you can cover with fleece early on.

Mice and birds: They will attempt to eat newly sown peas. Trap the former, and use some sort of barrier for the latter (see above).

Diseases

Early- and late-sown peas are at risk from mildew. Resistant varieties exist. Other diseases include fusarium wilt, and various foot and root rots, which cause plants to rot at the base. Otherwise, there's not a lot you can do, other than remove foliage/plants to prevent the spread of infection.

Harvesting and storing

Begin harvesting peas when pods have fattened. Early varieties are ready in late May, but the main pea season is June to July, ending in October. Pick mangetout when the pods are 5–7.5cm/2–3in long and you can just about make out the shape of the peas through the pods. Sugarsnaps are ready when they're plump, and snap cleanly. Peas freeze readily and can also be bottled (see Part 4). Allow some pods to dry on the vine to provide seeds to sow the following year.

Nutritional value

Vitamins: B1, C, K***; folate**; B3, B5*. Mangetout peas are the best vegetable source of biotin and have more than double the vitamin C of garden peas. **Minerals:** magnesium, phosphorus, iron, zinc, manganese* **Phytochemicals:** zeaxanthin, cryptoaxanthin, kaempferol.

Contain almost as much protein as broad beans and moderate amounts of fat, and are rich in dietary fibre. 83kcal, LGI

VARIETIES

Early (round-seeded): Douce Provence, Feltham First, Meteor
Early (wrinkle-seeded): Little Marvel, Kelvedon Wonder (mildew-resistant), Misty
Second early: Early Onward, Hurst Greenshaft (mildew-resistant), Jaguar (mildew-resistant) ▶

Maincrop: Onward, Cavalier (mildew-resistant), Ambassador (mildew-resistant)
Heritage: Alderman (tall), Champion of England (tall), Lincoln

Mangetout: Carouby de Mausanne, Oregon Sugar Pod, Sugar Sweet
Sugarsnap: Cascadia, Sugar Ann, Sugar Snap
Petit pois: Waverex

PEPPERS, including CHILLIES

Peppers (also called capsicums) can be either sweet or hot (also called chillies or chilli peppers). They belong to the same family as tomatoes and aubergines, and do best when grown under cover – although they will crop outdoors if conditions are favourable. Peppers, including chillies, start off green, but change to yellow, red or deep purple, and all shades in between as they ripen. The longer a sweet pepper remains on the vine, the sweeter it gets. A chilli pepper just gets hotter.

Planning and preparation

Soil should be fertile and well drained but moisture retentive for both, with pH 6–6.5. If growing outside, choose a sunny, sheltered spot, like a border next to a south-facing wall. A sweet pepper plant should produce around six to ten peppers, whereas a chilli pepper plant can produce scores of fruits.

Sowing and planting

Peppers won't germinate below 20°C/68°F and should be started off in a seed tray or modules. Place in a propagator or an airing cupboard. (Some hot peppers can take a month to germinate, so be prepared for a long wait! That may mean sowing as early as January/February.) If peppers are to be grown outdoors, delay sowing until March/April. When the first three leaves have formed, prick out the seedlings into bigger modules, or 7.5cm/3in pots, and then into 10cm/4in pots when they are a little larger – at all times ensuring that an even temperature in excess of 18°C/65°F is maintained during the day, and that night-time temperatures do not slip below 10°C/50°F. Finally, move into 23cm/9in pots, or grow-bags – three plants per bag. If growing outdoors, harden off well and do not plant out until late May or early June, when all risk of frost has passed. Space plants 45cm/18in apart.

Cultivation

Keep plants well watered, and, if growing indoors, damp down at least daily to keep humidity levels high. Many pepper varieties grow to around 1m/ 3ft 3in tall and will require cane support. Feed container-grown plants weekly with comfrey liquid, or another high-potash feed (as for tomatoes). Feed those in soil several times during the growing season. Mulch with compost, to reduce water loss from the soil. In the autumn, cover plants growing outdoors with fleece.

Pests and diseases

As a member of the Solanaceae family, peppers share the same pests and diseases as tomatoes (see page 191).

Harvesting and storing

Pick peppers from July to October. Harvesting sweet peppers while they are still green encourages plants to continue fruiting, but if left to ripen for an extra few weeks, they develop sweetness and colour. They will ripen on a windowsill if picked green. Leave chilli peppers to ripen on the plant. Peppers will keep fresh for a couple of weeks in a fridge and may be frozen or converted into chutneys, pickles and relishes (see Part 4).

Drying chillies: string up on twine and place on a wire rack somewhere warm, or in a cool oven or dehydrator. Take great care when handling chilli peppers in general, as the capsaicin – the phytochemical responsible for its fiery taste – is concentrated in the white pith surrounding the seeds, and it can easily irritate and burn. Eyes are especially sensitive.

Nutritional value

Vitamins: C***; E, folate*. Contains three times the RDA for vitamin C.
Phytochemicals: beta-carotene, lutein, zeaxanthin, **beta-cryptoxanthin**, **capsaicin** (chilli peppers only), coumarin, flavonoids
32kcal, LGI

VARIETIES

Sweet peppers (red): Bell Boy F1, Canape F1, Gypsy F1

Sweet peppers (yellow): Golden California Wonder, Orange Bell, Tequila Sunrise

Sweet peppers (purple): Purple Beauty

Chilli peppers: Cayenne, Hungarian Hot Wax, Jalapeno

Exceptionally hot chilli peppers: Habanero, Scotch Bonnet, Dorset Naga

Nicky's Nursery and The Chilli Pepper Company offer a wide selection of varieties (see Resources).

POTATOES

Nothing beats the taste of freshly dug potatoes, especially when they're organically grown. Nowadays, there are more than a hundred varieties to choose from, whether your preference is for floury sorts, for baking, roasting, mash or chips, or waxier kinds for boiling and salads. We feel that we must take some of the credit for this renaissance, having started 'Potato Days' when at HDRA, back in 1994. At that time you'd be lucky to find more than half a dozen varieties in seed catalogues.

As well as the traditional shopkeeper's 'reds' and 'whites', skin colour can vary from yellow to the deepest purple, with flesh to match. Potatoes are a great crop for 'cleaning' new land, because all the digging, earthing up and weeding gives the soil a good 'going over'. You can also grow them successfully in containers.

Planning and preparation

Potatoes prefer a slightly acid soil (pH 5–6) and an open site. Choose somewhere that spuds have not been grown for at least three years, to reduce exposure to soil pests and diseases. Potatoes are a nutrient-demanding crop, so dig the land thoroughly the previous autumn/winter, incorporating plenty of organic matter.

Potatoes are grown from 'seed', which are actually small tubers from the previous year that have been kept under conditions of dormancy in a cold store. Seed potatoes are classified as 'first earlies', 'second earlies' and 'maincrops', depending on how long they take to reach maturity. First earlies are harvested 11–13 weeks after planting, though some extremely fast-growing varieties may be dug after 8–10 weeks; second earlies take around 15 weeks; and maincrop potatoes (which can be split into early and late) stay in the ground for 16–20 weeks. It is inadvisable to plant home-saved tubers because of the risk of viruses and other diseases. Instead, buy 'certified' seed in January/February. A fun way of doing this is to visit one of the various 'Potato Day' events that are now held around the country in January/February, where you can buy tubers individually.

Place your seed potatoes in a tray or egg carton to sprout (chit), with the 'rose' end uppermost. Chitting isn't essential, but it encourages earlier cropping by two to three weeks. The 'rose' end gets its name because the cluster of embryonic shoots, or 'eyes', resembles a rose, apparently, although you need plenty of imagination to see it! Chitting breaks the tuber's dormancy, so that shoots are produced, and this occurs when temperatures exceed 4°C/39°F. A cool greenhouse or spare bedroom, kept at around 10°C/50°F, is ideal. Rub out all shoots, apart from two or three at the rose end. Those that remain should be about 2.5cm/1in long at planting time. Move the potatoes somewhere cool to check growth if the weather delays planting. There's no need to chit maincrop varieties, although it can result in heavier yields, but if you do, leave all eyes to sprout.

Potato yields can vary enormously, but a reasonable crop from ten plants of a first early variety should weigh around 7kg/15lb, whilst the same number of a maincrop variety will yield around 12kg/26lb.

Sowing and planting

Begin planting first earlies from mid-March onwards, as long as the soil is not too cold or wet. If in doubt, test the soil temperature, which should be at least 6°C/42°F at planting depth. Make a hole around 10–15cm/4–6in deep with a trowel or dibber, insert the tuber, shoots uppermost, and cover with at least 5cm/2in of soil. Space tubers 30cm/12in apart, in rows 45–60cm/18–24in wide. Earlier crops are possible by sowing in a polytunnel, cold greenhouse, or container under cover, from late January.

Begin planting second earlies in April, spacing as for first earlies, and continue until May. Maincrop potatoes can also go in from April onwards, but need more room – allow 40cm/16in between plants and 75cm/30in between rows. Plant them slightly deeper, with a 10cm/4in covering of soil.

Some gardeners prefer to grow potatoes in trenches, where they can concentrate manure or compost. A typical trench is the width of a spade and about 15cm/6in deep, with organic matter forked into the bottom with a layer of grass mowings, or comfrey leaves if available. Place the tubers on top, spaced as above, and cover with soil. Potatoes can also be grown using 'no-dig' methods (see page 53).

It's possible to have newly dug potatoes in the autumn/early winter (a special treat on Christmas Day) by sowing a fast-growing, early variety in July. They're something of a gamble, however (unless they're in a polytunnel or glasshouse), as you'll need to protect them from frost, and they're susceptible to blight (see below).

Cultivation

Potatoes are at risk from frost and should be covered with fleece or newspapers if the weather turns chilly. If damaged, growth is checked, but they will recover, sending up new shoots in due course. When the plants are about 15–20cm/6–8in high, pull up the soil on either side of the stems using a draw hoe to create a ridge running the length of the row. This will help to stop any tubers near to the soil surface from turning green. Where plants are closely spaced and earthing up is difficult, put down a thick layer of straw, topped off with grass mowings.

Keep plants well weeded at all times, and water if dry, especially when they are flowering. Maincrop varieties benefit from a fortnightly spray of high-potash, liquid comfrey or liquid seaweed fertilizer from late-June onwards.

If space is restricted, grow potatoes in a container. There are specially designed potato barrels, or you could use heavy-duty refuse sacks, punctured at the base. Plant up to five tubers in a 15cm/6in layer of multipurpose growing medium and periodically add more of the same stuff to the container until it is just below the rim, feeding at least monthly with organic chicken pelleted fertilizer.

Pests and diseases

Pests

Slugs: Keeled slugs nibble tubers, leaving them open to infection. Slug pellets are ineffective, as the attack is underground, but nematode biological controls are available (see page 89). Some varieties are more susceptible/resistant to slugs than others.

Wireworms: These are the larvae of click beetles, which lay eggs in grassland. On hatching, they drill knitting needle-like holes into tubers. Wireworms are a problem of newly cleared grassland, but can cause trouble for several years. Fork the land over in winter to expose them to birds.

Aphids: Peach-potato aphids feed on foliage and can transmit virus diseases via their saliva. Spray with an organically approved insecticide.

Potato eelworms: On allotments where inadequate crop rotation has occurred, eelworm, or 'potato sickness', can be a big problem. Pinhead-sized cysts can remain dormant in the soil for ten years. They hatch from June to August, causing the foliage to yellow and die prematurely. Avoid by growing resistant varieties.

Diseases

Potato and tomato blight: This is a devastating fungal disease that usually strikes between June and September. Earlies can sometimes avoid it, but it's almost inevitable in warm, wet summers. Brown blotches on the edges and tips of leaves indicate attack, and within a couple of weeks all the foliage dies. Rain washes spores onto the soil, where they infect the tubers, which rot in store. Remove and destroy affected leaves at once, if necessary cutting all the foliage to the ground. Don't compost, because spores may not be completely eliminated. Traditionally, potatoes were treated with Bordeaux mixture (a mixture of copper sulphate and lime) as a preventative measure, but concern about copper build-up in the soil means that this is no longer recommended. Fortunately, there are some resistant varieties: those with the prefix 'Sarpo', which were bred in Hungary by the Sárvári family and trialled in North Wales, are almost immune, and seem to be standing up well to the new and far more aggressive blight strain that has arrived in Britain (see our book *Organic Gardening: The Whole Story*).

Viruses: Mosaic and leaf roll viruses are transmitted by aphids, and are carried over to the next season via infected tubers (which is why growing certified seed, raised in places where aphids are absent, is so important). Plants exhibit mottled and/or curled leaves and remain stunted. Remove plants and destroy. There are no cures.

Blackleg: This is another tuber-transmitted disease. Stems blacken and leaves turn pale and curl. The problem is worse in waterlogged soils. Remove and destroy.

Scab: This is primarily a cosmetic disease, causing unsightly lesions that disappear when potatoes are peeled. It's worse on soils with a high pH, so surrounding tubers with grass clippings to create an acid environment when planting can help.

Other diseases: Potatoes can suffer from a number of other diseases that can result in internal browning and rots in store, for which there are no effective remedies. However, in general, growing organically means a healthier soil and more robust plants that are able to fight infection.

Harvesting and storing

Early potatoes are ready for harvest from June to July, when the tubers are the size of a hen egg. Carefully lift with a fork, inserting it approximately 30cm/12in from the centre of the plant, angled inwards (special broad-tined, potato forks minimize spearing). Lift maincrops in August and September, allowing a couple of weeks after the foliage has died, or been cut back, for the skins to harden. Leave on the ground surface for a few hours for the soil to dry, so that most of it can be brushed off, then store in hessian sacks, or double-thickness stout paper sacks. Don't wash them, as this will reduce storage life. Use any speared or otherwise marked tubers first – the slightest damage will result in rots that will quickly spread. Store in a frost-free shed. Alternatively, clamp (see page 247). Smallish, new potatoes can be frozen whole, as can partially cooked chips (see Part 4).

Nutritional value

Vitamins: B6, C**; E, folate*. Vitamin C is easily lost during cooking. Potatoes can also lose up to two-thirds of their vitamin C when stored over winter.

Minerals: potassium*

Phytochemicals: carotenoids, anthocyanins, hydroxycinnamic acid, flavonoids, protease inhibitors

Potatoes also contain some protein, and they are a good source of fibre. 75kcal; MGI (new potatoes have a low GI, but their starch builds up as they age)

VARIETIES

Earliest earlies: Orla, Lady Christl, Rocket, Swift

First earlies: Accent, Arran Pilot, (Sutton's) Foremost

Second Earlies: Celine, Charlotte, Estima, Kestrel, Nadine

Maincrop: Desiree, Maris Piper, Nicola, Pink Fir Apple, Roseval

Eelworm-resistant: Accord, Argos, Lady Balfour, Maxine, Valor

Blight-resistant: Cosmos, Lady Balfour, Orla, Sarpo varieties, e.g. Sarpo Mira, S. Axona or S. Una, Verity

Heritage: Belle de Fontenay, British Queen, Duke of York, Epicure, Golden Wonder, King Edward

Rare and unusual: Mr Little's Yetholm Gypsy, Highland Burgundy Red, Shetland Black

Alanromans.com and Edwin Tucker & Sons Ltd sell a superb range of varieties (see Resources).

PUMPKINS and WINTER SQUASHES

Pumpkins and winter squashes are greatly underrated vegetables, which is a pity because they are so easy to grow. They have firm, flavoursome, orange-coloured flesh, and will store for months – unlike summer squashes, which have pale, watery insides and must be eaten young.

Planning and preparation

Winter squashes require a well-composted soil (pH 5.5–6.8) in full sun, but as they take up a lot of space, it makes sense to create individual planting holes, approximately 30cm/12in square and deep, filled with compost. Trailing sorts can sprawl across the ground or be trained up wires or trellis.

An average pumpkin weighs 2–3kg/4½–6½lb, but some of the smaller types weigh just 500g/1lb or less. Expect four to five fruits from a typical butternut squash. If you want a real whopper, choose Atlantic Giant – the current world record stands at 767kg/1,689lb!

Sowing and planting

Sow in late April, two seeds to a 7.5cm/3in pot, on a window sill or in a propagator set to 15°C/59°F. Thin to the strongest, then plant out at the two-leaf stage, but not before the end of May, making sure to harden off fully. If sowing outside, wait until the end of May or early June. Space trailing sorts 1.8m/6ft each way, and bushy varieties 1.2m/4ft. If growing up trellis, position one plant every 1.2m/4ft. Squashes will grow perfectly happily in containers or grow-bags – one plant per bag.

Cultivation

Protect newly transplanted plants with fleece for a couple of weeks until they're established. For further cultivation details, see 'courgettes and marrows' (page 144). If giant fruits are required, remove all flowers once the first couple of fruits have started to develop.

Pests and diseases

Slugs can be a nuisance (see page 87); otherwise powdery mildew and cucumber mosaic virus are the main problems (see page 144).

Harvesting and storing

Leave pumpkins on the vine for the skins to harden for as long as possible, but remove before the first hard frosts arrive. Cut with secateurs to leave around 7.5–10cm/3–4in of stem attached, to minimize the risk of rot. Leave outside to ripen for 10 days, but bring indoors if the weather is unfavourable. Store at around 10°C/50°F, where they should keep for six months; a spare bedroom is ideal – if it doesn't cause family rows! Check periodically for signs of rot.

Wash the seeds of hull-less varieties to remove the pith and leave for a week to dry on a tray in an airing cupboard.

Eat raw or lightly roasted. Squashes can be frozen and used in jams and pickles (see Part 4).

Nutritional value

Vitamins: C, E**, B1*
Phytochemicals: alpha-carotene, beta-carotene, beta-cryptoxanthin, lutein, lignans, phytosterols
13kcal, MGI

VARIETIES

Pumpkins

Halloween types: Connecticut Field, Jack O'Lantern, Mars F1

Giant: Atlantic Giant, Hundredweight
Small: Baby Boo, Jack Be Little, Small Sugar
Hull-less seeds: Baby Bear, Lady Godiva, Triple Treat

Winter squashes

Butternut types: Avalon F1, Butternut, Sprinter F1
General: Crown Prince F1, Queensland Blue, Uchiki Kuru
Small: Blue Ballet, Little Gem Rolet, Sweet Lightning F1
Heritage: Delicata, Golden Hubbard, Rouge vif d'Etampes, Turk's Turban

RADISHES

Most people know this pungent-tasting, scarlet, globe-shaped ingredient in summer salads. It's one of the quickest and easiest vegetables to grow. Fewer, however, are aware of the white-skinned, cylindrical mooli radishes from the Far East, which can grow over 30cm/12in long, and are more often eaten cooked. Then there are the large, pink or black, winter-hardy European sorts, which can provide roots from October to April for a grated salad or cooked side dish. Most unusual of all are the crunchy edible pods of varieties like Rat's Tail or Munchen Bier. Radishes are a great crop for children to grow, and do well in containers.

Planning and preparation

If they are to grow well, radishes need a fertile sandy loam, pH 6.5–7.5, ideally one that has been composted or manured the previous year. Choose an open position for early and late sowings, and light shade for those in mid-summer. On heavy soils, incorporate grit and organic matter. For mid-summer crops, choose bolt-resistant varieties.

Because summer-sown radishes grow so quickly, they're a useful intercrop or row markers for slow-growing vegetables, such as parsnips or parsley. Ten plants of summer-cropping varieties should produce around 150g/5oz of roots, and the same number of winter-hardy sorts should produce around 2.25kg/5lb, whilst mooli radishes can weigh up to 0.5kg/1lb each.

Sowing and planting

Summer radishes: Begin sowing outdoors in March, when the soil temperature has reached at least 5°C/41°F. Continue every 10–14 days until September to provide a succession of crops throughout summer and autumn. Sow seeds 1cm/½in deep *in situ*, aiming for around 2.5cm/1in between plants, in rows 15cm/6in apart. You can extend the season at each end, sowing in late February and October, by using cloches or growing in a cold frame, polytunnel or cold greenhouse.

Mooli radishes: Wait until late June/July, because early sowings will almost certainly bolt. Space rows 25cm/10in apart, with 10cm/4in between plants, or sow seeds in a grid formation, spacing them 18cm/7in apart in each direction (within the row and between each row).

Winter radishes: Sow in July or August to prevent bolting, leaving 15cm/6in between plants and 30cm/12in between rows, or sow seeds in a grid formation, spacing them 23cm/9in apart in each direction (within the row and between each row). If allowed to run to seed the following spring, they'll produce masses of edible pods – not to be confused with varieties that are grown especially for their pods (see below), which crop much more quickly.

Cultivation

Hoe regularly to keep weeds under control, and water in dry weather to prevent the roots from becoming woody and/or running to seed. Inadequate, or late, thinning can also be responsible for plants bolting.

Pests and diseases

Radishes are members of the brassica family and, in theory, are prone to attack by a wide spectrum of pests and diseases (see cabbages). In practice, however, because of their rapid growth, they escape most of them, and flea beetles are the only real problem (cover the crop with fleece). From mid-summer onwards, cabbage root flies can occasionally be troublesome.

Harvesting and storing

Harvest spring- and summer-sown radishes from April to November. Pick as soon as they're ripe, approximately four weeks after sowing in mid-summer, and eat fresh. Mooli radishes take about seven to eight weeks to grow and are ready in August/September. Most will stand for up to a month when mature, but some varieties can be left in the ground during the winter. Dig winter-hardy types in October/November and store in sand or leave in the ground, covered with a protective mulch (see carrots). Radishes don't freeze well.

Nutritional value

Vitamins: C**; folate*
Phytochemicals: glucosinolates, protease inhibitors, flavonoids and allyl isothiocyanates (these give radishes their peppery, pungent taste)
12kcals, LGI

ROCKET

Also known as salad rocket, roquette, Italian cress and arugula (in the USA), rocket has become wildly popular in recent years. Wild rocket is a perennial plant with pungent, mustard-flavoured leaves; whereas cultivated varieties are more-productive, less-bitter annuals. You can crop rocket almost all year round, and it'll grow happily in a container on a windowsill.

Planning and preparation

Prefers a slightly shaded position and a light, moisture-retentive soil that has been composted within the past year.

Sowing and planting

Sow seeds outside, 1cm/½in deep, every fortnight from March to September. Space rows 20cm/8in apart and plants within the rows 10cm/4in apart, or space the plants 15cm/6in apart in each direction (within the row and between each row). Early and late sowings need protection, using cloches or fleece. It's possible to sow outside of these times if growing in a cold greenhouse or polytunnel. Choose a bolt-resistant variety for sowings in July and August, otherwise the plants will invariably run to seed.

Cultivation

Keep the soil moist at all times, otherwise there is a serious risk of bolting. This also reduces flea-beetle damage.

Pests and diseases

Include within the brassica rotation. The major pest is flea beetle (see cabbages). This is less of a problem with sowings after mid-summer.

Harvesting and storing

Pick several leaves at a time from each plant (which crop for around 40 days), so that they can recover and produce fresh growth. If flowering stalks are removed, the plant will usually respond by making smaller leaves. Flowers are edible – yellow from the wild form, and white from cultivated sorts. Outdoor-grown rocket can be picked from April to December.

Nutritional value

Vitamins: A, C, folate**
Minerals: iron, calcium, potassium, magnesium, phosphorus
Phytochemicals: carotenes
13kcal, LGI

SHALLOTS and SPRING ONIONS

Shallots are smaller than onions, and keep for longer, providing a useful bridge during April and May, when stored onions have finished and the new season's crop is not quite ready. Spring, or salad, onions are picked when green and young, before they've bulbed up. Japanese bunching onions are similar, resembling slim leeks, but are hardier and more productive. Small shallots are often preserved in vinegar as 'pickled onions'.

Planning and preparation

Prepare the ground the previous winter by digging in compost or manure. If the soil is acid, raise the pH to 6–7 using dolomite limestone several weeks prior to sowing or planting. Tread the land firmly. Store shallots somewhere light and cool until ready for planting. Ten shallots should produce a crop weighing around 800g/1¾lb.

Sowing and planting

Shallots: Plant in mid-February, or December/January if soil conditions permit. In cold districts, wait until March/April. Follow the guidance on the packet – e.g. Red Sun is likely to bolt if planted before March.

Push the sets into the soil until three-quarters buried – on heavy soils take out a shallow drill – spacing them 15cm/6in apart, in 23cm-/9in-wide rows. Alternatively, sow seeds in a grid formation, spacing them 18cm/7in apart in each direction (within the row and between each row). Tie cotton above the rows to stop birds from disturbing the sets, and re-plant those that become loosened by the birds – they like to tug them out.

Shallots can also provide an early bite of green leaves – plant in October/November, at 2.5cm/1in intervals each way, and cut in the spring when 10cm/4in high. This won't affect the crop.

Spring onions and Japanese bunching onions: Sow outside from March onwards, when the soil temperature has reached 5°C/41°F. Repeat sowings at two- to three-week intervals, until July, in shallow drills (1cm/½in deep), spacing seeds approx-imately 1cm/½in apart in rows 10cm/4in wide. Winter-hardy spring onions, sown from mid-August to early September, will stand through most winters, especially if protected with cloches.

Cultivation

If sown too thickly, thin out spring and bunching onions and eat the thinnings. Keep well weeded and watered. If not given sufficient water, shallots are especially prone to bolting in hot summers.

Pests and diseases

Shallots are usually trouble-free, but, as members of the *Allium* genus, they do share the same pests and diseases as onions (see page 163). The same applies to salad onions, which can also suffer from rust, which disfigures the leaves in hot summers.

Harvesting and storing

Shallots: Lift from July, when the foliage has died down. Clean off any soil and loose skin, and place somewhere to dry. Separate the individual bulbs and store as for onions, where they should last for up to nine months. Small sets can be pickled (see Section 4) or kept for planting the following year.

Spring onions and Japanese bunching onions: Harvest from March to September, when plants are 15cm/6in tall. Select alternate plants, so allowing the remaining ones to grow bigger in the extra space left behind.

Nutritional value

Similar to onions (see page 163).
20kcal, LGI

VARIETIES

Shallots
Standard: Golden Gourmet, Red Sun, Topper
French: Longor, Mikor, Vigarmor

Spring onions
Summer harvest: Apache (purple), Crimson Forest, White Lisbon
Winter hardy: De Rebouillon (bolt-resistant), Performer, White Lisbon Winter Hardy
Japanese bunching onions: Ishikura, Shimonita, Summer Isle

SPINACH

Spinach is fast-growing, and with careful planning can be cropped all year round, but it needs good soil and frequent water, otherwise it runs to seed. New Zealand spinach is a different species, with milder-tasting leaves, which thrives on poorer soils. It won't bolt, even in a drought.

Planning and preparation

Spinach needs fertile, well-drained soil that has been recently composted or manured (pH 6.5–7.5). Choose an open position in winter, and light shade in summer – alongside tall vegetables like broad beans, for example. Extend the season by growing in a polytunnel, cold greenhouse or using cloches. Because it grows so quickly, spinach is a good plant for intercropping. Ten plants should produce around 1–2.5kg/2¼–5½lb of leaves.

Sowing and planting

Spinach germinates when the soil has warmed to 7°C/44°F, usually from mid-March onwards. Sow seeds thinly outdoors, 2cm/¾in deep, in drills 30cm/12in apart. Thin to 7.5cm/3in between plants when they're large enough to handle, and to 15cm/6in several weeks later. Earlier sowings can be made under cover from late February onwards.

Continue sowing at three- to four-week intervals, until the end of May. You can sow in June, but there's a strong risk of bolting. Sow winter-hardy varieties from mid-August to early September. Avoid waterlogging on heavy soils by sowing along a 7.5cm/3in ridge. Expect to lose some plants over winter – if possible use cloches or grow under cover.

Sow New Zealand spinach in May, either in modules for transplanting out at 60cm/24in intervals, or by station-sowing three seeds in the ground at the same spacing, then thinning to the strongest. Protect with cloches until all risk of frost has passed.

Cultivation

Keep soil permanently moist, watering daily if necessary, and remove all weeds. New Zealand spinach sprawls over the ground, making a dense, weed-suppressing mat.

Pests and diseases

Because it grows so quickly, spinach usually avoids trouble, although slugs and birds will eat young plants. Pale yellow spots on leaves, with mould underneath, indicate attack by downy mildew. This is most common in wet weather. Remove infected material to prevent fungal spores from reaching the soil, where they can infect subsequent sowings. If the problem persists, grow resistant varieties.

Eliminate aphid infestations, as they can carry cucumber mosaic virus, causing 'spinach blight', which makes the leaves turn limp and yellow, and roll inwards. There is no cure, and plants must be removed and destroyed.

Harvesting and storing

Begin picking spinach five to eight weeks after sowing, from the end of May to October, selecting 'baby' outer leaves for salads. Alternatively, leave to grow larger for cooking. Up to half the leaves can be removed at once, or entire plants may be cut just above the base, leaving the stumps in the ground to re-sprout. Pick overwintering spinach from October to April/May, one or two leaves at a time. You'll find that it puts on a real spurt from March onwards. Spinach quickly deteriorates and should not be kept in a fridge for more than a few days, but it can be frozen (see Part 4).

New Zealand spinach is ready from June, until it is killed by frost in October/November. It produces masses of green shoots – cut off 5–7.5cm/2–3in of the fleshy, arrowhead-shaped tips. Tiny yellow flowers are produced along the stem, from which plants readily re-seed the following year.

Nutritional value

Vitamins: A, C, K, folate***; E**; B6*. Spinach contains five times the RDA for vitamin K.

Minerals: calcium, manganese**; magnesium, potassium, iron*. Spinach contains high levels of oxalic acid, which reduces the availability of calcium, iron and several other minerals to the body.

Phytochemicals: beta-carotene, lutein, zeaxanthin, phenolic acids and phytosterols. Spinach is ranked among the top five vegetable antioxidants. It is also rich in omega-3 fatty acids.

25kcal, LGI

VARIETIES

Summer sowing: Emilia F1 (red), Matador, Tetona F1

Summer and winter sowing: Medania, Monnopa (low oxalic acid content)

Winter: Galaxy F1, Giant Winter

Downy mildew-resistant: Galaxy F1, Palco F1, Scenic F1

Heritage: Bloomsdale, Giant Winter, Viroflay Giant

Non-bolting: New Zealand Spinach

SWEDES

Modern varieties of swede are a great improvement on the coarser varieties of old. They are less demanding to grow than turnips, and can be 'forced' to provide a welcome source of green salad leaves in the depths of winter.

Planning and preparation

Swedes need a fertile, well-drained soil, with a pH of 5.5–7, that has been recently composted or manured. Lighten heavy soils by adding leafmould, compost or a bagged soil conditioner.

Before sowing, tread the soil until firm. Swedes belong to the brassica family, so include them with other 'greens' when planning your crop rotation. Ten plants should produce 7–10kg/15–22lb of roots.

Sowing and planting

Early sowings run the risk of plants running to seed before they have made decent roots, and are more susceptible to powdery mildew, so delay until mid-May for gardens in the north, or until early June to early July in the south. Station-sow seeds, 2cm/¾in deep, 23cm/9in apart, with three seeds per station, and thin to the strongest when the seedlings are 2.5cm/1in high. Swedes need plenty of room, so space rows 38–45cm/15–18in apart, or sow seeds in a grid formation, spacing them 30–35cm/12–14in apart in each direction (within the row and between each row). Alternatively, sow two seeds into 4cm/1½in modules, remove the weakest and transplant as soon as the roots have filled the space. Protect the plants with fleece or fine-mesh netting, as they are particularly vulnerable to attack by flea beetles and, to a lesser extent, cabbage root flies.

Cultivation

Keep weed-free at all times and water regularly in dry weather to prevent the roots from turning woody. You should aim to keep the soil in a permanent state of dampness, to avoid checks to growth.

Pests and diseases

Swedes suffer from the same pests and diseases as other brassicas (see cabbages, p.132). Powdery mildew can be a problem in hot, dry summers, when leaves can become covered with a white coating, then turn yellow and die. Plants are more able to resist attack if they're kept well watered. Spraying with potassium bicarbonate helps to control infections (this approved organic fungicide is chemically similar to baking powder). Most modern varieties have some resistance to powdery mildew.

Harvesting and storing

Dig swedes as needed, from October onwards, and lift at the end of December. Store in moist sand, thereby avoiding problems of harvesting if the ground is frozen. On light soils they may be left in the ground, if protected by a 15cm-/6in-thick layer of straw.

For a supply of leaves for winter salads, replant roots in pots in January, covering with inverted pots (or place in the dark), and keep them somewhere warm (see chicory for details, p.142). The blanched leaves should be ready for cutting after three or four weeks, when about 10cm/4in high.

Nutritional value

Vitamins: C***; B1, B6, folate*
Phytochemicals: carotenoids, dithiolthiones, isothiocyanates, flavonoids, coumarin, other phenolic compounds, terpenes
24kcal, HGI

SWEET CORN

Home-grown corn-on-the-cob tastes so much sweeter than shop-bought sweet corn because the sugar in the kernels starts to convert to starch immediately after the cobs have been picked. It's not that difficult to grow, weather permitting, but if you live in the north of the UK, it's safest under cover. Varieties have been developed with bi-coloured (usually yellow and white) kernels, and for producing 'baby' sweet corn, or corn for popping.

Planning and preparation

Sweet corn requires a sunny and sheltered spot, and it's a nutrient-demanding crop, too, requiring a rich, moist soil (pH 5.5–7) to which compost or manure has been added the previous winter. Most varieties grow more than 1.2m/4ft high, some to over 2m/6ft 6in; though mini corn varieties are shorter, and are suitable for containers. Warm the ground using black polythene for several weeks prior to planting. Research has shown that, if you leave the polythene in place, and plant through slits, you can advance maturity by as much as a month.

Pollination occurs when pollen from the male tassels at the top of the plant is blown by the wind onto the female 'silks' that hang from the end of the immature cobs, so plant in a grid formation, rather than in rows, to ensure maximum fertilization. Mini corn is the exception to this rule, as the baby cobs are harvested before pollination occurs. Many modern varieties of sweet corn are labelled 'supersweet', and stay sweet for longer after cutting than traditional varieties, although some people find them somewhat sickly-sweet. They are also less hardy, and will cross-pollinate with other sorts, losing this retained sweetness characteristic. To overcome this problem, seed catalogues usually advise planting supersweet varieties 8m/25ft from other corn, but this is scarcely practical in most gardens. Even then there is no guarantee, as wind-blown pollen is able to travel much further than this. So, if you want to grow supersweet corn, choose one variety only, or select ones with markedly different flowering times. Fortunately, 'tendersweet' varieties also retain their sweetness, but without the cross-pollination complications.

Each sweet corn plant should produce one or two cobs.

Sowing and planting

Sweet corn will not grow if soil temperatures drop below 10–13°C/ 50–55°F, so there's little point in sowing seeds before mid-April. Use large modules, 7.5cm/3in pots or root trainers, with one seed in each, planted 2.5–4cm/1–1½in deep. Place in a propagator at 20°C/68°F, or in an airing cupboard. Grow on under cover and transplant after three to four weeks, in late May or early June, when all risk of frost has passed, hardening off first and covering with fleece or cloches. Set out plants in a grid formation (preferably four rows of four plants, minimum), planted at 35–45cm/14–18in intervals in each direction, with taller varieties going in at the wider spacing. Baby sweet corn can be planted in rows 45cm/18in apart with 15cm/6in between plants, or in containers.

In southern England, you can sow outside from mid-May onwards, but there's a risk that in a poor summer the plants won't have had the time to grow to maturity before they're killed by autumn frosts. Station-sow two seeds at a time, leaving gaps as above, and cover with bottle cloches, then remove the weakest.

Cultivation

Hoeing damages the shallow roots of sweet corn, so control weeds by mulching, or by hand-weeding. In more exposed situations, stake plants when they are about 75cm/30in high, and earth up around the stem to encourage additional rooting. Water until the plants are established, and then again when tassels appear, as this will increase the number of kernels in each cob. Also apply a comfrey or seaweed liquid feed at this time. If side shoots, or 'tillers', appear at the base, don't remove them. If you wish to aid pollination, tap the tassels. Mini corn produces unfertilized, immature cobs, but these will grow to full size if the plants are pollinated, so, to be safe, cut off any tassels that appear.

Pests and diseases

Sweet corn makes a tasty snack for mice, rats and squirrels (which scamper up the stems) as well as badgers (which trample them down). You may need to devise effective barricades! Otherwise, the only other potential pest is the frit fly, which attacks young seedlings. Its eggs, which are laid in the central shoot, develop into creamy-white maggots, causing wilting and premature death. However, once they have five or six leaves the plants are no longer attacked by the frit fly, so protect outdoor-sown crops with fleece. Frit fly shouldn't be a problem with module-grown plants under cover. Sweet corn is usually disease-free, although it can suffer from various smuts, for which there is no cure.

Harvesting and storing

Pick cobs from July to October, when the tassels have turned dark brown and the cobs are around 18–23cm/7–9in long. Peel back the sheath to expose the first few kernels, and pierce one of them with your thumbnail. If it oozes a thin and watery liquid, it's not quite ripe. If it's creamy, it's just right. If it's solid, you're too late! To pick, hold onto the central stem and twist the cobs until they part from the plant, or snap downwards.

Harvest mini corn when the cobs are around 10–15cm/4–6in long, before the tassels have formed. Leave cobs of popcorn varieties as long as possible on the plant to go hard.

Ideally, cook sweet corn within 30 minutes of picking it, although supersweet and tendersweet types (some of which can be eaten raw) retain their sweetness in the fridge for about a week. Surplus sweet corn can be dried, bottled or frozen (see Part 4).

Nutritional value
Vitamins: B1, B3, B5, B6, C, E, folate*. Baby sweet corn is particularly rich in folate.
Minerals: phosphorus, magnesium*

Phytochemicals: zeaxanthin, lutein (it gives corn its yellow colour), phytosterols, protease inhibitors, phenolic acids, limonene, saponins. Sweet corn is also a useful source of protein.
111kcal, MGI

VARIETIES
Standard: Earliking F1, Kelvedon Glory F1, Sundance F1
Supersweet: Earlibird F1, Northern Extra Sweet F1, Sweet Nugget F1
Tendersweet: Lark F1, Swift F1
Bi-coloured: Honey Bantam F1, Luscious F1, Mirai bicolour F1
Mini corn: Minipop F1, Minor F1, Snobaby F1
Popcorn: Popcorn Peppy F1, Popcorn Robust F1, Red Strawberry
Heritage: Black Aztec, Golden Bantam, Stowell's Evergreen

SWEET POTATOES

This nutritionally rich, tropical vine, with tuberous roots, is best grown under cover. New varieties, however, are being bred for our shorter summers, and, with the climate warming up, they may become more common in future.

Planning and preparation
Sweet potatoes need a rich, free-draining soil, pH 6–7, enriched with compost or manure the previous year. To be certain of a reasonable crop, grow them in a greenhouse, polytunnel, cold frame or under cloches. Containers – tubs or potato barrels – are ideal. If you decide to grow them outside, choose a sheltered spot in full sun, and warm the ground under polythene before planting. Sweet potatoes have a trailing habit, and will scramble over the ground, forming additional tubers wherever they root, though you can train them up trellis, or over a wigwam, as for runner beans.

Each plant should produce at least six reasonably sized tubers, weighing 1.5kg/3¼lb in total.

Sowing and planting

Sweet potatoes are grown from cuttings called 'slips'. Mail-order seed companies sell varieties that have been bred to cope with British conditions, and send unrooted slips out from late April onwards. They usually arrive in a withered condition and should be put into a container filled with warm water and covered with a polythene bag to maintain humidity. Leave for a day or so in the warm, in bright light, until they've revived, and then pot up into 15cm/6in pots, spacing them approximately 7.5cm/3in apart around the edges. Place somewhere warm and bright, to grow on, and transfer to individual 7.5cm/3in pots when rooted.

Alternatively, produce your own slips from shop-bought tubers. Conventionally grown sweet potatoes are sprayed with anti-sprouting chemicals, so always buy ones that are organically grown. You should easily get ten slips from a single tuber. In late March/early April, plant tubers into a suitably sized pot (the type of growing medium is unimportant) and cover with a polythene bag to sprout. Put them somewhere warm, 20°C/68°F minimum. When the shoots are 10cm/4in tall, and have several leaves, pull them away gently from the tuber and pot up as above. Transfer them to individual pots when they've developed roots. You can also produce slips from tubers, half-submerged in a glass of water, but always make sure that they're kept warm, humid and in bright light.

Don't plant out before the soil has warmed to 14°C/57°F, and not before the end of May. If grown outside, cover with cloches for the first few weeks. Bury plants 10–13cm/5–6in deep, including at least half the vine, and space them 30cm/12in apart, in rows 75cm/30in wide. Tubers will rot in soil that is cold and waterlogged, so plant along 15cm-/6in-high ridges to reduce this risk. Alternatively, plant individually in containers.

Cultivation

Make sure that the soil remains moist at all times, and feed a couple of times from July onwards with comfrey liquid. Feed container-grown plants every fortnight.

Pests and diseases

Sweet potatoes may be attacked by various flying pests, viruses and fungal diseases (especially root rots in cold, wet soils), but on the whole they usually avoid trouble. Slugs appear to dislike them!

Harvesting and storing

Leave as long as possible before harvesting, as the tubers bulk up considerably during the final weeks. Begin in September, and continue until the first frosts. They have extremely delicate skins, so lift carefully. Tubers should be eaten within a fortnight, otherwise they will start to rot. Store in a dry place, where the temperature exceeds 14°C/57°F. They are 'cured' commercially, however, by keeping them in the light for two weeks at 25°C/77°F and 90 per cent humidity (they don't go green like potatoes). During this time, the skins harden and the eating quality improves, as the starch turns to sugar.

Nutritional value

Vitamins: A, C***; B1, B5*. Orange-fleshed varieties contain up to four times the RDA of beta-carotene, the vitamin A precursor; white varieties contain none.

Minerals: potassium, copper, manganese*

Phytochemicals: alpha-carotene, beta-carotene, lutein, **zeaxanthin**, lycopene, flavonoids and phenolic acids. Purple varieties are rich in anthocyanins. In the USA, sweet potatoes are considered to be the most nutritionally valuable vegetables of all.

87kcal, MGI

VARIETIES

Beauregard Improved, Georgia Jet, T65

TOMATOES

Home-grown tomatoes are a world away from insipid supermarket offerings. The choice is immense, in colours (from red and yellow to purple, black and even striped) and in shapes (from marble and plum to meaty beefsteaks). Although they're best grown under glass, they'll also crop outside in a sunny, sheltered spot, or even in a window box or a hanging basket.

Planning and preparation

Tomatoes are split into two main types, based on how they grow. Those that stop growing naturally at a pre-determined size are called 'determinate' – these 'bush' types develop side branches, sprawl over the ground and don't require any support. On the other hand, those that have a tall, vigorous main central stem and are trained up canes or twine are called 'indeterminate', or 'cordons'. The growth of these must be controlled, by pinching out side shoots and 'stopping' the central stem when it's reached a certain size. As a general rule, most indeterminate varieties are grown in glasshouses, though many of them can also be grown outdoors. Most determinate (bush) varieties are grown outdoors, but they, too, fare better under cover.

Specialist suppliers list a huge number of varieties – some have hundreds. Cherry and 'currant' tomatoes are the smallest and sweetest; plum-shaped tomatoes are used to make sauces and pastes; whilst some beefsteak tomatoes weigh in at over 450g/1lb each.

Tomatoes need warm, sunny conditions, so best results are achieved under cover in a glasshouse, polytunnel or cold frame. Outdoors, they're at the mercy of the weather – in a cool, wet summer they'll ripen poorly and are unlikely to escape blight. So, if you plan to grow tomatoes outside, choose the sunniest and most sheltered spot in the garden. Soil should be fertile (with compost added several months before planting), well drained and with a pH of 5.5–7. Tomato yields vary considerably according to type and variety, with indoor plants giving the heaviest crops. Ten plants should produce fruits weighing around 20–35kg/44–77lb.

Sowing and planting

Start all tomato plants the same way. Sow seeds in gentle heat, preferably in a propagator at 20°C/68°F, because they germinate when soil temperatures reach 16°C/61°F. Place them 2cm/¾in deep in modules, or in 7.5cm/3in pots, or in seed trays. Keep a close eye on windowsill-raised plants, and transplant them before they become pale and 'leggy'.

Sow seeds of plants destined for a heated glasshouse in January; for unheated glass or a polytunnel in March; and for outdoor plants in early April. When they have made three leaves, pot them on into 9cm/3½in pots, maintaining adequate warmth at all times.

Transplant into their final positions when they are 15–20cm/6–8in tall, and the first flowers show. This should be in late February or early March, for heated glasshouse plants. (Ensure that night-time temperatures never fall below 10°C/50°F.) Plants grown under cover, without heat, must wait until late April or early May, and outdoor tomatoes should not be planted out until June, after hardening off.

Space cordon plants 45cm/18in apart, in rows 75–90cm/30–36in wide. Bush varieties can go closer, at 45–60cm/18–24in each way, and dwarf varieties even nearer, at 30cm/12in between rows and plants. Use 23cm/9in pots if growing in containers; never plant more than two cordon tomatoes in a grow-bag.

Plant deeply, with the first leaves brushing the soil surface. This will encourage additional rooting from the stem.

Cultivation

Indeterminate (cordon) plants require support. In glasshouses, this usually involves stretching a taut, horizontal wire from end to end, immediately below the ridge. Attach stout twine, reaching down to the ground, for the plants to spiral upwards. Alternatively, use 2.4m/8ft canes, tying the main stem to the cane every 30cm/12in with soft twine. Train outdoor tomatoes up 2m/6ft 6in stakes or canes.

Remove side shoots (which angle out from leaf joints) when they're about 2.5cm/1in long. (If allowed to grow to 15cm/6in, they can be taken as cuttings to make new plants.) Pinch out, or 'stop', the main stem when glasshouse-grown plants have made seven or eight fruiting trusses. (If the main stem reaches the roof before this happens, train it horizontally along the top wire.) Stop outdoor plants after three to five trusses.

Determinate tomatoes – bush/dwarf sorts – limit their own growth and require no support or side-shoot removal. Place straw under the foliage, or plant through black plastic, to protect fruits from rain splash and to deter slugs.

All tomatoes benefit from a mulch of compost and/or wilted comfrey leaves. Plants growing in soil should not need extra fertilizer treatment (unless they're growing poorly) other than an occasional liquid comfrey, or seaweed, feed from late July onwards. Feed container-grown plants weekly.

Water plants regularly at the transplanting stage, until they are well established. You shouldn't need to water outdoor plants except in extended periods of dry weather, but beware of over-watering after a long, dry spell, as ripe fruits are likely to split. Container-grown plants, and those grown under cover, must be watered daily, and in some cases twice daily. Tomatoes in grow-bags are particularly at risk from drying out.

Although frequent watering and heavy feeding result in heavier yields, this is usually at the expense of taste (which is one reason why supermarket tomatoes are so often appalling). Instead, adopt a less forced approach – grow 'hard'– to get the finest flavour.

As the plants grow, remove any lower leaves that turn yellow. Ignore leaves that are tightly curled – this is a natural physiological response to hot conditions (leaf area is reduced, thereby limiting transpiration losses) and is self-rectifying.

Shade glass structures using netting, or a paint-on product such as 'Cool-glass', to protect against scorch and conditions such as greenback (see below).

Pests and diseases

Tomatoes belong to the *Solanum* genus, sharing many pests and diseases with potatoes. Outdoor tomatoes suffer

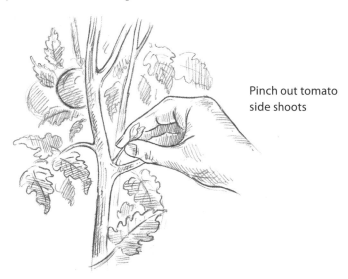

Pinch out tomato side shoots

fewer problems than those under cover, on the whole, but can be annihilated by blight. Look out for tomato moth, a new pest from South America, which arrived in Britain in 2009. It mines the leaves and burrows into fruit. Unfortunately, no control strategies have been devised, as yet.

Pests

Aphids: Curled, disfigured leaves and shoots, on which tiny 'greenflies' are clustered, indicate attack by peach-potato aphids. Their sticky, sugary excretions fall onto the fruits, encouraging the growth of sooty moulds. Remove affected leaves and/or spray with an organically approved insecticide. Sponge the mould off carefully with soapy water.

Glasshouse whiteflies: Small, white, delta-shaped insects have larvae that live underneath the leaves as dark oval 'scales'. These feed on plant sap, and their sugary excretions are colonized by black moulds. Hang up yellow, sticky traps, which attract the adults; spray with insecticidal soap (which also kills larvae); or use the highly effective biological control *Encarsia* (see page 88). Growing French marigolds amongst indoor crops doesn't destroy whiteflies, but it does deter them – one of the few companion-planting remedies that works! A more unorthodox remedy is to 'hoover up' the adults with a battery-powered vacuum cleaner early in the morning, when they're sluggish – extremely satisfying!

Glasshouse red spider mites: These tiny creatures feed on foliage, causing leaves to mottle, turn yellow/bronze and die. Fine, silky webbing can often be seen under the leaves. The problem is worse in hot, dry conditions, so spraying the foliage with water twice a day to increase humidity helps to reduce attack. In addition, introduce the predatory mites *Phytoseiulus*, which prey on adults (see page 89).

Tomato moths: Caterpillars attack leaves, and in severe cases can completely shred them. Pick off by hand, or spray with an organic insecticide.

Potato eelworms: Occur from May to August. Leaves turn yellow, then black, and plants are stunted with small fruits. Tiny pinhead-sized cysts can be seen on the roots (see potatoes, page 174). This is especially problematic on allotments where inadequate crop rotations are practised. There is no cure.

Diseases

Potato and tomato blight: A devastating fungal disease that occurs mainly in July and August in wet and humid weather. It is worse on outdoor crops, but can also strike indoor tomatoes. Leaf edges turn grey/brown and fruits develop brown, marbled patches before they rot. Remove and destroy all foliage. Tomatoes can catch blight from potatoes, so keep them apart (but within the constraints of the rotation!). Varieties with some blight tolerance include Ferline F1, Legend and Koralik.

Tobacco mosaic virus (TMV): Causes

pale green mottling of leaves and stunted growth. The virus is spread on hands and tools, so wash them carefully after handling infected foliage. Remove and destroy affected leaves/plants. Resistant varieties include Nimbus F1 and Shirley F1.

Tomato greenback: This is a glasshouse disease brought on by excessive heat. Fruits remain unripe, and stalks are girdled by a hard leathery ring. It is less likely to occur in structures that have been shaded. Resistant varieties include Alicante, Matina and Shirley F1.

Blossom end rot: This condition is brought on by a deficiency of calcium caused by acid conditions and irregular watering. Fruits turn leathery at the base and then rot. It's worse on acid soils, and in grow-bags. Water more frequently, and apply ground or dolomite limestone to soils, to increase pH.

Fusarium wilt: Lower leaves wilt, as water is unable to circulate properly. There's no cure. Resistant varieties include Ferline F1, Incas F1, Super Suncherry F1.

Magnesium deficiency: Not a disease as such, but equally damaging. Leaves turn yellow and develop ugly brown blotches, but the veins stay green. Common when too many high-potash feeds have been used, which 'lock-up' magnesium. Also a problem on acid soils. For a quick fix, dissolve 100g/4oz Epsom Salts (magnesium sulphate) in 5 litres/1¼ gallons of water, and spray the plants every two weeks. Increase soil alkalinity with ground limestone.

Other diseases: Tomatoes can also be affected by stem rot, verticillium wilt, botrytis and a number of other diseases, none of which is curable. Glasshouse growers can overcome certain soil-borne diseases by growing plants that have been grafted onto resistant rootstocks.

Harvesting and storing

Pick tomatoes as they ripen, twisting them carefully from the vine with the calyx attached. Heated glasshouse tomatoes begin cropping in May/June; those in polytunnels and unheated glass, from early July. Outdoor tomatoes are ripe from the end of July/early August and continue until October, when they are killed by frost. Keep picking fruits to encourage further setting. Any unripe tomatoes at the end of the season can be ripened in warm drawers – ensure there is a gap between each fruit. Tomatoes will keep in a fridge for several weeks. They can also be bottled, frozen, dried and converted into sauces, ketchups, pickles and chutney (see Part 4).

Nutritional value

Vitamins: C, E**; B6, folate*
Phytochemicals: beta-carotene, lycopene (it gives tomatoes their red colour), flavonoids, phytosterols, terpenes, rutin. Up to 85 per cent of the lycopene in our diet comes from tomatoes and tomato products. Cherry tomatoes are especially rich in flavonoids. Tomatoes rank as one of the top five antioxidant vegetables. 17kcal, LGI

see varieties overleaf

VARIETIES

Tall outdoors: Alicante, Ferline F1, Outdoor Girl

Tall glasshouse: Alicante, Cherry Belle F1, Shirley F1

Cherry: Gardener's Delight, Suncherry F1, Sungold F1, Tommy Toe

Currant: Broad Ripple Yellow Currant, Goldrush, Sweet Pea Currant

Beefsteak: Big Boy F1, Buffalo F1, Super Marmande

Bush: Red Alert, Sub-Arctic Plenty, Totem F1

Plum: Incas F1, Roma Improved, San Marzano

Heritage: Ailsa Craig, Brandywine, Harbinger

Tomatoes for hanging baskets: Gartenperle, Tiny Tim, Tumbling Tom

Unusual: Black Russian (chocolate), Tigerella (striped)

Simpson's Seeds and Seeds-By-Size sell a large number of varieties (see Resources, p.304).

TURNIPS

These fast-growing brassicas provide leafy greens and tasty roots for much of the year. Turnips can be globe-shaped or flattened, with yellow or white flesh.

Planning and preparation

Turnips are more demanding than swedes, requiring a well-composted soil, pH 5.5–7, preferably in partial shade. Freshly manured ground can cause the roots to fork. When planning crop rotations, include turnips with cabbages and other brassicas. Ten plants should produce roots weighing 1.1kg/2½lb of early varieties; and 3kg/6½lb of maincrop.

Sowing and planting

Begin sowing in early March, in a cold greenhouse or under cloches, when the soil warms to 5°C/41°F: turnips are extremely sensitive to cold and may bolt. Outdoor sowings can begin later in the month, continuing every three to four weeks until July, to provide a succession of crops. Cover them with fleece to provide protection from flea beetle and cabbage root fly attack.

Sow seeds 2cm/¾in deep, directly into the soil (turnips dislike being transplanted), in rows 23cm/9in apart. Begin thinning when the seedlings are 2.5cm/1in tall, and large enough to handle, initially to 2.5cm/1in, then 5cm/2in and finally 10–13cm/4–5in. The discarded plants make tasty salad greens.

Sow maincrop varieties from July until mid-August in wider, 30cm/12in rows, progressively thinning, as before, to 20cm/8in.

Make a final sowing with an early

variety in late August or early September. Space rows close together – 15cm/6in is adequate – and allow 5cm/2in between plants. This will provide mini turnips and green tops the following spring.

Cultivation

Don't let the soil dry out, especially in hot weather, because plants may bolt and become woody. Too much water, on the other hand, will lead to bigger, but less-flavoursome, roots. Keep well weeded at all times.

Pests and diseases

Turnips are susceptible to the same pests and diseases as other brassicas (see cabbages). Seedlings can be decimated by flea beetles, if not protected by fleece. Their larvae will also feed on the roots.

Harvesting and storing

Lift early varieties when they're golf-ball sized, from late May until September. Pull maincrop varieties from October, or leave in the ground until Christmas. After that, the quality deteriorates. Like carrots, they may be lifted and stored, with the leaves removed, in moist sand. Eat the leaves of any that sprout in store – they are surprisingly tender.

Autumn-sown turnips will provide mini roots, and a supply of fresh greens, in March and April, or earlier if covered with cloches (cut them 2.5cm/1in above ground when they are 10–15cm/4–6in high, and they'll re-sprout). Turnips can be frozen and used in pickles and chutneys (see Part 4).

Nutritional value

Vitamins: C**
Phytochemicals: dithiolthiones, isothiocyanates, flavonoids, coumarin, phenolic compounds, terpenes, other organo-sulphur compounds. Turnip greens contain lutein and zeaxanthin. 23kcal, HGI

VARIETIES

Early (E): Primera F1, Purple Top Milan, Snowball
Maincrop (M): Green Top Stone, Market Express F1, White Globe
Heritage: Golden Ball (E/M), Laird's Victory (M), Veitch's Red Globe (E)

UNUSUAL VEGETABLES

CARDOONS

This spectacular 2m-/6ft 6in-high plant, resembling a giant globe artichoke, is usually grown in herbaceous borders for its foliage and striking, thistle-shaped flowers. It's hard to imagine any part of it being edible, but you can, in fact, eat the blanched leaf stalks.

Grow as an annual, station-sowing three seeds in April into individually prepared planting holes, 30cm/12in square and deep, spaced 1m/3ft 3in apart. This is obviously not a plant for small gardens, and two to three cardoons should be sufficient. Keep well watered and weeded. In September, before they begin flowering, tie the leaves together at the top (they are prickly, so wear gloves). Choose a dry day and wrap corrugated cardboard tightly around the stems. Three weeks later, dig up the plants and trim off the outer stems and leaves – you can eat only the inner stalks and hearts, but they are delicious.

CELTUCE

This is not a cross between celery and lettuce, as some people think, and in America it's known as 'asparagus lettuce'. It looks like a cos lettuce that's bolted, and most of the leaves are not worth eating, apart from the youngest at the top. However, the stem does have a pleasant flavour and crunchy texture, and may be eaten raw or cooked – hence the celery connection. Grow it as you would a lettuce, sowing seeds 1cm/½in deep in modules from April to June. Plant out at 30cm/12in intervals, and harvest when plants are around 45cm/18in tall – this is a lettuce you want to run to seed!

SALSIFY AND SCORZONERA

These two sadly neglected root crops are described in *Jane Grigson's Vegetable Book* as having a 'succulence unusual in vegetables', with the additional note that they're both delicious, but that 'scorzonera has a slight edge'. Both have long, slender roots, although salsify is creamy white in colour, like a parsnip, whereas scorzonera is brownish-black.

Sow the large seeds of both, 1cm/½in deep, and 5cm/2in apart in drills 15cm/6in wide. Salsify may be sown in April, but it's better to delay sowing scorzonera until May, because earlier sowings may bolt. Thin to 10cm/4in. Neither crop is particularly demanding, or much troubled by pests or diseases. Harvest from mid-October, as and when needed, taking care to avoid snapping the roots as they are prised from the ground. Both roots can be left *in situ* or lifted and stored in sand as for carrots. Scorzonera is a perennial, so if the roots are not thick enough, leave them in the ground to grow for another season. Both crops are rich in vitamin C and potassium. They can be fiddly to prepare (scorzonera bleeds when raw, like beetroot). However, when cooked (after scrubbing), the skin detaches quite easily.

Salsify varieties: Mammoth Sandwich Island

Scorzonera varieties: Duplex, Hoffman's Long Black, Maxima, Russian Giant

SEAKALE

Create a permanent bed for this long-lasting perennial brassica, which provides delicious, blanched leaves every spring. It's usually grown from rooted cuttings called 'thongs', planted 60cm/24in each way in late March. Make a hole with a dibber and insert the thongs, bud end uppermost, so they're covered by 2.5cm/1in of soil. Don't attempt to force plants in their first season, but the following autumn (when the foliage has died back), cover them with a 30cm/12in plant pot which has had its drainage holes blocked, or use a rhubarb, or sea kale, forcer. Harvest the blanched leaves in March and April. Seakale roots can be lifted and forced, like rhubarb, for an earlier crop.

You can also grow seakale from seed, although this will take an extra year. Sow seeds 2.5cm/1in deep in a seed bed and thin to 15cm/6in. Transplant to their final positions the following spring. Although sea kale belongs to the cabbage family, it tends to escape most brassica pests, however, clubroot can sometimes be a problem. Mulch every spring with compost/manure and apply the occasional seaweed spray – seakale is a coastal plant and prefers light, sandy soil.

Varieties: Lilywhite (seeds); Angers (thongs)

CHAPTER 8

Fruit

However little space you have in your garden for growing fruit, you can always fit something in, whether it's a 'family' apple tree on the lawn, strawberries in a hanging basket, a 'hedge' of blackberries, or morello cherries on a north-facing wall. Nothing beats the pleasure of tasting a home-grown juicy peach – it knocks the spots off anything you can buy. So get planting!

APPLES

Everyone has room for at least one apple tree in their garden, even if it's in a container. So why not give it a go?

Planning and preparation

Apple trees live for at least 20 years, so consider the following when selecting which will suit your particular circumstances:

- How much space do you have?

- Will the trees be in the open, or against a fence or wall?

- Do you want eating (dessert) apples or 'cookers'?

- How many people in your family like apples?

Size and shape of tree

Fruit trees are grafted onto rootstocks. This regulates the flow of nutrients and restricts their size. The graft is made 15cm/6in or so above ground, and usually shows as a slight bulge in the stem.

If space is tight, buy trees that have been grown on the most dwarfing rootstock, called M27, which will grow only 1.5–1.8m/5–6ft high. M9 is next in size, producing trees 1.8–3m/6–10ft tall. Although they'll start bearing fruit within a year or two, the disadvantage with both these rootstocks is that they have shallow roots and must be staked permanently.

M26 is the most popular dwarfing rootstock, which produces trees that grow to 2.4–3.5m/8–11½ft, along with MM106, which is semi-dwarfing, allowing trees to grow to 3.5–5.5m/ 11½–18ft tall. Trees grafted onto M26 and MM106 take an extra year to start cropping, but stakes are not necessary after three years.

If you have space for a traditional orchard, buy 'standard' trees on M25 or MM111 rootstocks, but be warned – these trees are big!

Most trees planted in the open are shaped like a goblet, with four to six branches radiating from a central stem, 60–75cm/24–30in above ground. This form is known as a 'bush'. When you

work out how far apart to plant bush trees, assume that the tree's spread will be the same as its height.

When space is more restricted, train trees flat against a wall, fence, or posts and wires. Grow them as single stems (cordons), espaliers (with horizontal tiers) or fans. Space cordons 60cm–1m/ 24–39in apart and fans/espaliers 3–4m/10–13ft apart. Supports should be at least 1.8m/6ft high, though it's possible to grow single-tier espaliers that are only 45cm/18in high. These 'step-over' trees make an attractive decorative edge to the vegetable plot or border.

The youngest (and cheapest) trees are called 'maidens', and they consist of a single stem. Sometimes they will be 'feathered' with tiny branches. Grow these if you want cordons, or if you are confident about pruning the tree into

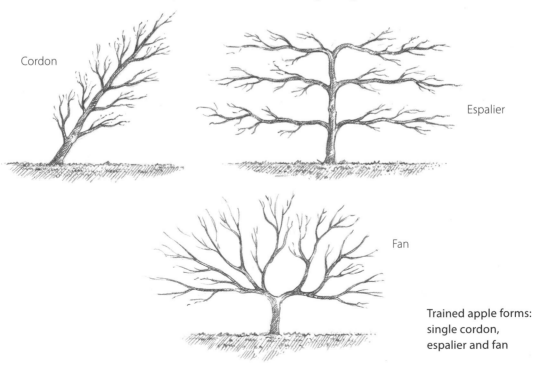

Cordon

Espalier

Fan

Trained apple forms: single cordon, espalier and fan

the shape you want. Otherwise, choose two-year, or older, trees, which will have been trained into particular shapes – bush, espalier or fan, etc.

A typical dwarf bush tree should produce around 14–25kg/30–55lb of fruit; a cordon 2.5–3.5kg/5½–8lb; an espalier 9–12kg/20–26lb; and a standard in excess of 50kg/110lb.

Choice of variety

There are hundreds of varieties of apples to choose from (see pages 304–305) – the National Fruit Collection at Brogdale in Kent has almost 2,000. Every year, in October, there are Apple Day events up and down the country, where you can taste different varieties. Select ones that have resistance to scab and mildew. These are two of the most serious diseases, so avoid any varieties that are susceptible. Cox's Orange Pippin, whilst undoubtedly delicious, is difficult to grow successfully.

Specialist nurseries supply their trees from November to March and they are delivered without soil on their roots (bare-rooted). Far fewer varieties are grown in containers for sale in garden centres, so choice is much more restricted, but you can plant them all year round.

There are three main harvesting periods. Early varieties ripen from July to early September, but don't keep well, and must be eaten at once. Mid-season varieties ripen during September and October, and most store for several months. Late varieties are picked in October (with a few in November) and ripen in store, some lasting until May. If you want to eat home-grown apples for as long as possible, choose a spread of varieties.

Pollination

Most apples must be fertilized with pollen from a different variety, apart from a handful of varieties that are self-fertile. In urban areas, this is often achieved by bees carrying pollen from neighbours' gardens, but to be sure of getting a crop it's best to plant two or more trees that flower at the same time. Apple varieties are divided into groups according to flowering period. They're usually given a number from 1 (the earliest to flower) to 7 (the latest). Choose trees with the same, or adjacent, numbers. Trees that are labelled 'triploid' (Bramley's Seedling is a good example) require two other, non-triploid, varieties for successful pollination.

Where there is only space for one tree, grow a 'family tree', which will have three varieties, all with compatible flowering periods, grafted onto a single rootstock.

Position

Choose a spot in the garden in full sun, and preferably protected, so avoid frost pockets. The soil should be at least 60cm/24in deep, fertile, well drained and slightly acid (pH 6.7). Enrich sandy soils with a good supply of compost or well-rotted manure. Carefully remove all weeds, especially intractable perennials, like couch grass and bindweed. If planting in a lawn, strip off an area of turf at least 90cm/3ft in diameter.

Planting

Plant bare-rooted trees from November to March, when they've shed their leaves. Dig a hole that's large enough to accommodate the root system comfortably, and knock a 1.2m-/4ft-long stake 30–45cm/12–18in into the ground, slightly off-centre on the windward side (the tree goes in the centre). Loosen the base with a fork and sprinkle on approximately 120g/4oz of bonemeal, and a similar amount of hoof and horn fertilizer. Add 'Rootgrow' – a formulation that will encourage rapid formation of mycorrhizal fungi (see page 47), and hence much more effective rooting.

With the tree in place, carefully back-fill the hole with a mixture of top soil and compost/manure, treading the roots and shaking the stem as you go, to eliminate air pockets. Plant it so that the soil surface is level with the mark on the trunk where it changes colour – indicating the planting depth in the nursery. The graft union should be at least 10cm/4in above ground. Saw off the stake just under the lowest branches, and secure with a tree tie to avoid chafing. If rabbits are a problem, slip a spiral plastic guard over the tree to prevent them from chewing the bark. Water thoroughly.

Treat container-grown trees in a similar fashion, first immersing the pot in a bucket of water until it ceases to bubble. Carefully tease out the roots around the edge.

Plant restricted forms (cordons, fans and espaliers) against a support system that has horizontal wires, stretched taut, 60cm/2ft, 1.2m/4ft and 1.8m/6ft above ground. If using posts, space them every 3.6m/12ft. Plant cordons at an angle of 45 degrees, with the graft union uppermost, attaching them to 2.4m-/8ft-long canes that have been secured to the wires. When growing against a wall, plant trees at least 30cm/12in from the brickwork.

tree tie

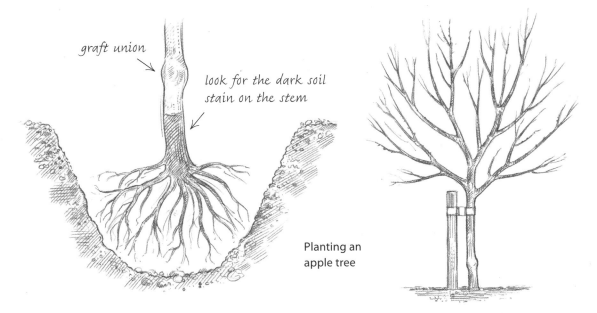

graft union

look for the dark soil stain on the stem

Planting an apple tree

Pruning and cultivation

Concentrate on getting the shape right during the early years in the life of a tree. Any good supplier will provide details of formative pruning – but there's nothing mysterious or difficult about it. The main thing is being able to recognize new season's growth (which is paler and more flexible than old wood) and to differentiate between the slender, oval-shaped buds that will grow into shoots and the rounder buds that will become fruits. Most trees bear their fruits on short spurs, formed from side shoots (laterals) growing out from the branches, although a few 'tip-bearing' varieties form theirs only at the end of these shoots. This obviously influences how the trees are pruned.

As a general rule, bush trees are pruned in the winter, whereas cordons and other more restricted forms are pruned from mid-July (southern counties) to early September (northern parts of the UK).

Keep trees well weeded, and water during dry periods, especially from July to September when fruits are swelling. Mulch with compost or manure, ensuring that the mulch does not come into contact with the bark.

During early summer, some tiny fruits fall as part of the 'June drop'. Thin out the fruits left to one per cluster, removing those that have no stalk ('king' fruits) or are otherwise misshapen. Aim to space fruits every 10–15cm/4–6in. Failure can result in trees fruiting in alternate years only (biennial cropping).

Pests and diseases

Apples can suffer from a large number of pests and diseases. Those listed below are the most widespread.

Pests

Codling moth: Female moths lay eggs in June and the resulting caterpillars tunnel into the fruit in July, resulting in 'maggoty' apples. In late summer, they crawl out to find a home under loose bark to spend the winter as pupae, emerging as moths the following spring. There are several ways of disrupting this life cycle.

Hang tent-shaped codling moth traps from branches in mid-May, leaving them on until the end of July. These have sticky pads soaked with pheremones – chemicals released by females to attract males. The poor, smitten males make a bee-line for the

Codling moth trap

pads, become stuck, and die before they can mate. As an extra precaution, tie a band of corrugated cardboard around tree trunks in July to trap maggots searching for overwintering quarters – remove and destroy in December. Alternatively, spray in late September and October with a nematode biocontrol called *Steinernema carpocapsae*, which parasitizes the caterpillars.

Apple sawflies: Eggs are laid on the tiny fruitlets in May, and caterpillars burrow inside. Affected apples usually fall to the ground in June. Remove and destroy any fruits with tell-tale 'frass'– the excrement from feeding maggots. Fork over the ground lightly in winter to expose pupae to the weather and birds.

Aphids: Eggs overwinter on trees and hatch in March. The insects feed on the leaves and young buds, causing distortions. Remove affected leaves by hand, or spray with an organic insecticide.

Winter moths: Caterpillars feed on buds and young leaves, producing tattered leaves. Tie grease bands around tree trunks in late October to catch the wingless female moths as they attempt to reach the branches to lay their eggs.

Diseases

Scab: Symptoms are brown/green blotches on leaves, and corky brown lesions on fruit. The fungus overwinters primarily on fallen leaves, so collect them and make leafmould. The disease is worse when spring is cool and wet. Although disfigured, the apples are perfectly safe to eat. Avoid scab by planting resistant varieties such as Ashmead's Kernel, Discovery or Egremont Russet.

Powdery mildew: Symptoms are a powdery white coating on leaves, shoots and flowers, which is worse in hot, dry weather. Remove and destroy affected material. Spray with potassium bicarbonate or sulphur as a cure (certain varieties, such as Cox's Orange Pippin, are 'sulphur shy' and mustn't be sprayed). In winter, prune and destroy any shoots that have been distorted by mildew. Avoid powdery mildew by planting resistant varieties like Adam's Pearmain, Bramley's Seedling or Jupiter. Some varieties, like Ashmead's Kernel, are resistant to scab and mildew.

Canker: Deep lesions, distortions and cracking appear on shoots and older wood, which can die. The problem is worse on heavy, wet soils. Cut out cankerous wood in winter. Avoid canker by planting resistant varieties like Annie Elizabeth or Newton Wonder.

Harvesting and storing

Apples are ready to pick when they part easily from the tree when lifted slightly, or twisted, from late July to the end of October. Store undamaged apples in slatted boxes (you can purchase apple racks) in a frost-free place, ensuring that fruits don't touch. Check from time to time, and remove any that are rotten. Some late varieties will keep until May. Apples can be bottled, juiced, frozen or used in jams, pickles, relishes, sauces and ketchups (see Part 4).

Nutritional value

Vitamins: E, C*

Phytochemicals: quercetin, proanthocyanidins, anthocyanins, caffeic acid chlorogenic acid, phloridzin, catechins, phenolic acids

47kcal, LGI

VARIETIES

Dessert ('eaters')

Early: Discovery, Epicure, Irish Peach

Mid-season: Blenheim Orange (triploid), Egremont Russet, Red Devil

Late: Ashmead's Kernel, Bright Future, Pixie, Tydeman's Late Orange

Culinary ('cookers')

Early: Emneth Early, Grenadier, Rev. W. Wilks

Mid-season: Bramley's Seedling (triploid), Golden Noble, Howgate Wonder

Late: Annie Elizabeth, Edward VII, Lord Derby

High vitamin C: Bramley's Seedling, Golden Noble, Ribston Pippin

Chris Bowers & Sons and Keepers Nursery have an excellent range. Bernwode Fruit Trees specialize in heritage varieties. R. V. Roger Ltd supplies trees grown in the north (so hardier). Walcot Organic Nursery sells only organically grown trees.

BLACKBERRIES and HYBRID BERRIES

Cultivated blackberries are larger than their wild relatives, though not always as well flavoured. These cane fruits are the easiest to grow of all the soft fruits, and are rarely troubled by pests and diseases. Even birds usually leave them alone. Most hybrid berries, of which over a dozen sorts exist, are based on crosses between raspberries and blackberries.

Planning and preparation

Choose a site in full sun, although blackberries can stand partial shade. Don't plant where the ground is badly drained. Improve the soil by adding compost or manure, and remove all perennial weeds. Blackberries dislike alkaline soils, the ideal pH being 6.5.

Blackberries are self-fertile, and, as they flower late, frost damage rarely occurs. If space is limited, choose one of the newer, upright, thornless varieties. Blackberries with thorns tend to be more vigorous – Himalayan Giant is an absolute brute and makes a perfect burglar-proof hedge!

Black and hybrid berry canes need a support framework of wires, attached to a wall or fence. Alternatively, erect freestanding posts, cross-section

75 × 75cm/3 × 3in, spaced every 3.6m/12ft. Fix the lowest wire 90cm/36in above ground and then at 30cm/12in intervals, with the topmost wire at 1.8m/6ft.

A single blackberry plant should produce 4.5–14kg/10–30lb of fruit, depending on the variety.

Planting

Blackberries are usually supplied in pots, and can be planted at any time; but if they're bare-rooted, plant between November and March. Space plants 1.8–4.5m/6–15ft apart, depending on the variety. Dig a hole large enough to accommodate the pot/roots – 60cm/24in across and deep should be adequate. Sprinkle in a handful each of bonemeal and hoof and horn, and backfill with a mixture of compost and soil. Plant with the new, fat buds on the crown just below the surface.

Pruning and cultivation

Immediately after planting, cut all growth to 20cm/8in above ground. New canes will shoot from the stumps and, later, from below the soil. Attach them to the wires, either with twine or by weaving them in and out. They won't fruit in their first season, because blackberries fruit on wood that's at least one year old. Keep plants well weeded and watered, and mulch with compost near to, but not touching, the base.

During successive years, canes made during the previous season will flower and fruit. At the same time, new canes are produced to replace them. When tying in canes, separate the old from the new wood, to avoid confusion and congestion (see illustration overleaf). After the berries have finished fruiting, cut back all the old wood to ground level.

Create new plants by layering. Lay the tip of a new, young stem next to the ground and anchor it with wire hoops (see illustration overleaf). In a few weeks, when it has rooted, detach and pot up.

Pests and diseases

Although blackberries and hybrid berries share the same pests and diseases as raspberries, they're mostly problem-free. Yellowing between the leaf veins (chlorosis) can occur on alkaline soils. This indicates iron deficiency, so treat with liquid seaweed fortified with sequestered iron.

Harvesting and storing

Pick blackberries and hybrid berries when ripe, from July to September. They'll keep in a fridge for a few days. They can be bottled, frozen or used in jams, jellies and syrups (see Part 4).

Nutritional value

Vitamins: E***; C, K**; folate*
Minerals: manganese***
Phytochemicals: salicylate, ellagic acid, tannins, lignans, carotenoids, anthocyanins, ellagitannins, quercetin, gallic acid
25kcal, LGI

see varieties overleaf

Layering blackberries

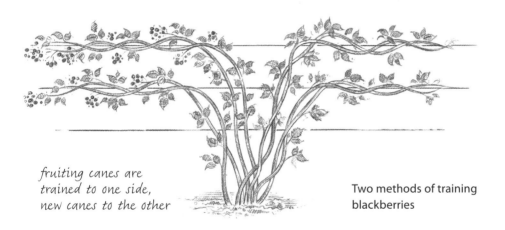

fruiting canes are trained to one side, new canes to the other

Two methods of training blackberries

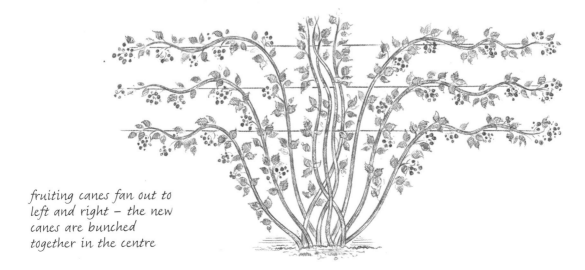

fruiting canes fan out to left and right – the new canes are bunched together in the centre

BLACKCURRANTS

This easy-to-grow fruit contains masses of vitamin C.

Planning and preparation

Blackcurrants are bush fruits, growing 1.2–1.5m/4–5ft tall. They need a fertile, well-drained, preferably heavy, and slightly acid soil (pH 6.5). On light soils, add plenty of well-rotted manure or compost to the planting area. Blackcurrants flower in March/April, and frost can destroy the crop, so choose a sunny, and preferably sheltered, spot. They're freestanding and don't need support.

Most blackcurrants fruit during July, but some crop until the end of August. As they're self-fertile, there are no pollination problems, and a single plant should produce 2–5kg/4½–11lb of fruit, depending on the variety.

Planting

Plants are either supplied 'bare-rooted', for planting between November and March, or in containers, for planting all year round. Space plants 1.5m/5ft apart (except for the compact variety Ben Sarek, which can go much closer, at 1m/3ft 3in intervals). Dig a hole large enough to accommodate the roots, or plant ball, and sprinkle a handful of bonemeal into the bottom. Plant the bush 5cm/2in deeper than it had been in the nursery (look for the soil stain) to develop a more extensive stool (the name for the shoots arising from the base of the plant). Backfill with equal amounts of topsoil and compost or manure.

Pruning and cultivation

Immediately after planting, cut the stems to leave just two buds on each. New shoots will sprout from these buds, and from underground, but the bush won't crop in its first season. Mulch with compost and/or wilted grass mowings, to conserve moisture and to suppress weeds. Although blackcurrants put down deep roots, they also develop a dense network of fibrous roots close to the soil surface, so avoid hoeing.

In subsequent years, when frost threatens in early spring, cover plants with fleece to protect the flowers, removing it during daytime. Renew the mulch, and water in dry weather. Blackcurrants mainly fruit on wood made the previous season, so prune during winter dormancy, taking out approximately a third of the older wood, which will be thicker, much darker, or almost black. Birds eat blackcurrants, so it's advisable to net them.

To propagate blackcurrants, take 25cm-/10in-long cuttings in October. Trim the tip just above a bud, and remove all but four buds near the top. Push firmly into sandy soil, so that around 10cm/4in of the cutting, including all the buds, are showing. See illustration overleaf. Dig up and replant in 12 months, when the cutting has rooted.

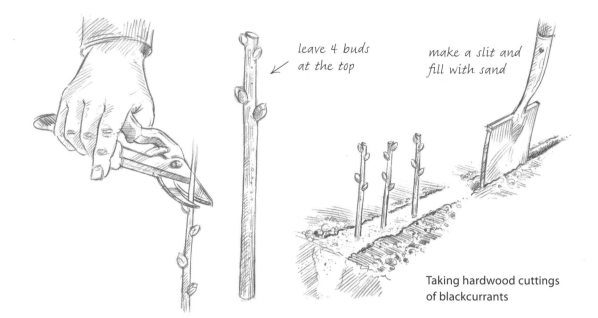

leave 4 buds at the top

make a slit and fill with sand

Taking hardwood cuttings of blackcurrants

Pests and diseases

Pests

Blackcurrants can be attacked by aphids, capsid bugs and a type of leaf midge. These rarely cause serious problems.

Blackcurrant gall mites: They live in buds, which become swollen, round and fail to open – hence the popular name 'big bud'. Check the bushes in winter, and remove and destroy affected buds. The mites can also transmit 'reversion' virus, which is difficult to spot. The plants drastically lose vigour, fail to make much new growth, and yields fall. The only solution is to dig up and destroy affected plants. Resistant varieties include Seabrook's Black, Ben Hope and Foxendown.

Diseases

Blackcurrants suffer from several fungal diseases, the worst being American gooseberry mildew (see gooseberries), although most modern varieties of Blackcurrants have some resistance.

Leaf spot: Small brown blotches appear on leaves from May onwards. Pick affected leaves and destroy. Spores overwinter on fallen leaves, so gather up and convert into leafmould.

Grey mould: Leaves wilt and branches die back. Prune affected wood.

Harvesting and storing

Blackcurrants ripen from early July, and are ready to pick when the colour has turned from dark blue to glossy black. Wait until entire strings have ripened before picking. Blackcurrants will keep in a fridge for about a week and can be frozen, bottled, juiced or used to make jams and jellies (see Part 4).

Nutritional value

Vitamins: C***; E**. Blackcurrants contain five times the RDA for vitamin C.

Minerals: copper, potassium, manganese*
Phytochemicals: anthocyanins, phenolic compounds
28kcal, LGI

Foxendown (resistant to most diseases)
Late: Ben Alder, Ben Hope, Ben Tirran, Jet (extra late)
Heritage: Baldwin (late), Boskoop Giant (early), Seabrook's Black (mid-season)
High vitamin C: Baldwin, Ben Sarek, Seabrook's Black, Wellington XXX

VARIETIES

Early: Ben Connan, Titania
Mid-season: Ben More, Ben Sarek,

BLUEBERRIES

Called 'superfoods' because of their beneficial nutritional qualities, blueberries have become enormously popular in recent times. They're easy to grow, but only in an acid soil – which is why many people use containers.

Planning and preparation

Blueberries are closely related to bilberries, which grow wild on acid heathland, sharing their love of moist, nutrient-poor acid soils (pH 4.5–5.5). This is one of the few crops where digging in compost or well-rotted manure is a bad idea! It's pointless trying to grow blueberries on alkaline soils, but you can acidify light, sandy soils with a 60:40 blend of ericaceous, lime-free, compost (formulated for azaleas and rhododendrons) and untreated bark chippings. Use the same mixture in containers.

Choose a spot in full sun or partial shade, and space plants every 1.5m/5ft, although certain varieties can go closer at 75cm/30in. Blueberries grow as bushes and do not require support. Although some varieties are self-fertile, all will crop better if pollinated by another variety. If you have the space, grow two or more plants. Plants live for up to 50 years, and should produce 2–5kg/4½–11lb of berries each season.

Planting

Most container-grown blueberries come in 2-litre pots and can be planted all year round. Dig a hole approximately 60cm/24in across and deep, and backfill with the ericaceous growing media mixture already mentioned. Water well, using collected rainwater, because most tap water is hard (alkaline) and should be avoided at all costs. If growing in containers, choose a pot slightly larger than the one from the nursery, and add water-retaining granules.

Once planted, if bushes do not grow well, and if the leaves turn yellow whilst the veins stay green, the soil is insufficiently acid. Correct with sulphur chips or wettable sulphur, but take care to follow the manufacturer's instructions precisely.

Pruning and cultivation

Prune the tips of branches, and remove flower buds immediately after planting. Blueberries fruit on older wood, so for the first couple of years there is not much pruning to do. On mature bushes, prune any time between November and March. Remove old stems that are no longer capable of cropping, weak growth, and branches that cross or point downwards.

Keep the soil moistened and well weeded at all times. Mulch with leafmould, well-rotted sawdust (left outside to weather until dark and crumbly), pine needles, or peat that has been dredged from northern reservoirs. Periodically treat with sulphur chips at a rate of 250g per sq. m/8oz per sq. yd. Feed container plants with 50g/2oz of ericaceous organic fertilizer in April and July. Never use high-potash tomato feeds, or equivalent.

As they outgrow their pots, periodically 'pot-on' container-grown plants, so that they eventually end up in tubs that are around 60cm/24in across and deep. Insulate with bubblewrap or hessian sacking in winter, to prevent freezing. Don't move indoors, because plants that have had insufficient exposure to the cold crop poorly.

Propagate blueberries by taking layered cuttings as for blackberries (see page 205), or hard cuttings as for blackcurrants (see page 207), in October, or softwood cuttings (see page 111) in the spring.

Pests and diseases

Blueberries are largely free of pests and diseases, but net them to keep off any hungry birds. The fruits, along with the leaves and shoots, are also attractive to rabbits, badgers and deer.

Harvesting and storing

Blueberries fruit from July to late September, and most varieties stay ripe for four weeks. Pick when berries are blue/black and have a waxy bloom. They'll keep for two to three weeks in a fridge, and can be frozen, or made into jams and jellies (see Part 4).

Nutritional value

Vitamins: E, K*; C**
Minerals: manganese*
Phytochemicals: anthocyanins, proanthocyanidins, resveratrol, flavonols, tannins, phenolic acids, lignans, chlorogenic acid.

Blueberries have the highest antioxidant ability of all fresh fruit.
57kcal, LGI

VARIETIES

Bluecrop, Chandler, Herbert, Sunshine Blue (tolerates pH 6.5, grows only 90cm/36in high)

The Dorset Blueberry Company and Chris Bowers & Sons (see Resources, p.304–5) sell a good range of varieties.

CHERRIES

Cherry trees used to be too big for the average garden, but that situation has been transformed with the arrival of self-fertile varieties and dwarfing rootstocks, which make container growing possible. There are two main types of cherry – sweet cherries to eat fresh, and acid cherries for use in cooking.

Planning and preparation

Sweet cherries are naturally vigorous, and when grafted onto a rootstock called F12/1, grow over 6m/20ft tall, making them impossibly large for all but the biggest gardens. Most cherries are grafted onto a semi-dwarfing Colt rootstock, and are trained as bushes, cordons or fans, growing to 3–3.6m/10–12ft. Gisela 5 is far more restricting: trees grafted onto it rarely grow more than 1.8–2.4m/6–8ft high, allowing them to be comfortably grown inside a fruit cage. Acid cherries are less vigorous and are usually grafted onto Colt or Gisella 5.

Cherries need a fertile, well-drained and slightly acid, soil, pH 6–6.5. Choose a sunny and sheltered spot, to minimize the risk of frost damage when they flower in April. Select a south- or west-facing wall for sweet cherries, whereas acid cherries will cope on an east-, or even a north-facing wall.

Most of the older varieties of cherry bear fruit only if pollinated by another 'compatible' variety that flowers at the same time, so cherry varieties are classified into 'compatibility groups' based on their flowering period and suitability as pollinators. Most specialist fruit-tree suppliers will advise you on suitable pollinating partners. Alternatively, many modern varieties are bred to be self-fertile, which is useful, especially if you have space for only a single tree.

Planting

Most trees are 'bare-rooted' and should be planted between November and March. Container-grown trees can be planted at any time. Plant cherries as you would for apples (see page 201). Space plants grown on Colt, 4–4.5m/13–15ft apart, and those on Gisela 5, 2.4–3m/8–10ft apart.

When growing fan-shaped cherries against a wall or fence, fix horizontal wires at 15cm/6in intervals (every two courses of bricks), starting 38cm/15in above ground. Attach bamboo canes to the wires, fanning out from the central stem, and tie the branches to these. Train cordons as you would apples.

Pruning and cultivation

Trees are usually supplied as one-year-old 'maidens', or as older trees that have been shaped into bushes or fans. Concentrate on creating the main structure of the tree during the first few years. Your supplier should be able to provide formative pruning details.

Sweet cherries fruit on wood that's several years old, and pruning involves eliminating dead and diseased branches and those that are growing awkwardly or crossing each other. Acid cherries fruit on one-year-old wood, and so more intensive pruning is required. Cut out the short fruiting side shoots of fan-shaped trees after they have finished cropping, and tie in the new shoots, which will fruit the following year. Don't prune during winter months to avoid silver leaf disease (see 'diseases').

Keep trees well weeded, and per-manently mulched with compost or manure. Water during dry spells in June/July, to reduce fruit splitting.

Pests and diseases

Pests

Birds: Bullfinches and blue tits destroy flower and leaf buds in winter; blackbirds and other species eat ripe cherries. Netting is the only effective solution.

Cherry blackflies: Black aphids attack young leaves and shoots from March onwards, causing distortions and depositing sticky 'honeydew' on foliage. Remove damaged shoots and/or spray with an organic insecticide.

Pear and cherry slugworms: Slug-like grubs skeletonize the leaves and eat the fruits from June to September. Pick off and squash (not for the squeamish!), or spray with an organic insecticide.

Diseases

Silver leaf: Shows as a silvery sheen on the leaves, which progressively kills branches. Prune back affected branches until the brown stain on the cut surface disappears. If the entire tree becomes infected, grub-up and burn. Avoid pruning from early September to mid-May when sap flow stops, which allows the fungus access into the tree.

Bacterial canker: Cankers, exuding gum, form on branches, which subsequently die, often killing the tree. The disease is worse on waterlogged sites. Prune affected wood, but not in winter.

Harvesting and storing

Sweet cherries ripen during June/July; acid cherries in August/September. Pick when they've turned deep red, leaving the stalks attached. Cherries can be frozen, bottled or jammed (see Part 4).

Nutritional value

Vitamins: C**
Phytochemicals: beta-carotene, anthocyanins, limonene
48kcal, LGI

VARIETIES

Sweet cherries
Self-fertile: Celeste, Lapins (Cherokee), Summer Sun, Sunburst
Require pollinators: Early Rivers, May Duke, Merton Glory, Napoleon Bigarreau
Acid cherries: Morello, Nabella – both self-fertile

FIGS

Figs aren't difficult to grow – the tricky part is getting them to fruit successfully. However, they're well worth the effort. Fresh figs are scrumptious, and with the climate warming up, they are sure to become more widely grown in the UK in the future.

Planning and preparation

Figs need a sheltered, sunny position, and are usually cultivated as 'bushes' in the open, or as 'fans' against a south-facing wall. They can also be grown in containers. Two crops are possible each year, if they are grown in a glasshouse. Figs are self-fertile (flowers are hidden inside the embryonic fruitlets), so they don't need a pollinating partner.

Figs grow on their own roots, free from the restricting influence of rootstocks, and reach a height of 8m/26ft, if allowed to grow unchecked. To restrain them, plant into a pit 60cm/24in square and deep, the sides lined with paving slabs, and half-filled with broken bricks or other rubble, well tamped down. Alternatively, use a container slightly larger than the pot in which the plant arrives.

If growing against a wall, stretch horizontal wires 30cm/12in apart to a height of 2.4m/8ft. Space trees 4.5m/15ft apart. A mature fig should yield around 7–9kg/15–20lb of fruit.

Planting

Plant bare-rooted trees from November to March (the later the better), and container-grown plants at any time. Fill the pit or container with soil, to which a bucketful of compost and a handful of bonemeal has been added, and plant the fig at the same depth as it was grown in the nursery (look for the soil stain on the stem).

Pruning and cultivation

For the first couple of years after planting, concentrate on building up the basic framework of the tree – your supplier should be able to provide details of the pruning methods required. Once the tree has begun cropping – usually after three years – prune as detailed below.

In September, when all the fresh figs have been picked, remove any immature fruits that are gooseberry-sized or larger (these are unlikely to survive the winter), leaving only those that are the size of a pea. These will swell and ripen the following year, but only if protected. However, all the young fruits, irrespective of size, can be left on glasshouse-grown trees; the larger ones will provide an earlier crop.

In November, before the first hard frosts arrive, drape fleece over trees to protect the young fruits. Don't remove until the following spring. If possible, transfer container-grown trees to a polytunnel or cold greenhouse. In the early spring, before the sap starts to flow, remove dead or diseased branches, and any that are growing awkwardly. Thin out a proportion of wood to reduce congestion, and to allow sunlight to ripen the figs. Later, in June, pinch back new shoots after five or six leaves to encourage the formation of new fruits at the tips: next year's crop.

Never allow the roots to dry out – which means watering frequently in dry weather – though ease off in the final stages of ripening. Mulch trees with compost, and feed every two weeks with comfrey liquid, or other high-potash fertilizer. Container-grown plants will need to be re-potted every few years.

Pests and diseases

Figs are largely problem-free, although you should net ripe fruits to foil bird attack. Woodlice can be a real nuisance as the fruits near perfection, but there's not much you can do about it. Figs grown under glass can suffer from red spider mite attack (see tomatoes, p.192, for control methods). The coral spot fungus, which produces striking pink pustules on branches, is also an occasional problem. If it strikes, cut out and burn infected wood.

Harvesting and storing

Figs ripen from late July to September. Pick when they've developed their full colour, are soft to the touch and begin to split. Although they'll keep in a cool place for a week or two (but only for several days in a fridge), they are luscious when fresh.

Nutritional value

Phytochemicals: flavonoids, polyphenols, coumarin
74kcal, MGI

VARIETIES

Green: Bourjasotte Grise, Brunswick, White Marseilles
Purple: Brown Turkey, Rouge de Bordeaux, Violetta
(Only Brunswick and Brown Turkey will reliably make a crop outside.)

Reads Nurseries sell over 40 different varieties (see Resources, p.305).

GOOSEBERRIES

Baked in a crumble and devoured with lashings of home-made custard, stewed as a fool, turned into jam, or simply eaten straight from the bush, there are many ways to enjoy this delicious fruit.

Planning and preparation

Gooseberries are usually grown as bushes in the open. They can also be grown as upright cordons, trained against a fence or wall (with single, double or triple stems growing 1.8m/6ft tall) or trained as fans. They can even be grown in containers. Gooseberries crop in the second year after planting and live for more than 15 years.

Plants need a well-drained, reasonably fertile and slightly acid soil (pH 6.5), although they're very forgiving, and will grow practically anywhere. Improve the soil by adding compost (but not manure, which encourages lush growth, susceptible to mildew). They prefer a sunny spot, but will tolerate some shade. Gooseberries will grow happily against an east-facing wall, but they flower in March and April, so avoid frost pockets.

Space bush trees and fans 1.2–1.5m/4–5ft apart, single cordons 38cm/15in apart, double cordons 45cm/18in apart and triple cordons 75cm/30in apart. When growing cordons and fans, attach horizontal wires 60cm/2ft and 1.2m/4ft above ground to walls and fences. A gooseberry bush should produce around 2.5–4.5kg/5½–10lb of fruit, and a cordon 1–3kg/2¼–6½lb.

Planting

Plant bare-rooted gooseberries between November and March, and container-grown plants at any time. Dig a hole slightly larger than the root mass and sprinkle a handful of bonemeal and seaweed meal into the bottom. Look for the soil stain on the stems of bare-rooted bushes, and plant to this depth. Tie-in cordons and fans to bamboo canes lashed to the wires. Bushes need no support, although half-standard gooseberries, which have a 1.1m/3½ft stem, must be staked.

Pruning and cultivation

Immediately after planting, cut all branches back by half their length, to an outward-facing bud, and any side shoots to two or three buds. Gooseberries fruit on wood that's one year old and older. In subsequent years, prune in winter and summer. Although winter pruning can be done at any time between November and March, it's best to leave it as late as possible, to foil bullfinches, which can easily strip bushes of their buds. The objective is to open up the bush by removing branches that are dead, diseased or crossing. Cut out any mildewed shoots and trim back half the new growth (which is lighter in colour) made by branch leaders the previous year.

If the variety has an 'upright' growth habit, prune just above an outward-facing bud; if it's 'spreading', prune to an upward-facing bud. Cut back all side shoots (which is where the goose-berries form) to three or four buds.

Treat cordons in the same way, shortening the new growth on the central leader by half and cutting back all the side shoots to three or four buds.

Summer pruning takes place in late June, and involves pruning the tips of all side shoots so that only five or six leaves remain. This has the virtue of eliminating any aphid infestations (which can cluster at the tips) and mildewed shoots. Pull up any suckers.

For weed control, mulching is the best method because gooseberries have shallow roots that can be damaged by hoeing. Use straw, wilted comfrey or grass clippings, which will also conserve moisture. Put compost around the base of the bushes each spring, and feed every other year with a high-potash organic fertilizer.

If frosts threaten at flowering time, protect fruits with fleece. Water plants in dry weather to assist fruit ripening, but don't over-water, because this will encourage aphid and mildew attack. From May onwards, thin out fruits and use for cooking. This assists ripening and encourages larger berries.

Propagate gooseberries by taking hardwood cuttings in October as you would for blackcurrants (see page 207).

Pests and diseases

Pests

Birds: Net your fruit, because bull-finches destroy buds in winter and blackbirds and other species eat the fruit in summer.

Gooseberry sawflies: This pale green caterpillar, with black spots and a black head, can completely defoliate bushes within days. Damage occurs from late April to early September. To control sawfly, inspect weekly and remove affected leaves while the caterpillars are still small and congregate together. Otherwise, spray with an organic insecticide. The key dates are late April, early June, early July and early September.

Gooseberry aphids: Small grey-green aphids infest young shoot tips in spring. Remove as part of summer pruning and/or spray.

Diseases

American gooseberry mildew: From April onwards, leaves and shoots become covered with a white powdery coat. Shoots later become stunted and disfigured, and fruits can also be affected badly. The disease is worse in wet, humid conditions. Prune out infected growth, and maintain an open shape. Sulphur can be used as a preventative, but certain 'sulphur-shy' varieties (e.g. Careless, Lord Derby) are damaged by it. When bushes are attacked, a potassium bicarbonate spray can sometimes be effective, although it's more reliable as a protective measure. The varieties Green

Gem, Howard's Lancer, Keepsake, Leveller and Whinham's Industry are all susceptible. See right for resistant varieties.

Gooseberries can also be attacked by several other diseases, including silver leaf (see page 212), botrytis (dieback) (see page 91) and coral spot (see page 214).

Harvesting and storing

Harvest gooseberries from early July until August. You can pick them earlier, or when thinning, for culinary purposes. They're completely ripe when they've developed their full colour, and are slightly yielding to the touch. They'll keep for a couple of weeks in a fridge and can be bottled, frozen, or made into jams and jellies (see Part 4).

Nutritional value

Vitamins: C**
Phytochemicals: kaempferol
19kcal, LGI

VARIETIES

Dessert
Green: Green Gem, Gunner, Howard's Lancer
Red: Bedford Red, Lancashire Lad, May Duke, Pax (spine-free and mildew-resistant)
Yellow: Bedford Yellow, Early Sulphur, Leveller
White: Langley Gage, White Lion, Whitesmith

Culinary

Greenfinch, Invicta, Jubilee (all mildew-resistant)
Careless, Keepsake

Worcesterberry is a blackcurrant/ gooseberry hybrid, which is mildew-resistant and is larger and thornier than the gooseberry.

Rougham Hall Nurseries and R.V. Roger sell an excellent range of varieties (see Resources, p.305).

GRAPES

Outdoor-grown grapes are invariably smaller than those produced under glass, and are more suitable for winemaking than eating. 'White' varieties are more reliable than 'red'. Muscat, which are the finest flavoured, and 'vinous' dessert grapes, must be grown indoors, and require some heat in spring. If you have a cold glasshouse, grow 'sweetwater' varieties. Red grapes contain more protective phytochemicals than white.

Planning and preparation

Grapes need full sun and should ideally be planted against a wall facing south or south-west. Outdoor vines are only really a proposition in southern Britain, unless you have an exceptionally favourable microclimate. Elsewhere, you need a glasshouse. Vines aren't that fussy about soil fertility; the important thing is to ensure that the ground is well drained – sandy gravels, pH 6.5–7, are ideal. Lighten heavy soils using compost and grit. Vines can also be grown in containers.

In the open, erect a system of stout posts and wires, using 1.8m-/6ft-long posts, sunk 60cm/2ft into the ground, spaced every 2.4m/8ft. Attach three horizontal wires 45cm/18in, 75cm/30in and 105cm/3½ft above ground. Space rows at least 1.8m/6ft apart. When growing grapes against a wall, or in a glasshouse, fix wires 15–23cm/6–9in from the surface, at 30cm/12in intervals.

Vines are self-fertile and extremely long-lived. They begin cropping after three years. A mature vine should produce fruit weighing 2.5–7kg/5½–15lb.

Planting

Plant bare-rooted vines, inside and out, from November to March, and container-grown plants at any time, spacing them 1.2–1.5m/4–5ft apart. Glasshouse vines can also be rooted outside, but then directed indoors close to ground level – remove a pane of glass and feed the plant through. This reduces the need for watering.

Pruning and cultivation

After planting, shorten the main shoot, or 'rod', to 60cm/24in, and all side shoots to one bud. Subsequent pruning depends on the specific method of training. The 'Double Guyot' method is usually used when vines are grown in the open on posts and wires, whereas most indoor grapes, and those trained against a wall, involve 'rod and spur' methods. Ask your supplier for details.

Vines fruit on the current year's wood, so in November remove all side shoots that have fruited. From March to September, tie-in new fruiting laterals and eliminate unwanted foliage.

Mulch vines with compost. Feed glasshouse vines weekly with a high-potash organic liquid fertilizer, from fruit formation until the grapes begin to change colour. At midday, sharply tap the rods when the flowers are open, to ensure pollination. Give indoor vines a good soaking with water every fortnight; outdoor vines can be left unwatered, except in a drought.

Pests and diseases

Grapes grown outdoors attract birds, so net them. Grapes (inside and outdoors) are susceptible to fungal diseases, especially powdery mildew and grey mould, so for the former spray with sulphur as a preventative and cut out any diseased and distorted shoots. There's not much you can do about grey mould, apart from picking off affected fruits.

Glasshouse-grown grapes can also be attacked by glasshouse red spider mites and whiteflies (see page 89 for biocontrols). Mealybugs are another problem – waxy-white bugs cluster in inaccessible places, feeding on plant sap and producing sticky 'honeydew'. Introduce predatory ladybirds called

Cryptolaemus as the best defence (see page 89).

Harvesting and storing

Start picking outdoors in September, and continue until the end of October. The longer the grapes remain on the vine, the sweeter they become. Cut grapes with secateurs, on either side of the bunch to provide a handle. Avoid touching the grapes, which will damage the delicate 'bloom'. Grapes will remain fresh for several months once picked, if the stem is inserted into a jar of water, refreshed weekly. Grapes don't freeze well, but can be juiced, dried, made into jellies and, of course, converted into wine (see Part 4).

Nutritional value

Vitamins: K*
Minerals: copper*
Phytochemicals: quercetin, ellagic acid, anthocyanins, flavonols, catechins, proanthocyanidins, **resveratrol** (red grapes only)
60kcal, LGI

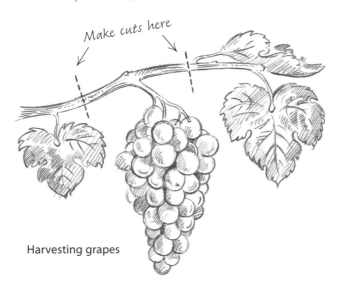

Make cuts here

Harvesting grapes

PEACHES, NECTARINES and APRICOTS

Traditionally, peaches have had a reputation for being difficult, since they're susceptible to frost, and to peach leaf curl disease, and they need plenty of sun. But all that changed with the arrival of resistant varieties, and genetically dwarfing types suitable for growing in tubs. Peaches are the hardiest of these 'stone' fruits, followed by nectarines (which are smooth-skinned peaches). Apricots, which flower in February, are the most sensitive. Apart from the method of pruning, which differs for apricots, they can all be grown in the same way.

Planning and preparation

Peaches, nectarines and apricots are usually grown as fans against a south- or south-west-facing wall, or as bushes in the open. They can also be grown under glass (with or without heat, depending on the variety) but take up a large amount of space. Trees generally live for more than twenty years, and begin cropping after three years, although patio trees fruit earlier. A typical mature fan tree should bear 30–40 fruits, a bush tree more than double that, and a patio plant as many as 20.

They're self-fertile, so don't need pollinating partners. Peaches and nectarines are usually grafted onto a rootstock called St Julien A, which is semi-vigorous. The Montclaire rootstock is an improvement, combining high productivity, lessened susceptibility to frost and medium vigour. Apricots are usually grafted onto St Julien A, although they may also be grown on Pixy, or Torinel, rootstocks, which are less vigorous. Fan trees will usually grow 2.4m/8ft tall and need to be spaced 4m/13ft apart; bush trees need 4.5m/15ft between plants.

Peaches and nectarines require a rich, moisture-retentive soil, pH 6.7–7. Apricots can cope with more alkaline conditions (pH 6.5–8), but are hopeless on light, sandy soils. In all cases, dig in plenty of compost or manure, and ensure good drainage – waterlogging is invariably a death sentence.

Planting

Plant container-grown trees at any time of the year, and bare-rooted trees from November to March. Add a good handful of bonemeal, and a sprinkling of mycorrhizal fungal preparation to aid rooting (see apples, page 201). Stake bush trees securely. Fix horizontal support wires on walls, 15cm/6in apart, starting 30cm/12in above ground.

Pruning and cultivation

Spend the first few years building up the framework. Ask your supplier to provide details of appropriate pruning techniques. Peaches and nectarines fruit on one-year-old wood. When trees begin cropping, prune fans in the spring to create replacement shoots, which will fruit the following year. Prune again in September, after the crop has been picked, removing wood that has fruited. Bush trees need hardly any pruning at all. Formative pruning for apricots is the same as for peaches, but thereafter the aim is to build up short, fruiting spurs that are one year old, and older. Never prune stone fruit during the winter, because spores of bacterial canker and silver leaf disease can enter the cut surfaces.

The risk of frost (except for plants under glass) makes the flowering period hazardous, so cover trees outdoors at night with sacking or fleece, removing it during the daytime. Pollinating insects are likely to be absent, so hand-pollinate at midday, when flowers are fully open, transferring pollen from the stamens to the stigmas with a soft artist's brush, or a cotton bud.

Mulch around trees with a layer of compost, and feed with comfrey or other high-potash liquid feed, every fortnight from May to August. Water well in dry weather, especially as fruits are swelling, but ease off during the final stages of ripening. Glasshouse-grown trees must be watered at least twice a week, or daily in very hot weather.

Begin thinning fruits, which tend to cluster in pairs, from May/June onwards, when marble-sized. Aim to leave one fruit every 10cm/4in. Don't pull them, as this may damage the shoots, but cut them in half with a sharp knife through the unripe stone. The damaged fruitlets will subsequently wither and die. Repeat when fruits are walnut-sized, to leave peaches every 20cm/8in and nectarines every 15cm/6in. Apricots are smaller and can be spaced every 7.5–10cm/3–4in.

Patio plants have a roughly 90cm-/3ft-diameter 'mop' head, atop a 90cm/3ft stem. Virtually no pruning is required, and trees can be brought indoors from Christmas to April, making it possible to grow them as far north as the Scottish borders.

Pests and diseases

Pests

Birds: Destroy flower and leaf buds in winter and ripe fruit in summer. Netting is the only effective solution.
Wasps: They take advantage of skin damage caused by birds. Set baited traps near trees.
Aphids: Peach-potato aphids overwinter as eggs on peaches. These hatch out and commence feeding in March. In May, winged forms migrate to potatoes. Remove badly affected foliage and spray with an organic insecticide.
Glasshouse red spider mites: For control, see page 89.

Diseases

Peach leaf curl: Can affect peaches and nectarines badly, but not apricots. Fungal spores, present in winter rain, cause young leaves to turn red, pucker and eventually fall, sometimes killing the tree. The traditional remedy is to spray with Bordeaux mixture at the end of

January; then two weeks later (before the flower buds open); and again just before leaf fall. A much better alternative is to erect a polythene canopy over the trees to prevent rain from splashing the leaves. Leave in place from early December to May. Glasshouse-grown trees are rarely troubled.

Other diseases: Peaches and nectarines are attacked by silver leaf disease and bacterial canker (see cherries, page 212), although apricots are rarely affected. Treat powdery mildew with sulphur, as for grapes. In heavy, wet, cold soils, apricots can suffer from dieback, for which there is no cure.

Harvesting and storing

Fruits can be harvested from July until late August. Although they may look ripe, wait until they're slightly yielding to the touch, and come away cleanly from the tree, before picking. Apricots can be stored for longer than peaches and nectarines, and will keep for several weeks in tissue-lined boxes, in a cool, dark place. All types of fruits can be bottled, dried, frozen or incorporated into pickles (see Part 4).

Nutritional value

Vitamins: C***
Phytochemicals: Beta-carotene, lutein, cryptoxanthin, lycopene, anthocyanins, rutin

Peaches – 33kcal, LGI; Nectarines – 40kcal, LGI; Apricots – 31kcal, MGI

VARIETIES

Peach: Avalon Pride (resistant to leaf curl), Hales Early, Peregrine, Rochester
Nectarine: Fantasia, Humboldt, Lord Napier
Apricot: Alfred, Flavourcot, Moorpark, New Large Early, Tomcot

Patio trees
Peach: Bonanza, Garden Lady
Nectarine: Nectarella, Terrace Ruby
Apricot: Aprigold, Champion

Reads Nursery sell a good selection of trees (see Resources, p.305).

PEARS

Pears are susceptible to a large number of pests and diseases, often fail to crop, and frequently rot in the blinking of an eye. Even so, they're worth all the trouble for that first juicy mouthful!

Planning and preparation

Pear trees frequently live for more than fifty years. If planted on their own roots, they take several decades to begin fruiting and grow to 15m/50ft. To overcome these handicaps, they're usually grafted onto two semi-vigorous rootstocks obtained from quince trees – Quince A and Quince C. Bush pears grafted onto Quince C grow

2.4–5.5m/8–18ft high, whilst those on Quince A grow slightly larger (3–6m/10–20ft). Trees usually take at least four years before they start cropping.

Plant bush trees on Quince C, 3–4m/10–14ft apart, and those on Quince A, 3.5–4.5m/11½–15ft apart. Cordons can go closer, at 75–90cm/30–36in apart, and espalier/fans at 3.5–4.5m/11½–15ft apart. If you don't want to wait that long, try a 'leg tree', which bears fruit in its second year. These intensively trained cordons were developed for commercial producers, but they're also available to gardeners.

In order to set fruit successfully, most pears must receive pollen from another, varietally different, pear tree that flowers around the same time. A few varieties, like Conference and Concorde, can set fruit without a pollinator, but will produce a better crop with one. Joséphine de Malines and Jargonelle, are 'triploid' varieties and require two pollinators.

Planting

Plant pears as you would apples (see page 201), choosing a sunny and sheltered spot away from frost pockets. If your site is exposed, grow Conference, Concorde or Winter Nelis.

Pruning and cultivation

Like apples, most pears fruit on short spurs and the training methods are the same (see page 202). A few, notably Jargonelle and Joséphine de Malines, are 'tip bearers' and must be pruned differently. Ask your supplier how to do it.

Keep trees well weeded, and water during dry periods – pears prefer soil to be permanently moist, but not water-logged. Mulch with compost, and feed with a nitrogen-rich organic fertilizer if growth is poor,

Pears require less thinning than apples – aim for two fruits per cluster when thinning after the 'June drop'.

Pests and diseases

Pears share many problems with apples, including aphids, winter moth, scab, canker and powdery mildew, to name but a few (see page 203).

Pests

Pear midges: Fruitlets swell rapidly in late spring, then fall to the ground. The yellow/white grubs hibernate in the soil. Remove and destroy affected fruits. Fork over the ground lightly in winter to expose the pest's cocoons to birds and the weather.

Pear leaf blister mites: Leaves become blistered and turn red/yellow in spring. Remove and destroy.

Pear and cherry slugworms: Slug-like grubs skeletonize the leaves from June to September. Spray with an organic insecticide, and rake the soil in winter, as for pear midge.

Diseases

Fireblight: This is a serious disease that can cause the death of the tree. Symptoms arise from July to October, when leaves, flowers and shoots wilt, then blacken, as if scorched by a bonfire. Wounds exude a slimy white liquid. Cut back all affected branches to unstained wood. If necessary, dig up and burn the entire tree, because the disease is highly contagious.

Harvesting and storing

Judging the right time to harvest pears can be tricky. Pick prematurely, and they are hard and tasteless; delay too long and they rot from within, becoming 'sleepy' – soft brown and mealy. As a general rule, wait until you can detach the fruit from the tree with a gentle twist of the hand. Pick early and mid-season pears, which ripen in August and September, before they are fully ripe. Eat within a couple of weeks.

Leave varieties that mature in October until you start noticing windfalls. Pick and store in a cool shed (ideal temperature 3–7°C/38–44°F). Some varieties keep into the New Year, but most are over by Christmas. They're ready to eat when the skin softens near the stalk. Pears don't freeze well, or dry easily, but they can be bottled, made into jam and used in pickles (see Part 4). They make excellent wine and perry.

Nutritional value

Vitamins: C, E*
Phytochemicals: anthocyanins, proanthocyanidins, ferulic acid, caffeic acid, chlorogenic acid
40kcal, LGI

VARIETIES

Early: Glow Red Williams, Jargonelle, Merton Pride, Williams Bon Chrétien
Mid-season: Conference, Fertility Improved, Louise Bonne de Jersey
Late: Concorde, Josephine de Malines, Packham's Triumph, Winter Nelis

PLUMS and GAGES

Plums are the easiest of the stone fruits to grow, and will crop in most parts of the country. Gages have a superior flavour, but are more sensitive to the weather and less prolific. Damsons are hardiest of all. Plums are one of the few fruits that are not suitable for container growing.

Planning and preparation

Choose a sheltered spot away from frost pockets. Improve the soil with compost or manure – it should be rich and moisture-retentive, pH 6.5–7. Plums are usually trained as 'bushes' in the open (or as standards, or half-standards, if space permits), but they can also be grown as cordons, or as fans against a fence or wall. Gages need the warmth of a south- or west-facing wall, but culinary plums and damsons can take an east- or even north-facing aspect.

There are two main sorts of rootstocks

for plums: St Julien A, which is semi-vigorous, with trees 4–4.5m/13–15ft tall; or Pixy, which is semi-dwarfing, with trees 2.4–3m/8–10ft tall. Space bush trees on Pixy 2.4–3m/8–10ft apart, and fans every 4.5m/15ft. Bush trees on St Julian A require more room – 3.5–4.5m/12–15ft; leave 5m/16½ft between fans. Cordons are grown only on Pixy and should be spaced every 90cm/3ft. A few varieties are self-fertile and can be grown on their own. Others require a pollinating partner that flowers at the same time. Check with your supplier, as certain varieties are incompatible with others, even though they flower simultaneously.

Planting

Trees are usually supplied 'bare-rooted', and must be planted from November to March. Plant trees bought in containers at any time. For details of preparing planting holes, stakes and support wires (for fans and cordons), follow the advice for apples (see page 201).

Pruning and cultivation

If you buy one-year-old 'maidens' you'll be able to train them to your requirements. Branches on bush trees usually start 75cm/30in above ground. If they begin at 1.2–1.4m/4–4½ft, the tree is called a 'half-standard'; at 1.8–2.1m/6–7ft, it's a 'standard'.

Bought trees that are older will already have been partially trained. Plums fruit on wood that is one to four years old, the pruning objective being to build up a supporting network of branches that are well endowed with fruiting spurs, like an apple. Your supplier should provide details of appropriate training methods.

Once they've begun producing fruit – usually after three years – eliminate only dead, diseased and awkwardly placed shoots, plus a small proportion of very old wood. Prune only between June and August, to minimise the risk of silver leaf disease, which is the main killer of stone fruit. At the same time pull up (do not use secateurs) any suckers (shoots springing from the base of the tree).

Plums flower in March and April, so cover them with hessian sacking, or fleece, on frosty nights, removing it the following day. Bees, and other pollinating insects, are often few in number at this time of the year, so it is worthwhile hand-pollinating (see page 221).

Keep trees well watered, with regular applications, rather than infrequent dousings, which can cause fruits to split. Plums appreciate additional nitrogen, so feed with blood, fish and bonemeal, pelleted chicken manure, or other organic fertilizer. A mulch of compost/manure around the base of the tree (but not touching it) will help to conserve moisture and suppress weeds. Weed carefully, by hand not hoe, to avoid damaging the shallow, surface roots.

Shortly after the natural drop in midsummer, thin out the plums to leave a 5–7.5cm/2–3in gap between each. This improves the size and flavour, and helps to prevent biennial bearing, when the tree carries a heavy crop one year and none the next. Heavily loaded plum branches are quite brittle, so use wooden props to prevent them from snapping. The variety 'Victoria' is particularly prone to breakages, and this provides an entry route for the silver leaf fungus.

Pests and diseases

Pests

Birds: They can destroy flower and leaf buds in winter and ripe fruit in summer. Netting is the only effective solution.

Wasps: They can take advantage of skin damage caused by birds. Set baited traps near trees.

Plum fruit moths: This is the plum equivalent of maggoty apples caused by codling moth, and the remedy is the same. Hang up a pheromone trap from mid-May until early August to trap hapless male moths, thereby ensuring that eggs remain unfertilized and don't become maggots.

Plum sawflies: They're similar to apple sawflies and occur at about the same time.

Aphids: Plums are attacked by mealy plum aphids, which are green and waxy and live on the underside of leaves; and leaf curling plum aphids, which are yellow-green and cause leaves to curl tightly. The leaf-curling sort are active as early as late January, but the mealy plum aphid doesn't usually attack before May/June. Squash the aphids and

remove foliage and spray with an organic insecticide, in both cases.

Diseases

Brown rot: Look for soft brown areas on fruits that ultimately shrivel and stay on the tree as 'mummified' fruits. Also causes withering on shoots and leaves. Remove all affected tissue and fruits. Collect any fallen fruit and destroy.

Plums also suffer from silver leaf disease and bacterial canker (see cherries, page 212) and from a variant of apple scab and powdery mildew (see apples, page 203)

Harvesting and storing

The harvest period for plums, damsons and gages runs from late July until early November. Dessert plums and gages are ripe when they have developed a bloom and pull easily from the tree. Eat within a few days. Pick culinary sorts and damsons while they are still slightly unripe. Plums will keep for a couple of weeks in a cool place if the stalks are left attached. They can be bottled, frozen or used in jam, chutney and pickles, and make a delicious crumble (see Part 4).

Nutritional value

Vitamins: C, E, K*

Phytochemicals: lutein, ferulic acid, hydroxycinnamic acid, tannins, proanthocyanidins, other flavonoids and phenolic compounds. Plums and gages have high antioxidant activity.

36kcal, LGI

VARIETIES	Gages
Plums	Cambridge, Denniston's Superb, Oullins Golden Gage
Dessert: Coe's Golden Drop, Jubilee, Kirke's Blue, Opal	
Culinary: Belle de Louvain, Czar, Early Rivers	**Damsons**
Dual purpose: Marjorie's Seedling, Severn Cross, Victoria	Farleigh, Merryweather, Shropshire Prune

RASPBERRIES

Raspberries are easy to grow and provide a delicious alternative to strawberries. They thrive under cool, damp conditions and flower late, so usually miss the frosts. Summer-fruiting raspberries crop throughout July and early August, and autumn-fruiting raspberries crop from the end of August to the end of October – making a nice long picking season if you have both.

Planning and preparation

Raspberries need a moisture-retentive, but well-drained, slightly acid soil, pH 5.5–6.5. Although they prefer full sun, they'll crop in partial shade. A month before planting, make sure that all weeds, especially perennials, are removed. Dig a trench 45cm/18in wide and 23cm/9in deep and backfill with a mixture of soil and compost/manure.

Autumn-fruiting raspberries can be grown unsupported, whereas summer-fruiting types grow more than 1.5m/5ft tall and need a support framework of posts and wires.

Drive 2.3m/7½ft posts into the ground, to a depth of 45cm/18in, every 2.4–3m/ 8–10ft. Attach three horizontal wires at 75cm/2½ft, 1.05m/3½ft and 1.7m/5½ft above ground using wire staples, and straining bolts at one end to tauten them.

Brace end posts adequately with angled wooden struts. Space plants 38–45cm/ 15–18in apart, in rows 1.5–1.8m/5–6ft wide. If possible, orient rows in a north–south direction, to reduce shading from adjacent plants. In small gardens, simply train a couple of raspberries on either side of a single post.

Plants live for 10–12 years, and whilst summer-fruiting types will fruit one year after planting, autumn-fruiting types crop that same year. All raspberries are self-fertile, so need no pollinating partners. Summer-fruiting varieties should produce 0.9–1.4kg/2–3lb per plant; autumn-fruiting varieties 350g/¾lb per plant.

Planting

Don't plant raspberries too deep, or the roots will rot. A 5–7.5cm-/2–3in-deep covering of soil is adequate. Add a sprinkling of bonemeal to the planting hole, spread out the roots and lightly cover with soil, then tread down firmly. Bare-rooted plants must be planted between November and March, but container-bought plants can go in at any time.

Pruning and cultivation

Unless already shortened by the supplier, prune newly planted raspberries to a bud 23cm/9in above ground. In spring, canes will break into leaf, followed by new shoots from below the soil surface. When this occurs, cut the original canes (summer-fruiting varieties only) to the ground. Although this eliminates all the berries, it also strengthens the new canes, giving more fruit the following year. Tie the new canes to the wires.

In February, cut back canes that have grown excessively to just above the top wire. In June, pull up any suckers that are growing too far from the wires. At the same time, prune out any weak and spindly canes. Cut all the old canes to the ground immediately after fruiting, and tie in new canes.

Autumn-fruiting raspberries crop on the upper part of the current season's wood, so they should be pruned in February to about 15–23cm/6–9in above ground. There is no need to thin canes in summer.

Scatter pelleted chicken manure and a high-potash organic fertilizer (kali vinasse) along the rows, at a rate of 125g per sq. m/4oz per sq. yd, early in March. Later that month, apply a mulch of compost close to, but not touching, the canes. Raspberries are surface-rooting, so weed carefully, preferably by hand. Control weeds between rows by putting down an impermeable fabric, straw, or grass clippings over newspapers.

Raspberries need plenty of water to fruit well, so water heavily in dry weather. They also benefit from seaweed sprays every two to three weeks, from May until fruiting.

You can propagate raspberries by digging up and transplanting rooted suckers, but as old canes are invariably infected with virus diseases, we wouldn't recommend it.

Pests and diseases

Pests

Birds: Blackbirds love summer-fruiting raspberries, so a fruit cage is absolutely essential for these, but because of the availability of elderberries and other hedgerow bounty, autumn-fruiting raspberries are often left alone.

Raspberry beetles: Small yellow maggots feed inside the berries, causing hard encrustations and deformed fruit. The traditional remedy involves spraying plants in flower, when adult beetles are laying their eggs, but timing is difficult and pesticides can also kill bees. Instead, hang a raspberry beetle trap amongst the canes before flowering, in April/May. It mimics the raspberry flower scent and lures beetles to a watery death.

Raspberry aphids: There are two sorts, in different shades of green. Both attack young shoots and foliage from March onwards. Remove badly infested growth and/or spray with an organic insecticide. Aphids can transmit virus diseases (see below). Most 'Glen' varieties used to be resistant, but are no longer.

Diseases

Cane blight: Dark, cracked patches appear low down on canes and the leaves shrivel. Cut back and destroy all affected canes to ground level. If the patches on the canes are dark purple, the problem is spur blight.

Raspberry mosaic virus: This is the commonest of several viruses that can infect raspberries. Most of them are transmitted by aphids. Symptoms include leaf mottling and poor, stunted growth. There is no cure: dig up and destroy affected plants. Always buy accredited, virus-free plants.

Raspberries can be infected by other fungal diseases, including grey mould, cane and leaf spot and powdery mildew.

Harvesting and storing

Early varieties of summer-fruiting raspberries ripen in the first half of July; mid-season varieties follow from the middle of the month; and late varieties begin at the end of July/early August. Plants crop for around three weeks. Harvest autumn-fruiting raspberries from the end of August until early October.

Raspberries are ripe when they've developed their full colour and pull cleanly off the core ('plug') when squeezed gently. Pick on dry days only, or the fruit rots. Autumn-fruiting raspberries are more difficult to detach, and frequently come away with the plug attached. When picking berries on the lower half of the canes, crouch down and look upwards. It's amazing how many you can miss if you don't do this! Wearing an apron with a large pocket in the front to hold a storage container frees one hand to push the canes gently apart to reveal otherwise hidden gems. Raspberries will keep in the fridge for several days, and can be frozen, bottled and processed into jam and jellies (see Part 4).

Nutritional value

Vitamins: C***; E, folate*
Minerals: manganese*
Phytochemicals: ellagic acid, quercetin, gallic acid, anthocyanins, cyanidins, pelargonidins, catechins, kaempferol and salicylic acid. One of the best fruits for antioxidant activity.
25kcal, LGI

VARIETIES

Early: Glen Moy, Malling Jewel
Mid-season: Glen Ample, Glen Prosen, Malling Admiral
Late: Leo, Octavia, Tulameen
Autumn: Autumn Bliss, Himbo Top, Joan Squire
Yellow: Allgold (autumn), Fallgold (autumn), Golden Everest (mid)

RED and WHITE CURRANTS

It's a mystery why these strikingly beautiful fruits, with their long, pendulous garlands of currants, aren't more popular, not least because they are so easy to grow. Redcurrant jelly and lamb are just made for each other! Or try it with deep-fried Brie.

Planning and preparation

Although the fruits are closely related to blackcurrants, they're grown and pruned as if they were gooseberries. In the open, they're formed into goblet-shaped bushes on a short stem (or grown as half-standards); but they also come as single, double or triple cordons, and fans against a wall or fence.

Like gooseberries, they're not fussy about soil conditions, so long as it's well drained and slightly acid, pH 6.5. Even so, they will grow better if the soil is improved with compost. Like most fruit, red and white currants do best in full sun, but they'll also tolerate shade – redcurrants are just the thing for a north-facing wall.

Space bush trees 1.5m/5ft apart; single cordons 38cm/15in, double cordons 60cm/24in and triple cordons 90cm/36in apart. When growing cordons and fans against walls and fences, space them 1.8m/6ft apart and attach them to two horizontal support wires 60cm/2ft and 1.2m/4ft above ground.

Red and white currants are self-fertile, so will grow on their own. They last upwards of twenty years, and a single red/white currant bush should produce around 3.5–4.5kg/8–10lb of fruit; a cordon 0.9–1.4kg/2–3lb.

Planting

Plant bare-rooted currants between November and March, and container-bought plants at any time. Dig a hole slightly larger than the root mass and sprinkle in a handful of bonemeal and seaweed meal. Look for the soil stain on the stems of bare-rooted bushes, and plant to this depth. Tie-in cordons and fans to bamboo canes lashed to the wires. Bushes need no support, although half-standard forms, which have a 1.1m/3½ft stem, must be permanently staked.

Pruning and cultivation

Red and white currants fruit on one-year, and older, wood and are pruned in exactly the same way as gooseberries (see page 215).

Currants have shallow roots, which can be damaged by hoeing. Mulch with straw, wilted comfrey or grass clippings. Every spring, put a layer of compost around the base of the bushes, and feed with high-potash organic fertilizer in alternate years.

If frost threatens, protect fruits with fleece at flowering time. Water plants in dry weather to assist fruit ripening, but don't over-water, because this will encourage aphid attack.

Propagate red and white currants as you would blackcurrants (see page 207).

Pests and diseases

Red and white currants can be attacked by the same pests and diseases as blackcurrants (see page 208), although, fortunately, they are unaffected by American gooseberry mildew.

Birds: These are the biggest menace – redcurrants are their absolute favourites, and who can blame them? If you want any sort of a crop you must grow them under netting in a fruit cage. Winter protection of fruit buds from bullfinches and other birds is also recommended.

Red currant blister aphids: Light yellow aphids cluster under leaves in spring, causing red blisters. Remove badly affected leaves and squash/spray the remainder.

Harvesting and storing

Early varieties of redcurrant fruit in the first half of July; mid-season varieties occupy the remainder of the month; and late varieties fruit in August. White currants fruit in July. Plants crop for around three weeks.

Harvest when the fruits have achieved their full colour, and yield slightly to the touch. Red and white currants hang on well when ripe, so a few days' delay in picking is unimportant. Snip complete strings, and separate the currants at home, 'combing' them with the prongs of a fork. They freeze well and can be bottled, juiced and used in jams and jellies (see Part 4). Currants are high in pectin (a setting agent) and have traditionally been used in combination with low-pectin fruits to make jam.

Nutritional Value

56kcal, LGI

VARIETIES

Redcurrants
Early: Fay's Prolific, Jonkheer Van Tets, Junifer, Laxton No. 1
Mid-season: Red Lake, Rednose, Stanza
Late: Redpoll, Redstart, Rovada

White currants
Blanca, White Grape, White Pearl (Transparent), White Versailles

RHUBARB

Strictly speaking, rhubarb is a vegetable, but everyone thinks of it as a fruit. Forced rhubarb is ready from February, and provides a welcome source of delicate young stems for desserts, long before other fruits ripen. No garden should be without a clump or two.

Planning and preparation

Rhubarb grows best in richly manured, well-drained, acid soil, pH 5–6. Don't consign it to an out-of-the-way corner in semi-shade: instead, establish your patch in the open, in full sun, wherever possible. It's mostly grown from 'crowns', which are rooted divisions taken from mature plants, but it can also be raised from seed.

Rhubarb is a long-lived perennial plant, and is usually established in permanent beds, with crowns spaced every 90cm/3ft. Dig the bed thoroughly, removing all perennial weeds. Fork in a generous load of compost, or well-rotted manure, and add bonemeal at 500g per sq. m/1lb per sq. yd.

Plants spread, and can become congested as they get older. For this reason, some gardeners prefer to dig them up and replace them after four to five years, although they'll carry on cropping undisturbed for at least fifteen years.

Planting

Plant rhubarb in November or December, although any time before the end of March is acceptable. If you're propagating from an existing plant (which must be at least three years old), slice into the root with a spade and chop out a chunky section that has a dormant bud, or 'eye'. Plant with the bud slightly raised above soil level and tread in firmly.

Alternatively, sow seeds 2.5cm/1in deep in a seed bed in April, in 30cm-/12in-wide rows. Thin to 15cm/6in. Later, as the plants get bigger, thin again to 30cm/12in, and move into their final positions the following spring.

Cultivation

Cover established plants with a generous layer of compost or manure in midwinter, topping it up with wilted

comfrey leaves from time to time during the spring and summer. In November, after the foliage has died down, lightly fork bonemeal, at 250g per sq. m/8oz per sq. yd, into the bed.

Keep the bed well watered and weeded throughout the growing season. Cut off any flowering stalks at the base, because these depress vigour.

There are several ways of forcing rhubarb, to obtain out-of-season, exquisitely blanched stems. In December, dig up a crown and replant it in a tub, trimming the roots to fit. Place somewhere dark and warm (a temperature of 8–16°C/46–61°F is ideal) and check that the soil does not dry out. The stems should be ready for pulling in about five weeks. Discard the crown when it has finished cropping.

Alternatively, force plants *in situ*. Cover the crown in January or February with a terracotta rhubarb forcer, old chimney pot or other container that is at least 45cm/18in deep. Alternatively, pile up dead leaves or straw over crowns to a

Traditional terracotta rhubarb forcer

depth of 30cm/12in. Pull stems in four to six weeks. Don't force the same crowns for at least two years.

Pests and diseases

Rhubarb is invariably trouble-free. Birds don't touch it, and there are few pests. It can suffer from a number of virus diseases, which cause mottling, spotting and blotching of the leaves, but there are no cures. Dig up and destroy affected plants. Forced rhubarb in pots is sometimes attacked by grey mould fungus (improved ventilation helps), and slugs, too, enjoy the protected environment, occasionally causing minor damage.

Harvesting and storing

Rhubarb doesn't come into full production until three years after planting, so refrain from picking in the first year (tasting the odd stick or two in late spring is permitted!), and finish after May in year two. Forced rhubarb is ready from February onwards, and the earliest varieties of outdoor-raised plants begin cropping in April. Most finish by July, in time for the start of the main soft-fruit harvest, but some late varieties continue into early September.

Pick only tender young stems, whose leaves have not fully unfurled. Pull from the base with a slight twisting action – don't use a knife. Discard the leaves, which are poisonous, and put them on the compost heap, where they'll cause no further problem.

Rhubarb can be frozen, bottled, made into jam and used in chutney (see Part 4). It goes well with ginger.

Nutritional value

Vitamins: C*
Minerals: calcium, manganese*
Phytochemicals: lutein, gallic acid, rutin, anthocyanins, phyto-oestrogens, polyphenols. Rhubarb leaves contain high amounts of oxalic acid and are poisonous.
7kcal, LGI

VARIETIES

Crowns
Early: Champagne, Stockbridge Arrow, Timperley Early
Mid-season: Cawood Delight, Reed's Early Superb, Stockbridge Harbinger
Late: Brandy Carr, The Sutton, Victoria

Seeds
Glaskin's Perpetual (low oxalic acid), Victoria

R V Roger Ltd and Brandy Carr Nurseries stock a good range of varieties. The National Plant Collection of rhubarb, which holds over forty varieties, is at RHS Harlow Carr, Harrogate, Yorkshire.

STRAWBERRIES

Strawberries are Britain's most popular fruit, and understandably so. Nothing can beat the taste of ripe, luscious, freshly picked, home-grown berries, or Eton Mess – a yummy mixture of strawberries, crushed meringue and whipped cream. And they are so easy to grow, even if you only have space for a container on a patio or windowsill. The main season runs from June to July, but by selecting a range of varieties you could be eating strawberries for much of the year.

Planning and preparation

There are two main sorts of strawberries – summer-fruiting varieties, which give a single crop, and perpetual, or remontant, varieties, which produce fruit continuously from August until the first frosts of autumn. A third sort, alpine strawberries, are a type of wild fruit, producing masses of miniature sweet but not juicy fruits, from June to October.

Summer-fruiting strawberries last three years before they need replacing, remontants only two, and because there is a risk of diseases building up in the soil if they remain for any length of time, they're usually included in the vegetable rotation, only returning to the same piece of land after at least three, preferably four or more, years.

Strawberries grow best in full sun, but can tolerate a certain amount of shading. They prefer an acid soil, pH 6–6.5, which is fertile and well drained, and will grow on clay soils, but it's safest to create a slight ridge, 5–7.5cm/2–3in high, to avoid waterlogging. Prepare a bed a month or so before planting, carefully removing any perennial weeds. Incorporate compost, leafmould or well-rotted manure, and add bonemeal at the rate of 500g per sq. m/1lb per sq. yd (the phosphate it contains is more important to strawberries than to any other soft fruit crop). Space plants 45cm/18in apart in rows 75cm/30in wide, though alpine strawberries can go closer, at 30cm/12in between plants and twice this distance between rows.

Always buy virus-free stock from a reputable source. Strawberries are self-fertile, so there are no pollination problems. They're usually sold as bare-rooted young plants, or 'runners', or pot-grown plants. Strawberries planted in mid-summer will fruit the following year. A single plant can produce 200–900g/7oz–2lb of fruits, depending on the variety.

Planting

July is the usual month for planting bare-rooted strawberries, although they can go in as late as mid-September. If planted after this time, however, don't allow them to fruit the following year. Dig a shallow hole with a trowel, create a slight mound in the centre, and spread the roots of the plant evenly over it. Backfill, pressing the soil firmly, and ensure that the 'crown', or centre of the plant, is at ground level. Plant pot-grown strawberries at any time. Water well, and until the plants are established.

You can buy specially designed straw-berry tubs or barrels with holes in the sides to accommodate up to thirty plants.

Alpine strawberries are almost always grown from seed. They're usually sown in the autumn and planted out the following spring but can be sown in March. At least thirty plants are required for a worthwhile crop, and they should be replaced every couple of years.

Pruning and cultivation

In April each year, lightly fork in 125g per sq. m/4oz per sq. yd of bonemeal and the same amount of kali vinasse. A month later, lay a straw mulch around and under the plants to suppress weeds and prevent soil splashing (barley straw is better than wheat). Alternatively, fit a 25cm-/10in-diameter 'strawberry mat' around each plant. Some gardeners grow their plants through slits in sheets of 150-gauge black polythene, or permeable weed fabric membrane, although adding compost in subsequent years is problematical.

In the event of frost, protect flowers with fleece; but don't worry if they become damaged, because new ones will be produced. Later in the year, plants send out long runners with young plants at the end, which root into the soil. These can be left in place to crop the following year, and will give a much greater crop of somewhat smaller berries. Alternatively, remove them. It's a simple matter to propagate from

runners – simply dig up those that have rooted into the soil and replant, or peg them down into 7.5cm/3in pots filled with growing media using opened-out paper clips. After about five weeks, when they have rooted, cut the runner away from the parent plant.

In dry weather, water regularly, trying to avoid splashing the fruits (early morning is best). Search out and remove any berries that are mouldy. Straw-berries benefit from a fortnightly foliar feed with liquid seaweed from April until the first fruits begin to ripen.

After they've finished cropping, cut back and compost all the foliage of summer-fruiting strawberries, to leave around 7.5cm/3in of stalks above the crown, At the same time, scatter a light layer of compost or leafmould. Remove only old leaves of remontant varieties.

To get earlier crops, cover rows with cloches (moving pot-grown plants under glass in February, to give strawberries in May). Fresh strawberries are possible almost all year round in a heated greenhouse, although disease is an ever-present risk. In recent years, American 'day-neutral' varieties have come onto the market, fruiting just 12 weeks after planting, but the flavour is nothing special.

Pests and diseases

Pests

Strawberry aphids: Pale green or yellow insects infest the undersides of leaves in spring. Squash or spray with an organic insecticide.

Slugs and snails: These devour the fruits. For control methods, see page 87.

Stem eelworms: Symptoms resemble those of viruses – leaves are crumpled and brittle and there is very poor growth. This is a problem of inadequate rotation. Dig up and destroy plants.

Diseases

Verticillium wilt: A fungal disease that causes wilting, then yellowing and shrivelling of leaves. Destroy affected plants. The varieties Bolero, Rhapsody and Florence are resistant.

Red core: A persistent fungal disease that causes the leaves to turn red/brown. The blackened roots have a red core. This is worse in the north of Britain. The varieties Symphony and Rhapsody are resistant.

Viruses: There are various types, transmitted by aphids and eelworms, all affecting leaves (which turn yellow and crinkle) and vigour. Dig up and burn.

Powdery mildew: See page 91. Bolero, Cambridge Favourite, Florence and Rhapsody are resistant.

Strawberries also suffer from botrytis (grey mould) and several other diseases, for which there are no cures.

Harvesting and storing

Early varieties of summer-fruiting strawberries crop during June, mid-season varieties from mid-June to mid-July and late varieties throughout July. Pick strawberries on a daily basis, preferably early in the morning, when they are dry and cool, nipping off the stalks so they remain attached to the fruits. Strawberries will keep for several days in a cool place, but are best eaten fresh. They freeze poorly, turning to mush when thawed – a notable exception being the Totem variety. Strawberries can be bottled or made into jam (see Part 4).

Nutritional value

Vitamins: C***; folate*. Strawberries contain almost double the RDA of vitamin C.

Phytochemicals: anthocyanins, ellagic acid, salicylic acid, quercetin, myricetin, kaempferol, caffeic acid, ferulic acid, coumaric acid, chlorogenic acid, gallic acid.

27kcal, LGI

VARIETIES

Early: Elvira, Honeoye, Gariguette
Mid-season: Cambridge Favourite, Hapil, Pegasus
Late: Florence, Rhapsody, Symphony
Perpetual (remontant): Aromel, Bolero, Mara des Bois
Heritage: Cambridge Late Pine (late), Cambridge Vigour (early), Royal Sovereign (mid)
Alpine: Alexandria, Baron Solemacher

Chris Bowers & Sons sells a good range of varieties (see Resources, p.304).

OTHER FRUITS

CAPE GOOSEBERRIES

Sow seeds in seed trays in March, and put in a propagator at 18°C/65°F. Pot on when large enough, and plant out in mid-May, covering with cloches until all risk of frost has passed. Space plants at 75cm/30in intervals in each direction, and support individually with 90cm/3ft stakes. Alternatively, grow in containers. Pinch out the growing points if plants fail to make flowers by the time they are 30cm/12in high. Feed fortnightly with liquid seaweed.

In cool areas, grow in a cold greenhouse or polytunnel. Fruits are ready for picking when the 'paper lanterns' are crisp and yellow/gold in colour, which is usually not before September. Gather any unripe berries at the end of the season and ripen on a sunny windowsill – they should keep until December.

CITRUS FRUITS

Most gardeners who grow citrus fruits do so in containers so that trees can spend the summer outside and the winter in a conservatory or glasshouse where the temperature doesn't drop below 7°C/44°F. You can grow citrus fruits from pips, if you've the patience, but expect to wait at least ten years for your first fruits. It's much better, and quicker, to buy a named variety from a specialist supplier – Reads Nursery (see Resources, page 305) have an excellent range. Lemons are the easiest of all the citrus fruits to grow, and they crop almost all year round.

All trees are self-fertile and begin fruiting after two to three years. Apart from a liquid feed every 7–10 days during the growing period, very little attention is required. Water infrequently using rainwater, letting the soil dry out almost completely before watering again. In winter there's hardly any need to water at all. Very little pruning is required. Trees suffer from the usual glasshouse pests that attack tomatoes and cucumbers (see page 89 for control methods).

KIWI FRUITS

This is a fruit that needs lots of sun to ripen the fruit, and plenty of space, because vines grow up to 9m/30ft. Train plants up some trellis attached to a south-facing wall, over a pergola, or on a post-and-wire structure as for blackberries, spacing vines every 3m/9ft. They can be pruned in a similar way to grapes. Kiwi fruit varieties are either all-male (such as Atlas or Tomuri) or all-female (such as Haywood or Abbot), and you need at least one male to pollinate six female plants. Alternatively, grow a self-fertile variety, like Jenny. Fruits are produced on lateral shoots and ripen in October, but need to be picked and stored for four weeks to develop their full flavour. They will keep for several weeks in a fridge but don't freeze well.

MEDLARS

This is another tree that needs a lot of room, growing up to 6m/20ft tall. It's not fussy about soil conditions, but prefers a sheltered site in full sun, as the leaves and flowers are easily damaged by the wind. Plant and prune it as you would a half-standard apple, until you achieve the desired shape. When mature, very little annual pruning is needed. Medlars are self-fertile, so only one tree is required, but make sure that you try the fruit before you plant one – medlars are definitely an acquired taste! Pick the curiously shaped, leathery fruits in late October and place them upside down, on a tray, in a frost-free shed, for three weeks to ripen. Fruits turn dark brown and soften, almost to the point of rotting, in a process known as 'bletting'. Scoop out the flesh and eat raw, or use in jams and jellies. There are very few varieties – Dutch, Nottingham and Royal being the more popular sorts. Keepers Nursery stock some unusual varieties (see Resources, p.305).

MELONS

There are three types of melon: musk, winter or casaba, and cantaloupe. None crops reliably outdoors in Britain, and all but the cantaloupes should be grown in a heated greenhouse, at a temperature of at least 18°C/65°F. Sow seeds of cantaloupe melons in late April, starting them off in 7.5cm/3in pots on a warm windowsill, or in a propagator at 18–21°C/65–70°F. Pot them on into 13cm/5in pots (all the while

maintaining adequate warmth) and plant out into a glasshouse, polytunnel or cold frame, or under cloches, in late May or early June. Plants can be allowed to scramble over the ground or up strings/nets, like cucumbers. Restrict the number of fruits to four or five per plant, ruthlessly eliminating other fruiting laterals. Water generously, avoiding splashing the stems, and feed weekly with a high-potash organic fertilizer. Harvest in August/September, when the skins have begun to soften, but sound hollow when tapped, and the fruits part easily from the vine. Sweetheart F1 is by far the most reliable variety, and definitely the one for first-time melon growers to try.

MULBERRIES

These make big trees, over 8m/26ft tall, so are suitable only for large gardens – as a specimen tree in a lawn, perhaps. Somewhat surprisingly, though, they can also be grown in large tubs. Once the basic shape of the tree has been formed, little pruning is required, and the large, dark crimson, raspberry-shaped fruits are harvested in August – just shake the branches and stand clear! Mulberries take eight years before fruiting, but thereafter crop prolifically, which is just as well as birds love them. Mulberries are self-fertile, so you need buy only one, but make sure you get a black one, not a white one. There are no varieties. They're delicious eaten fresh, and you can also freeze and bottle them.

QUINCES

Many people confuse the fruits of the pinkish-red-flowered ornamental shrub *Chaenomeles*, popularly called 'japonica' with that of the true quince, *Cydonia oblonga*. Both are edible, but japonicas are much smaller and can be easily trained against a wall or fence. The true quince is usually grown as a freestanding tree, and will reach a height of 4m/13ft. It's essentially a fruit of southern Britain – if growing it in the north, train it flat against a south- or west-facing wall. Follow the advice for cultivating a bush apple or pear (quinces do, in fact, resemble a rounded pear). Pick the fruits in mid-October and leave for four to eight weeks to ripen, until the colour changes from green to golden-yellow. They're not usually eaten raw, but do make exquisitely wonderful aromatic jellies and marmalades. Common varieties are Champion, Meech's Prolific, Portugal and Vranja. All are self-fertile.

CHAPTER 9

Herbs

Herbs are so useful, and so easy to grow, that they should be an essential part of every garden, even if there's only space for a collection of pots near the kitchen door.

Many herbs are perennials and will live for several years; others need to be re-sown each year. Quite a few of the most popular herbs hail from the Mediterranean and grow best on light, well-drained soils in full sun. Lighten heavy soils with plenty of compost and grit, or grow in containers instead.

The quickest way to establish herbs is to buy plants, or take cuttings from existing plants, but you can raise most of them from seed. In most cases, routine maintenance involves little more than an annual trim, usually after flowering. Pests and diseases are mercifully few, although rusts can be a problem with certain species, like chives, mint and tarragon. The only remedy is to remove and destroy affected foliage, or, in some cases, to destroy the entire plant.

Many herbs will happily grow on a windowsill, even out of season, providing a source of fresh leaves for most of the year. Failing that, you can dry or freeze most species. Below is our choice of the dozen most popular herbs, but if you'd like to try something a bit more unusual contact Jekka's Herb Farm for supplies of over 600 different sorts of organically grown herb plants and seeds (see Resources, p.304).

Basil

A tender annual with strongly aromatic leaves. Wait until June before multi-sowing in modules. Plant outside at the end of the month leaving 30cm/12in intervals in each direction. Spray weekly with liquid seaweed and water only in dry weather – once weekly should be sufficient. Harvest up to half the plant at a time, tearing the leaves rather than cutting them to release the flavour, and it will re-grow. Homemade pesto sauce. Mmmm!

Chives

The easiest herb of all to grow, coping happily with semi-shade. Station-sow four seeds, at 30cm/12in intervals each way, in late April or early May and thin to the strongest. When harvesting, cut all leaves to the ground – the plant will soon recover. Remove the flower heads before they have a chance to ripen, otherwise they self-seed everywhere. Every three years, dig up and split the plant, then replant the clumps. Widely used to brighten up all sorts of dishes. Garlic chives have a mild garlic taste.

Coriander

A sun-loving annual that can be grown for its seeds or foliage. Sow seeds thinly in April or May in rows 30cm/12in apart and thin to 5cm/2in if growing for leaves, or 25cm/10in if growing for seeds. Don't sow in seed trays or modules, as coriander dislikes being transplanted and will run to seed. Grow 'Cilantro' for leaves, and harvest when plants are around 10cm/4in high. Cut flower heads when seeds are about to fall and place in a paper bag for collection. Good for Eastern recipes.

Dill

Aniseed-flavoured annual belonging to the carrot family. Sow thinly *in situ* in 30cm-/12in-wide rows in April/May and thin to 20cm/8in between plants. For a succession of plants, sow every few weeks. You can harvest the feathery leaves within eight weeks of sowing. Dill readily self-seeds, but will cross-pollinate with fennel, so keep them well apart. Goes well with fish.

Fennel

A tall perennial, growing 2m/6½ft tall, and a relative of Florence fennel (see page 147). Available with either bronze or green foliage. Seeds need a temperature of 15°C/59°F to germinate, so don't sow before May unless using heat. Plant out at 60cm/24in spacings. Remove flower heads as they appear, to encourage foliage production, and cut back to ground level in early winter. May need staking. A lovely addition to green salads.

Marjoram

Pot marjoram has a milder flavour than the wild sort, which is also known as oregano. Sow seeds in April in modules and plant out at 20cm/8in spacings in May. Cut back to 5cm/2in above ground in the autumn, and divide plants every three or so years in the spring to stop them from becoming too woody. Amazing with lamb.

Mint

Spearmint is the 'garden' mint, traditionally eaten with roast lamb, but there are many other types. Buy plants rather than seeds, or grow from cuttings, which can be taken at almost any time. Mint is a 'thug' and will spread everywhere if given the chance, so plant it in a bottomless bucket, sunk into the ground with the rim just protruding above soil level. Remove runners before they manage to root. Peppermint makes a refreshing tea.

Parsley

One of the few herbs that need a good, rich soil and preferably a little shade. Sow seeds thinly in March/April in rows spaced 30cm/12in apart; a second sowing in July will provide plants for the winter. Germination is extremely slow. Thin plants to 15cm/6in apart. Keep plants well watered. Parsley is a biennial and will throw up a seed head in its second year, so grow new plants every year. There are two, commonly grown, distinctive forms of parsley: curled and flat-leaved sorts. Either is a great way of adding vitamin C to many meals.

Rosemary

It's difficult to grow this perennial from seed, so buy plants or take cuttings. Plants grow tall and bushy – it makes a nice hedge – so space them every 60–90cm/2–3ft. Trim after flowering in spring and replace every five years. Although rosemary is hardy, drape plants with fleece when temperatures drop considerably. Made for lamb.

Sage

There are many different types of sage, all with strongly aromatic foliage. Like rosemary, it's easiest to buy plants, or take cuttings, rather than grow from seed. Needs a sunny spot to do well. Trim back after flowering in summer. Sage tea is traditionally used for treating sore throats.

Tarragon

You can grow Russian tarragon from seed, but who would want to when you can grow French tarragon instead (though not from seed) which is so much nicer? The Russian sort comes from Siberia and is completely hardy, whereas French tarragon needs protection in winter. Remove flowers in summer, and renew plants every three years. Nice with chicken, or to flavour vinegar (see page 302).

Thyme

There are scores of different types of thyme, but only common and creeping thyme can be grown from seed. This is another case where it's best to propagate your own from cuttings, or buy plants from a specialist nursery. If growing from seed, you'll need heat to germinate them. The young plants should not go out until all danger of frost has passed. Summer is the best time to take cuttings. Trim plants after flowering in spring, and protect tender thymes in winter. Wonderful for parsley and thyme stuffing.

PART 4

Preserving the harvest

Every gardener wants to have something to pick each day of the year. This is easy enough during the summer months, when gardens are awash with produce, but far harder when winter turns into spring, and the last of the brassicas comes to an end.

Fruit and vegetables are at their flavoursome best, and nutritional peak, when they're freshly harvested, but if they can't be eaten fresh, the next best thing is to store them, or preserve them, during times of plenty. Fortunately, there are very few fruits or vegetables that can't be preserved successfully in one way or another.

CHAPTER 10

Storing

It's surprising how many crops can be stored through the winter outside, especially if given a little protection. To be sure of success, however, bring them indoors into a cool shed, adapted especially for the purpose.

Storage outside

Carrots, parsnips, turnips, swedes, celeriac, salsify, scorzonera, winter-hardy radishes and Jerusalem artichokes, leeks and celery can all be left in the ground and lifted as needed, although you can come unstuck if the ground is frozen for any length of time. There's also an ever-present risk of rodent attack. If you decide to leave vegetables *in situ*, it pays to lift a few, and cover them loosely with soil. This allows you to get at them easily if the ground becomes too hard to dig. From December onwards, you should cover crops with a 15cm/6in layer of bracken or straw, to insulate them from the worst of the weather, as splitting can occur when water penetrates cracks and subsequently freezes.

Potatoes, on the other hand, can be preserved outdoors by a traditional method called 'clamping', although clamps offer only poor protection from frost, and the crop may be attacked by rats. Nevertheless, to make a clamp, you need to spread a layer of straw or bracken on the ground and heap up the potatoes in the shape of a pyramid. Cover with more straw or bracken and leave for a couple of days for the potatoes to sweat. Shovel soil over the entire heap, patting it down with the back of a spade, until it is about 15cm/6in thick. Leave a few lengths of straw 'chimneys' poking through the soil cap, at the top, and at the base, so air can penetrate. If the soil used to cover the clamp comes from close by, take care not to leave a hole behind that could fill with water when it rains, flooding your clamp. It's better to construct several small clamps, rather than one big one, to avoid frequent opening and closing. That way, you can dismantle an entire clamp in one operation, bag-up the potatoes, and transfer them to a cool shed.

Storage in a cool shed

Potatoes, root crops, onions and garlic, winter cabbages and apples will keep for months if stored somewhere cool, well ventilated and frost free. Cellars have traditionally fulfilled this function, but few houses have them these days, so most people use a garden shed, garage or outhouse instead. Unfortunately, wooden sheds are invariably constructed from flimsy timber boards and must be insulated in order to give adequate protection during cold weather. If you intend to store a reasonable quantity of vegetables, you may wish to dedicate a shed specifically for the purpose.

To do this, you should cut slabs of insulation board (rolls of loft insulation are also fine) to fit between the ribs of the shed sides and roof, and line with sheets of plywood or hardboard to hold it in place. Fix the shed directly onto a concrete base, as this will help to keep it cool (timber floors are too warm), and locate it in the shadiest part of the garden. Any windows (the fewer, the better) should face north. Drill two or three ventilation holes at the top of each of the longer sides, and an equal number near the base of one side only, and cover them with wire mesh, or equivalent, to keep out birds and vermin. The air will be drawn in through the lower holes and out through the top, cutting down the stagnant air pockets that allow storage rots to flourish.

Potatoes

To store potatoes, you need to brush off most of the soil, taking care not to damage the skin. To prevent the tubers from turning green, store in jute, hessian or double-thickness paper sacks (they sweat in polythene or plastic bags). Potatoes prefer slightly warmer conditions than other roots: 5–10°C/41–50°F being the ideal temperature range. They become unpleasantly sweet if it drops below 4°C/39°F for any length of time. In freezing weather, cover the sacks with blankets, an old duvet or a thick layer of newspapers to provide extra insulation. Go through the potatoes every month, removing any that have gone rotten, because these will infect the rest. Look out for shoots and rub them out, because they act like wicks, drawing moisture out of the tubers and causing them to shrivel.

Root crops

Packing carrots, swedes, turnips, beetroot, celeriac and winter radishes in boxes of dry sand, coir or fine bark chippings is a tried-and-tested way of preventing them from drying out and shrivelling, and it's especially appropriate if your land is prone to waterlogging. Wooden tea chests make ideal containers (see page 305), but any substantial wooden box will do.

Select dry, unmarked roots, and brush, rather than wash, off excess soil. Twist off the green tops, to prevent 'bleeding' and to eliminate the 'wick' effect (see above). Place a layer of roots onto a shallow bed of sand, so that they are close together but not touching. Pour over additional sand until they're completely covered, then add another layer of roots, and so on until the box is full. This is best done with the box in its final position, because a tea chest filled with sand is extremely heavy. The optimum temperature range for storage is 0–4°C/32–39°F, but a few degrees higher won't make a great deal of difference.

Storing carrots in moist sand

Onions and garlic

Onions and garlic keep best under conditions of low humidity and within a temperature range of 2–4°C/36–39°F. They can be laid on slatted shelves or wire trays, but if hung as ropes from the roof of a shed, or outhouse, they take up far less space. Choose onions with dry, wispy leaves, because those with thick, green necks and stems (a condition that is worse in cool, wet summers) won't keep and should be eaten, or processed, first. Tie together both ends of a 1m/3ft 3in length of polypropylene twine to make a loop, and hang from a hook at a convenient height in the shed roof.

Pick up the bottom of the loop and raise it a finger's length, so that it's parallel to the two hanging strands. Thread the onion leaves through the two 'holes' so formed, then pull tight, clamping the bulb at the neck. Thread the leaves of the next onion through the loop with one hand, and rotate the bulb clockwise in a complete circle around both strands of twine with the other hand, gripping them together, so that the onion sits on the shoulder of the first bulb. Repeat with the next onion, this time rotating it anticlockwise. Continue, turning in alternate directions, until the rope is full, by which time

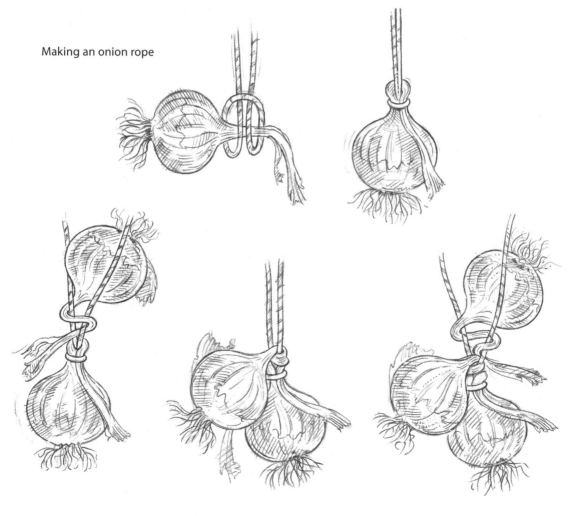

Making an onion rope

all the onions will be firmly clasped by the twisted twine. It's easy once you get the knack, and they look so attractive hanging in your shed, that it's a skill worth acquiring. If it really is too much bother, pack the bulbs into an open-meshed onion net and suspend from a hook.

Soft-necked garlic is usually plaited, without using string, though if you find it troublesome you can use the same technique as for onions, or alternatively, net them. As its name suggests, hard-necked garlic is stiff and can't be plaited. You can tie individual bulbs together with string, though it's hardly worth the effort, because the bulbs rarely store well beyond Christmas.

Winter brassicas

Winter cabbages will keep for several months, if hung up in nets in a cold shed or garage, and kept at a similar temperature to root crops. Brussels sprouts, too, will last perfectly well for up to a month, if they remain attached to the stem. Sever at ground level and store upright in the cool, in a dish of water.

Apples

How long an apple will keep in store depends to a large extent on the variety in question. Early-maturing apples don't keep at all; mid-season apples rarely last more than a month or two; and only late varieties make it into the New Year. Some, however, like Tydeman's Late Orange or D'Arcy Spice, will survive until April, or even May. The optimum temperature range for storing apples is 2–4°C/36–39°F, but this is only possible with refrigeration. Thankfully, fruits stored at 4–7°C/39–44°F will keep perfectly well. You can store them in the same building as your vegetables, but they appreciate moister air.

Check that apples have their stalks attached, and are blemish-free. Before storing, set them aside in a cool place for several days to sweat. Always label the apples carefully, and segregate early-ripening sorts from those that ripen later, because the ethylene gas they produce can prematurely ripen later varieties. Place them so that they're not touching (it's no longer considered necessary to wrap each fruit separately) in single layers in trays – the stackable wooden sort with triangular fillets at each corner that you can sometimes pick up free of charge from greengrocer shops are ideal. Pre-formed fibre trays, made from recycled card, designed to hold individual fruits, are usually available from the same source. It's also possible to buy purpose-built wooden apple stores, with up to ten sliding tray shelves, or if you're handy at DIY, you could knock one up from scrap timber. Check fruits from time to time and remove any that are rotten.

Storage indoors

Other vegetables, like peas and beans, marrows, pumpkins, squashes and tomatoes, along with pears, are best stored somewhere warmer and drier – a spare, unheated bedroom, larder or conservatory is ideal, providing that, if appropriate, you can get your partner's approval!

Peas and beans

Tasty drying varieties include White Emergo and Czar butter beans, the haricots Canadian Wonder and Barlotta Lingua di Fuoca, and the marrow-fat pea Maro, which makes great mushy peas. The Heritage Seed Library, run by Garden Organic, has a considerable collection of historic varieties, of which the Pea bean, Hutterite soup bean, Soldier bean and Carlin pea are well worth a try.

Leave on the vine for as long as possible, ideally until the pods have turned yellow and brittle. Harvest plants in their entirety to finish drying indoors, hanging from the roof of a shed or glasshouse. Shell the crop and spread the peas or beans out on a tray for a few days, then store in airtight glass jars. Dried peas and beans, rehydrated and used in soups, stews and casseroles, were an essential element of the British diet in earlier times, and are likely to become so again, as rising population and climate change inevitably usher in a more vegetarian diet.

Cucurbits and tomatoes

Marrows, pumpkins and squashes should keep for many months if stored at temperatures of 10–15°C/50–59°F. Ensure that fruits have a short length of stem attached, to prevent rots from penetrating the flesh. Cucurbits can be hung up individually in nets, or stored on the floor or shelves; but must be inspected regularly, and moved periodically, to prevent bruising at the contact point.

Store green tomatoes for several weeks, to ripen on trays, or in boxes. You can accelerate the process if you transfer some to a paper bag, and add a ripe banana.

Pears

Pears aren't an easy crop to store. They prefer warmer conditions than apples (ideal temperature 3–7°C/38–44°F) but they're notorious for being hard and unripe one day, and rotten the next. There's no need to wrap them, but leave gaps between individual fruits and inspect daily. Few will keep past Christmas, and because they cross-taint apples, it's best to keep them well apart.

CHAPTER 11

Freezing

Freezing is the most popular method of preserving fruits and vegetables, most of which will keep safely from one harvest until the next. Keen gardeners soon discover that a single freezer is not enough, though it's easy to get carried away and fill the freezer with far more food than you can eat!

What and how to freeze

Most vegetables freeze well, apart from those that have a high water content, like lettuces, cucumbers and other salad crops, which turn to mush when thawed. Others, like onions, can impart taint to foods, and should be double-packed. If freezer space is limited, freeze only those vegetables that cannot readily be preserved by other methods. Some vegetable varieties freeze better than others, which is perhaps something to consider when deciding what to grow. Almost all fruits can be frozen with little trouble, and this is the most popular method of preserving them.

Blanching

Almost all vegetables need blanching before freezing. This makes them taste better and last longer. Exceptions are spinach, kale and other leafy greens, because they coalesce, making it difficult for the steam to penetrate thoroughly.

Prepare vegetables prior to blanching in a form ready for eating. For example, cut runner beans into short strips, but leave French beans whole.

Blanching involves plunging food into scalding water for a few minutes, then cooling it rapidly in cold water prior to freezing, in order to improve the colour, flavour and texture of the food. It is used with many vegetables, but not with fruits. Blanching works by slowing down the internal enzymes that cause deterioration, softening the vegetables and making them easier to pack. It also checks vitamin loss. You can freeze vegetables without blanching, but they'll be less pleasant to eat, and won't last as long. If they remain in the freezer for no more than three months, however, this is unlikely to be noticeable.

To blanch, you'll need a large lidded saucepan that comfortably holds 4.5–9 litres/1–2 gallons of water, and a wire blanching basket, which you can buy for a reasonable cost if you plan to do a lot of freezing. If you have a chip basket, this will do instead, for all but the smallest vegetables. Fill the pan with water and bring to the boil – use approximately 4.5 litres/1 gallon water to every 0.5kg/1lb prepared vegetables. Place the vegetables in the basket, fully immerse in the boiling water and replace the lid. Begin timing as soon as the water has returned to the boil, using the times in the table on pages 256–8. When the correct time has elapsed, lift out the basket and dip it, and the vegetables, into a bowl of cold (ideally iced) water, leaving it there until the contents have cooled down. Lift out, drain and dry on kitchen towel or a clean tea towel. Change the water in the bowl frequently, to ensure that it stays cold if you're freezing a lot of vegetables. Over-blanching results in poorer texture, flavour and nutritional quality, whereas under-blanching increases enzyme activity, and is worse than not blanching at all.

Steam blanching is an alternative to blanching in hot water, and preserves more vitamins and minerals – but it takes longer. Time the blanching from the moment steam reappears from the steamer, after it has been placed over boiling water. Vegetables take half as long again to steam blanch, compared with blanching in water. Runner beans, for example, take three minutes, rather than two.

Open freezing

After blanching, some vegetables benefit from 'open freezing', which prevents food from solidifying into shapeless lumps. Spread whatever is to be frozen onto a tray, covered with greaseproof paper, leaving gaps between individual fruits or vegetables. Place carefully in the freezer. After a few hours, and before they've frozen fully, remove and pack into a bag or box. This will prevent the 'freezer burn' that occurs when food is exposed to freezing cold air.

Open freezing is especially suitable for free-flowing produce, like peas and beans, as well as currants and most berries (though these will not have been blanched). Freeze only tender, fresh young vegetables and fruits in tip-top condition. Tough, old runner beans belong on the compost heap! Aim to freeze foods immediately after picking, to maximize their freshness and nutritional content. If a delay is unavoidable, store in a fridge and freeze within 12 hours.

Many freezers have a fast-freeze button, and a dedicated shelf for food while it's being frozen. It usually takes about eight hours to freeze completely. Don't place unfrozen food next to food that's already frozen, because this can result in temporary partial thawing.

Containers

Airtight plastic boxes, and heavy-duty polythene bags secured with zips or wire twist-ties, make good containers for frozen fruit and vegetables. We prefer using rectangular-shaped boxes, which make optimum use of space in the freezer (unlike circular ones), and can be stacked after use, one inside another. They can be reused, season after season, for many years. When filling boxes, always leave sufficient headroom to allow for expansion when the food freezes – 1cm/½in is usually sufficient. Squeeze the air from polythene bags before sealing. Remember to label containers with a description of what each one contains and the date of freezing.

How to prepare vegetables for freezing

Vegetable	Method
Asparagus	Wash and sort spears according to thickness, and cut off any woody stems. Blanch thin stems for 2 minutes, and thick stems for 4 minutes. Alternatively, freeze the stems after cooking them.
Aubergines	Peel, dice or cut into 1cm/½in strips, then blanch for 4 minutes.
Broad beans	Shell. Blanch for 3 minutes. Open freeze.
French beans	Wash, top and tail. Blanch large beans for 3 minutes; small beans for 2 minutes. Cut large beans in half for ease of packing. Open freeze.

Vegetable	Method
Runner beans	Wash, top and tail, and string if necessary. Slice into slender 4cm/1½in long pieces. Blanch for 2 mins. Open freeze.
Beetroot	Select small beets, no bigger than 7.5cm/3in in diameter. Wash, then boil for 40–50 minutes until tender. Cool under running cold water. Rub off skins and slice or dice, then put straight into containers: no blanching is required. Tiny beets, less than 2.5cm/1in in diameter, can be frozen whole after blanching for 10 minutes.
Leaf beet and chards	Wash and cut stems into 1cm/½in pieces, blanch for 4 minutes, then open freeze. The leaves, on the other hand, should be blanched for only 2 minutes and frozen in portion sizes, like spinach.
Broccoli and calabrese	Trim off woody stems and outer leaves. Divide calabrese into sprigs. Blanch for 3 minutes. Open freeze.
Brussels sprouts	Remove outer leaves. Blanch for 3–4 minutes, depending on sprout size.
Cabbages	Remove outer leaves, wash and shred. Blanch for 1½ minutes.
Carrots	Scrub roots, peeling only if there's skin damage. Blanch small, whole carrots for 5 minutes; sliced or diced carrots for 2 minutes.
Cauliflowers	Wash, then break into sprigs, approx. 2.5cm/1in across. When blanching, add 1 teaspoon lemon juice to the water, to preserve the colour. Blanch for 3 minutes. Open freeze.
Celeriac	Wash, peel and cut into chunks. Don't blanch. Cook until tender, for use in soups or stews.
Celery	Scrub, remove leaves and strings, and cut into 2.5cm/1in pieces. Blanch for 3 minutes. Use in soups or stews.
Courgettes and marrows	Wash but don't peel. Cut into 1cm/½in slices. Blanch for 1 minute.
Florence fennel	Scrub and trim off the roots. Slice into 5cm/2in pieces. Blanch for 3 minutes.
Globe artichokes	Remove all the coarse outer leaves, stalks and the 'choke'. Blanch for 7–10 minutes. Alternatively, just freeze the hearts, after blanching for 5 minutes.
Hamburg parsley	Scrub well, but do not peel. Dice or slice. Blanch for 2 minutes.
Jerusalem artichokes	Scrub, slice, don't blanch, but cook until soft for use in soups.
Kales	Strip leaves from stems, wash, and blanch for 1 minute. Chop and put in bags in serving-sized quantities.

Vegetable	Method
Kohl rabi	Trim and peel. Freeze small roots whole or sliced or diced. Blanch for 3 minutes (whole) or 1½ minutes (sliced).
Leeks	Remove outer leaves, the root end and most of the green leaves. Clean, and cut into 2.5cm/1in chunks. Blanch for 2 minutes.
Onions	Peel and slice. Blanch chopped onions for 1½ minutes, or onion rings for just 15 seconds. Shallots and small onions may be blanched whole, for 4 minutes. Double-wrap to avoid taint.
Oriental vegetables	Remove outer leaves, wash and slice. Blanch for 2 minutes.
Parsnips	Trim, peel and dice. Blanch for 2 minutes.
Peas	Blanch shelled peas for 1½ minutes. Wash and trim mangetout and sugarsnap peas, then blanch for 3 minutes. Open freeze.
Peppers and chillies	Wash, remove the stems and caps, and scoop out the seeds and pith. Cut into halves and blanch for 3 minutes, or into strips and blanch for 2 minutes.
Potatoes	New potatoes (small) – clean or scrape and blanch whole for 4 minutes; chips – part-fry for 3 minutes, cool and freeze; roast potatoes and mash – cook thoroughly, then freeze.
Pumpkins and squashes	Cut flesh into cubes and then bake, steam or boil until tender. Pack and freeze.
Spinach	Wash, trim the stalks, and blanch for 2 minutes. Squeeze out excess water. Freeze in portion sizes as spinach hardens into a solid lump.
Swedes	Wash, peel and slice into chunks. Blanch for 3 minutes.
Sweet potatoes	Don't blanch. Cook in skins until tender, then cool and peel. Cut in half, slice or mash.
Sweet corn	Remove leaves and silks, and grade cobs according to size. Blanch small cobs for 4 minutes, medium cobs for 6 minutes and large cobs for 8 minutes. Wrap individually in kitchen foil or cling film, and pack in bags. Alternatively, use a knife to scrape off the kernels and open freeze.
Tomatoes	Freeze whole without blanching. Run under a hot water tap for a few moments when defrosting to remove the skins, which peel off easily. Only suitable for processing (being used in a cooked dish, or made into sauce). Alternatively, skin, cut into quarters and simmer in their own juice for 10 minutes. Cool and freeze.
Turnips	Trim, peel and dice small turnips. Blanch for 2½ minutes. Alternatively, cook and mash, then freeze.

Freezing fruit

Unlike vegetables, it's not necessary to blanch fruits in order to preserve them. Most recipes involve refined white sugar, implying that it acts as a preservative. Sugar is added as a sweetener, especially for tart fruits, and it helps to keep shape and texture (by drawing out the juices and making fruits firmer). It also retards oxidation, which causes discolouration – the brownness that occurs shortly after slicing an apple, for example. However, there are other ways of preventing discolouration – by using lemon juice or ascorbic acid (vitamin C) – so if, like us, you don't want to use white sugar, for dietary or nutritional reasons, that's fine!

If preserving for dessert use, choose only the best-quality fruit, free of blemishes, and not overripe. That doesn't mean that you have to waste windfalls, or other bruised or partially damaged fruit, however. Use them for processing, as jams, juices or purées. Wash fruit thoroughly, prior to freezing, and remove any damaged areas and non-edible parts – stalks, strings, gooseberry 'tops and tails' and suchlike. Take out the stones from cherries, plums and other stone fruit, which, if left in place, would otherwise taint the fruit.

Use the open-freezing method described above for berries (with the exception of strawberries), currants and cherries – none of which darkens when exposed to air. Alternatively, mix with organic, unrefined caster sugar in a bowl, using 125g/4oz sugar for every 500g/1lb fruit, then pack in containers and freeze.

Non-juicy fruits, and those that discolour when exposed to the air, are usually immersed in a syrup mix, as a way of maintaining their texture. This applies to apples, peaches, nectarines, apricots, plums, gages, damsons and melons. Pour 450g/1lb organic, unrefined caster sugar into a saucepan containing 1 litre/1¾ pints cold water, and slowly bring to the boil, stirring continuously, until all the sugar has dissolved. Allow to cool. Place the fruit in a plastic container, and cover with the syrup, allowing 1cm/½in headspace for expansion. If you don't wish to use sugar, unsweetened organic apple (or other fruit) juice is an acceptable alternative.

To prevent apples, and other fruits that have been halved or sliced, from discolouring, dip them in water containing the juice from two lemons for every 1 litre/1¾ pints. Alternatively, use 1 teaspoon ascorbic acid (vitamin C) or citric acid powders, per 1 litre/1¾ pints water.

It's almost impossible to prevent pears from discolouring – they turn black – and they also lose their delicate flavour when frozen, so we would caution against freezing. Bottle them instead (see page 269). If you must freeze them, use the syrup mix method. The same applies to strawberries, which readily turn to mush. This is fine if they're to be used as jam, but their appeal as a dessert is greatly diminished. Only the Totem variety retains its shape when thawed.

That leaves rhubarb, which can be treated as a fruit or a vegetable. Cut into 2.5cm-/1in-long chunks and open freeze, or pack in dry sugar. Alternatively, blanch for 3 minutes, and open freeze.

Another way of freezing fruit is to make purée. Prepare as appropriate, and place in a large pan with a tiny amount of water – just enough to prevent the fruit from sticking to the bottom. Heat gently, stirring from time to time, because the fruit breaks down into a pulp. Add organic, unrefined caster sugar, if desired – 125g/4oz sugar for every 500g/1lb fruit. When cool, press through a sieve or use a blender or food processor. Freeze in plastic containers, leaving room for expansion.

Freezing herbs

Herbs are easy to freeze, and retain their colour and taste, but unfortunately they do not keep their texture. Pick entire sprigs, wash and drain well, then pop into a plastic bag, and freeze. Alternatively, chop and place in an ice-cube tray, filling the individual cubes to the brim, then add water to the same level and freeze. Remove the frozen cubes from the tray, and pack in bags. To avoid tainting other foods in the freezer, double-pack the bagged herbs in plastic boxes. Remember to label them – all frozen herbs can look pretty much the same.

The usual advice is to dry 'woody' herbs, and freeze 'soft-leaved' sorts, like basil, chives, coriander, dill, fennel, mint and parsley, but in our experience, sage, tarragon and thyme freeze just as well. There's no need to thaw herbs when required for use. Crumble them while still in the bag, and add to soups, stews and other cooked dishes. They are no good for garnishing, because they become limp and soggy when thawed (with the curious exception of sage, which turns soft and fluffy). A frozen ice cube is equivalent to about a tablespoon of chopped herbs. Use in cooked food, or in drinks – floating ice cubes containing variegated mints, or herb flowers, make striking accompaniments to cocktails and cordials.

Storage times and thawing

As a general rule, fruits and vegetables can be stored in a frozen state for up to twelve months. After this time the texture and flavour slowly deteriorate. Puréed fruit is best eaten within eight months. When thawing fruit that is to be used as a dessert, place in a fridge and leave overnight, then serve chilled. This is not necessary if making jam. Cook vegetables from frozen, usually for 5–10 minutes, although it's best to thaw spinach and broccoli partially first. Don't forget that vegetables have already been partially cooked in the blanching process.

CHAPTER 12

Drying

Drying isn't as popular as it was in the past, thanks to freezers. But there are one or two circumstances where drying comes into its own – such as preserving herbs, making raisins and sultanas, storing sweet corn and chillies, or making fruit 'leathers'.

The principle is simple – by extracting moisture, the potency of yeasts, bacteria and other spoilage agents is diminished. The sugar and acidity of fruit also becomes more concentrated, further enhancing this protective effect. Aromatic oils, contained within herbs, fulfil a similar function.

In hotter climes than ours, food can be dried in the sun, but Britain is too damp and unpredictable for that, so drying inevitably takes place indoors, using supplementary heat.

Equipment

A domestic oven can be used for drying, the only snag being that it can take anything from a few hours to several days, which may lead to conflict in the kitchen! Harmony can be restored if you invest in a humidifier – an electrically operated device that blows warm air over stacked trays. Unfortunately, an Excalibur, currently the best on the market, will set you back a couple of hundred pounds, but it will dry meat – biltong or jerky – fish, mushrooms and other foods.

A cheaper alternative is to make your own drying box. It doesn't have to be anything fancy – a wooden container, the size and shape of a kitchen unit, with a few holes in the sides, at the top and bottom, works perfectly well. A couple of 60 watt incandescent light bulbs (not low-energy) fitted at the base, supply the heat.

You'll also need a supply of clean, air-tight, jars, to ensure that the contents stay absolutely dry.

Drying herbs

Pick herbs when they're dry and about to flower. Tie, or clip, individual sprigs to a line strung across a warm, dry room, or hang in an airing cupboard. (If tied in bunches, there's a risk that the inner leaves will go mouldy.) As an alternative to stringing, lay the herbs on wire racks, or newspaper, leaving sufficient space between each sprig for air to circulate freely. Leave until crisply dry – which can take anything from a few days to a week – then lightly crush, and store in jars somewhere dark, to prevent sunlight from bleaching away the colour

Sage, mint and other large- or soft-leaved herbs are best dried with an extra source of heat, to overcome problems with mould. Strip the leaves from the sprigs and blanch in boiling water for 1 minute. Transfer to chilled water, then drain and dry on kitchen paper. Spread the leaves on wire racks, and dry for an hour in a 45–55°C/113–130°F oven with the door open. Alternatively, dry them in an oven (with the door closed), as it's cooling down – though this method takes several hours. Dry parsley in an oven at 120°C/250°F for 1 hour, then turn off the heat and cool slowly until cold. Crush the leaves and store.

Drying fruit

Drying is essential if you want to eat your own raisins, prunes or sultanas, but although other fruits can be dried, they're invariably better if frozen or bottled. We'd recommend that you only consider drying apricots, peaches, plums and figs. To dry these, halve and stone apricots and peaches, but leave plums and figs intact. Place them on trays, lined with baking paper, and dry in an oven, with the door open, at its lowest setting. Maintain the temperature at, or around, 50°C/120°F for the first few hours; any higher and the skins will harden and seal. When they begin to shrivel, increase the temperature to 65°C/150°F and maintain for 2–3 days. They're ready when still soft, but no juices flow. Allow to cool for half a day, then store.

Making raisins from red grapes, or sultanas from white grapes, is fiddly, because they have to be split to remove the pips. This isn't a problem if you grow seedless grapes, but unfortunately the choice of outdoor varieties is limited, and the flavour, in most cases, is indifferent. Himrod or Lakemont make the best-flavoured sultanas. Try Beauty or Saturn, if you want raisins. Dry as above for stone fruit, but maintain the higher temperature for about eight hours.

Apples, too, can be dried in an oven. Peel, core and cut into 6mm/¼in thick rings. Dip immediately into water containing lemon juice to prevent browning, and thread onto bamboo canes, adapted to fit into the oven. Leave the door open and dry at 55°C/130°F for around six hours.

Fruit leathers

Strips of fruit leather, whose texture is like shop-bought fruit gums, but with a far superior taste, take some beating as a healthy snack. To make them, simmer your chosen fruit in a preserving pan, with an equal amount of chopped, unpeeled cooking apples. When soft, strain the pulp through a sieve. Return to the heat and continue simmering until the fruit has thickened. Pour a thin layer of fruit onto a tray lined with parchment baking paper and dry for up to 18 hours in an open oven at 60°C/140°F. The leather should peel away easily from the paper, and can be cut into strips or rolled for storage. It should keep for a couple of months in a jar in a larder, double that time in a fridge, and up to a year in a freezer.

Drying vegetables

Sweet corn: Boil cobs in unsalted water for 5–10 minutes, depending on size. Remove and dry, then place whole on wire trays in a cool oven to dry overnight. Strip off the kernels, and bottle.

Chillies: Split chillies in half, and scrape out the seeds and pith. Oven dry for 24 hours at 65°C/150°F, then tie, or thread, onto string and hang somewhere warm (an airing cupboard is ideal) for another week, to ensure they're completely dry. Pack in jars.

Tomatoes: Cherry tomatoes are the best for drying. Halve fruits and place, cut face uppermost, on fine-meshed wire trays. Sprinkle on a little salt, and dry in an oven, with the door ajar, for 10–15 hours at 65°C/150°F, until they're dry to the touch, but still yielding. Put them in a dish, and marinate in cider vinegar for half an hour. Drain, pack into sterilized jars, cover with olive oil and seal. These are better than shop-bought sun-dried tomatoes, in our opinion, though not as good as sun-blushed (but far fewer 'food miles' are involved).

Bottling

Bottling is making a comeback! As enthusiastic bottlers ourselves, this is good to know. Bottled fruit, served straight from the jar, makes a tasty, healthy dessert during the winter days, and bottled tomatoes, which can be popped straight into a pasta sauce or stew, are a useful addition to anybody's larder.

Bottling works by heating fruit and vegetables in covered jars to a sufficiently high temperature to destroy any bacteria, moulds or other spoilage agents. As the bottles cool, a vacuum is created, which prevents the contents from coming into contact with any further contamination. In the case of fruits, this can be achieved by sterilizing them at around 80°C/175°F using a water bath or pressure cooker (their inherent acidity also acts as a preservative). Vegetables are not naturally acidic, and only a few types are suitable for bottling, in part because of the need to heat them to temperatures greater than boiling point – typically 113°C/235°F – so you have to use a pressure cooker. Bottled fruits and vegetables will keep for years, as long as the seal holds, but aim to use them up within twelve months if you can, because the quality does deteriorate over time.

Equipment

Jars used for bottling have wide necks, and glass or metal lids that are fastened by screw-threaded metal rings or spring clips. Kilner jars are the best known, and have been made continuously in Britain since the 1840s, apart from a brief interruption during the last decade. Unfortunately, the supply of replacement rubber rings (used with glass tops) and metal discs dried up during this period, although alternatives have since become available online (see page 306). Happily, the company resumed production in 2009, in response to consumer pressure, and introduced new 500ml and 1 litre jars (equivalent to 1lb and 2¼lb respectively). Our only gripe is that the necks are narrower than before, making the jars less easy to fill; and the lids can't be used on old-style jars.

Good cookware shops often sell bottling jars that are similar to Kilner jars, made by the German manufacturer, Leifheit. These come in sizes from 500g/1lb to 3kg/6½lb, all with identical metal lids. For a more decorative jar, try the French brand, Le Parfait, which has a wide rubber ring, and a glass lid held on by a spring-clip. However, in our experience the lids can be difficult to close (especially when the jars are full of scalding fruit!), and even harder to open. It's worth checking out car boot sales, where you can often pick up jars for next to nothing.

For your water bath you'll need a large pan, preferably one with a lid, which is sufficiently deep for you to be able to immerse the jars fully in water. We use a 9 litre/2 gallon stainless-steel pan with vertical sides and a lid. This accommodates six 1 litre/1¾ pint jars and is more suitable than a bucket-style preserving pan. You can also buy thermostatically controlled electric sterilizers, which are specially designed for bottling. Don't forget that if you intend to bottle vegetables, you must have a pressure cooker. Last of all, you'll need a jam thermometer.

Before bottling, check that you have sufficient rubber rings and lids. Examine the jars' rims for chips (the slightest damage will prevent the lid from sealing successfully) and the rubber rings (including the rubber weld around the edge of metal lids) to see if they are in good condition, and not perished. Wash carefully, and sterilize everything in scalding water or in a dishwasher set at the hottest cycle.

Bottling fruit

Although we've mentioned bottling fruit in a water bath (using either hot or cold water) or in a pressure cooker, you can also do it in an oven. Our experiences with oven bottling, however, have been less than satisfactory, so we've not included details here. We prefer the cold-water bath method, which, in our experience, gives the most consistent results.

Whichever method you adopt, pick only the best-quality fruit, free from disease or other damage, remove all inedible parts and wash thoroughly. Halve or slice large fruits, like apples, pears or peaches, and dip them in a dilute solution of lemon juice to prevent discolouration (see page 259). Carefully pack the fruit into jars, gently poking it with a wooden-spoon handle to manoeuvre individual slices into gaps, until each jar is full to the brim. Cherries, plums and gages hold their shape better with their stones in, but remove them if you wish. Currants and berries, including strawberries, which bottle well, go in just as they are. For the purposes of bottling, consider tomatoes and rhubarb to be fruits.

Cold-water bath method

Once you've filled each jar with fruit, add cold water. If you prefer, use sugar syrup, which improves colour and sweetness, and maintains the fruit in good shape. To make syrup, dissolve 450g/1lb sugar in 1.1 litres/2 pints water.

For both liquids, tap the jars sharply to release any trapped air pockets, and ensure that the liquid comes to the brim. Replace the lids (complete with rubber ring, as appropriate), but screw down only loosely so that steam can escape. For jars with spring-clips, leave their lids held open at a slight angle. Ensure that jars are not in direct contact with the floor, and sides, of the preserving pan, or with each other, because they may crack. Stand them on a wire tray, wooden trivet or folded tea towel, and leave a gap of at least 5mm/¼in all round.

Place the pan on the hob, and fill it with cold water until it's almost level with the rims of the jars, but not so high that when it bubbles, water can enter the jars. With the lid in place, heat the pan slowly, so that the water temperature reaches at least 55°C/130°F after an hour. Raise it further during the next thirty minutes, to the temperature shown in the table below, and maintain it for the length of time specified. Then use a jug or saucepan to bale out enough water to enable you to grasp the jars easily with oven gloves. Place them on a wooden, or other, surface that is not cold to the touch. Screw the lids down firmly, or lever the spring-clip into place immediately, and leave to cool. You may find that, after an hour or so, you need to give the metal rings an extra turn. All this sounds very technical and complicated, but it's not, once you get into the swing of it, step by easy step.

Hot-water bath method

This is essentially the same as the cold-water bath method, except that you pour hot water, or hot syrup (minimum temperature 60°C/140°F), over the fruit. Fill the preserving pan with water that has been warmed to at least 38°C/100°F. Heat to 88°C/190°F over thirty minutes, and maintain at this temperature for the time shown in the table below.

Bottling fruit using the water bath method: times and temperatures

Fruit	Temperature (°C/°F)	Cold-water bath (minutes)	Hot-water bath (minutes)
Apples	74/165	10	2
Blackberries	74/165	10	2
Blackcurrants	74/165	10	2
Blueberries	74/165	10	2
Cherries	82/180	15	10
Figs	88/190	30	40
Gooseberries	82/180	15	10
Mulberries	82/180	10	2
Peaches, nectarines and apricots	82/180	15	20
Pears	88/190	30	40
Plums and gages	82/180	15	10
Raspberries	74/165	10	2
Red and white currants	74/165	10	2
Rhubarb	82/180	15	10
Strawberries	82/180	15	2
Tomatoes*	88/190	40	50

The above times are for 500ml/1lb and 1 litre/2¼lb jars. Larger jars will need extra time. Pears and figs contain less acid (which acts as a preservative) than other fruit, which is why they must be sterilized for longer.

* Use brine solution as an alternative to water in the jars, at the rate of 15g/½oz salt, dissolved in 1.2 litres/2¼ pints water. Add 10 minutes for 2 litre/4½lb jars.

Pressure-cooker method

Place the jars in the pressure cooker, on a trivet or cloth, and fill almost to the brim with hot water or syrup. Partially close the lids, as above. Add 2.5–5cm/1–2in water to the pressure cooker, close the lid and heat on the hob with the pressure valve open, until steam starts to escape. Close the valve and, within a 5- to 10-minute period, heat until the pressure reaches 5psi/0.34bar. Begin timing at this point – most fruits need just one minute, but increase this to five minutes for tomatoes and halved apples, pears, plums, figs, peaches, apricots and nectarines. Remove from the heat and allow the pressure to subside for ten minutes, before opening the valve. Lift out the bottles and tighten the lids.

Bottling vegetables

Use a pressure cooker for bottling vegetables. Prepare and blanch the vegetables as for freezing (see page 256), then pack into jars. Cover with hot water or hot brine (see note for tomatoes, page 269) and secure the lids loosely. Add water to the pressure cooker, and heat on the hob, with the pressure valve open, until steam starts to escape. Wait for a further 10 minutes, then close the valve, allowing pressure to build to medium (10psi/0.69bar). Time as follows:

40 minutes – asparagus, beetroot, celery
45 minutes – carrots
50 minutes – cauliflowers, peas, new potatoes, sweet corn
55 minutes – broad beans

Remove from the heat and allow the vessel to cool until the pressure returns to normal. Take out the jars and tighten the lids.

Testing and storing bottled fruit and vegetable jars

When the jars are completely cool (we suggest that you leave them overnight), test the bottles to ensure that a vacuum has been achieved. To do this, unscrew the metal rings (or release the spring clips) and lift each jar by its lid.

This can be a little unnerving! There's no need to raise them more than an inch/a few centimetres – you'll quickly discover which, if any, have failed! Refrigerate these, and eat within a week. Replace the rings/clips on the remaining jars and store somewhere cool and dark.

Opening jars and food safety

Insert the tip of a knife between the lid and the glass rim, and prise up gently, breaking the seal. Beware of twisting the knife and chipping the glass. Spring-clip jars usually have a rubber tab to pull, to release the vacuum. Even so, they can be difficult to open without the aid of a stout butter or oyster knife. Dunking jars in hot water for ten minutes sometimes helps.

As they age, the contents of jars tend to darken in store, but if this occurs early on it may be because they were not ripe enough, or the bottling temperature was too great. If the fruits rise or fall, they were probably bottled too quickly, although the keeping quality is not impaired. However, throw out anything that smells peculiar, looks mouldy or appears to be 'off' in any way. This applies especially to bottled vegetables, which can cause botulism – a potentially deadly form of food poisoning.

CHAPTER 14

Jams and jellies

There's something deeply satisfying about making jam – the wonderful aroma of the fresh fruit, as it bubbles feverishly in the pan, the mounting excitement as the sugar dissolves, the 'rolling boil' approaching, and the 'setting point' in sight – that fills you with heady anticipation.

It's not always as straightforward as that, however! For all its apparent simplicity, things can go wrong: for example, if you don't use enough sugar, or have over-ripe fruit, or insufficient acid. Happily, most of these problems can be avoided if you follow the simple rules below.

Equipment

You'll need a large, deep pan, with a wide base. If you intend doing a lot of preserving, invest in a good preserving, or maslin, pan. These hold around 8 litres/14 pints and are broader at the top, giving a greater surface area for evaporation. Most have a lip, a 'bucket-style' handle, for easier pouring, and a calibrated scale etched inside. Copper pans are exquisite to look at, and have excellent heat-conducting properties, but they can react with vinegar, and impart a metallic taint to pickles and chutneys. In addition, they will not work on electric induction hobs – a shortcoming they share with aluminium. Our advice, therefore, is to buy stainless steel.

You'll also need two spoons: a long-handled wooden one (preferably spatula-shaped, with a squared end for stirring) and a slatted sort for skimming scum. A jam thermometer will reassure you when the setting temperature has been reached, but it's not strictly essential. If you intend making jellies, a jelly bag and stand are useful, but a piece of muslin works just as well. (Traditionally, a square piece of muslin was used, each corner attached to the leg of an upturned stool.) Lastly, a funnel comes in handy when pouring jam into jars.

Save empty jars of shop-bought jam for re-use, or buy new jars from specialist suppliers. In the past, jars were sealed with discs of waxed paper, laid onto the surface of the jam, and covered with cellophane held in place by an elastic band, or string tied round the rim. You can still get hold of jam pot covers, in sizes to fit 225g/8oz and 450g/1lb jars, but modern jars are threaded, and have plastic, or metal, twist-lock lids with an impermeable seal around the inside. Kilner, and other wide-necked preserving jars can also be used for jams and jellies, if you have a large family, or eat a lot of jam!

Ingredients

All you need is fruit and sugar – and occasionally water, which helps some fruits to break down without burning. If the fruit contains insufficient acid to preserve it, or pectin (see page 274) to set it, mix it with another fruit that does. Certain vegetables can be turned into jam – marrows, pumpkins and carrots, for example – but they contain no acid or pectin, and so must be combined with other fruits, or have these ingredients added independently.

Sugar

You can use all sorts of sugar to make jam, but ordinary granulated is fine. We prefer Billington's unrefined, organic, granulated sugar, which still contains its vitamins and minerals. Preserving sugar has larger crystals, making it easy to stir, and is usually used with fruits that are high in pectin, whereas jam sugar, which is reinforced with pectin and citric acid, is used with fruits that don't have enough of their own.

As a general rule, medium- and low-pectin fruits should be combined with an equal weight of sugar, whereas those containing high amounts of pectin require one and a half times their own weight of sugar. In a typical jam, sugar makes up 65 per cent of the contents, of which 5 per cent is sugar present in the fruit.

Pectin

Pectin, the setting agent, is a gum that occurs naturally in the cell walls of fruits. The amount of pectin varies according to the type of fruit, and its condition. Cooking apples, such as Bramley's, blueberries, citrus fruits, acid cherries, all types of currants, damsons, gooseberries, and quinces are naturally high in pectin, whereas blackberries, sweet cherries, figs, medlars, peaches, pears, rhubarb and strawberries are low. Other fruits are somewhere in between.

Under-ripe fruit contains the most pectin, but levels decline as it ripens. Fruit that has 'gone over' has hardly any at all. Hence the advice in jam recipes not to use fruit that is past its best. If you're using fruit that has been previously frozen, you'll need to increase the pectin content by adding pectin stock (see below).

You can get round the problem of making jam with low-pectin fruit by combining it with one that is pectin-rich. Use blackberry with apple, for example. Alternatively, you could use jam sugar, buy apple pectin (in liquid or powder form), or make your own pectin stock. To do this, cook 1kg/2¼lb or so high-pectin fruit, like gooseberries, redcurrants or Bramley apples, on a gentle heat for an hour until the fruit has softened. Strain through a jelly bag, and pour the liquid into individual yogurt pots, each holding 100–225ml/4–8oz. Cover with cling film and freeze, then transfer to a plastic container when solid. Each pot should contain sufficient pectin stock for 1kg/2¼lb low-pectin fruit.

Acid

Acid, which is naturally present in fruit, plays an important role in setting jam and helping to prevent sugar from crystallizing. Most fruits that contain small amounts of pectin also have a low-acid content. You'll need to add extra acid, in the form of lemon juice or citric acid, to low-acid fruits, such as late-season blackberries, peaches, pears, dessert apples, sweet cherries and strawberries. To every 1kg/2.2lb fruit, add 2 tbsp lemon juice, ¼ tsp citric acid or 125ml/4fl oz homemade pectin stock.

Water

Most soft fruits are sufficiently tender to break down on their own and release their pectin, without additional water. Denser fruits, however, like apples and plums, need around half their weight of water, whilst blackcurrants, quinces, and other fruits with tough skins need their whole weight added in water. Add too little water, and the fruit may not soften sufficiently, trapping some of the pectin and potentially burning the pan; add too much, and the cooking time becomes longer, spoiling the taste.

Making jam

Select the best-quality ripe, or very slightly under-ripe, fruit. Remove all stalks and stones, and wash (if necessary), then gently dry on a tea towel or kitchen paper. Larger fruits, like apples, should be peeled and cut up. If peaches are dipped in boiling water for half a minute, and then transferred to cold water, their skins will slide off easily.

Smear a knob of butter over the base of the pan (this will lessen the amount of scum formed later on) and add the fruit, along with any water if required. Turn on the heat and bring to the boil, then simmer gently until the fruit is completely softened, stirring gently from time to time to prevent it from sticking to the bottom. This should take 10–15 minutes for berries, through to 45 minutes for blackcurrants (see recipes below). Add any extra pectin or acid now.

Pre-warm the sugar in an oven (this will help it dissolve more easily and not cool the fruit) and add it to the fruit, stirring on a gentle heat, until it has dissolved completely.

Turn the heat up to maximum, and bring to a 'rolling boil' as fast as possible – the surface should be a mass of foaming bubbles. Don't stir it while this is happening. After a few minutes, test to see if the setting point has been reached. This can take anything from three to twenty minutes from when the rolling boil commenced. Stir occasionally to prevent sticking.

To test, remove the pan from the heat and pour a teaspoonful of jam onto a cold saucer (preferably one that has been in the fridge icebox, or at least the fridge itself, for half an hour) and leave to stand for a minute. If the surface congeals, and crinkles when you push your finger through it, the jam has reached 'setting point'. If it remains fluid, return the jam to the boil for another few minutes. As an extra check, the jam thermometer should read 104.5°C/220°F or a degree higher. Jam that is under-boiled is runny, and does not keep; over-boiling results in dark, overtly sticky jam that has lost its fresh, fruity taste.

When the setting point has been reached, remove the pan from the heat, and skim off any scum with a slatted spoon. Although it sounds nasty, scum is mostly air bubbles produced by the processing, and can often be eliminated by stirring.

Leave to cool for ten minutes, then stir gently to distribute the fruit evenly throughout the pan. For easier filling, pour while still hot into a large jug and from there, via a funnel, into sterilized jars. Aim to fill them to within 5mm/¼in of the top, to minimize the air space. If using traditional jam jars, float a wax disc on the surface of the jam (with the waxed side facing downwards), and then cover the jar with cellophane (moistened on the upper side so that it tautens when dry), held on with an elastic band or string. Alternatively, use a jar with a special screw, or snap-top, lid. Neither of these options requires a wax disc. When using jars without discs, it's vital that the temperature of the jam is at least 77°C/170°F.

Label the jars, and store them somewhere cool and dark, where they should keep for up to 12 months.

Blackberry and apple jam

> 1.8kg/4lb blackberries
> 900g/2lb cooking apples
> 2.7kg/6lb sugar

Put the blackberries in a pan with 50ml/2fl oz water, bring to the boil and simmer until tender. Add the chopped apples, along with an extra 250ml/8fl oz water and cook slowly, until the fruit is soft. Mix together, add the sugar, and bring to a rolling boil.

Blackcurrant jam

> 1.4kg/3lb blackcurrants
> 2kg/4½lb sugar

Put the blackcurrants, sugar and 1.3 litres/2¼ pints water in a pan, and simmer until soft, and the pulp thickens. Add sugar and bring to a rolling boil.

Blueberry jam

900g/2lb blueberries

900g/2lb sugar

Put the blueberries and 5 tbsp water in a pan and simmer gently until the berries soften. Add the sugar at a low temperature and then boil up rapidly.

Cherry jam

Sweet cherries are low in pectin, so the amount needs to be boosted by adding pectin stock (see page 274) or using jam sugar, which has pectin and acid added. If making morello cherry jam, mix equal quantities of fruit and sugar and halve the amount of pectin stock.

1.8kg/4lb stoned dessert cherries

1.4kg/3lb sugar

1 tbsp lemon juice or 300ml/½ pint pectin stock

Bring the cherries and extra pectin to the boil and simmer until soft. The cherry stones impart extra flavour to the jam, so you could put these in a muslin bag and suspend it in the fruit, if desired. Add the sugar and bring to a rolling boil.

Damson jam

1.8kg/4lb stoned damsons

2.25kg/5lb sugar

Put the damsons and 300ml/½ pint water in a pan and bring to the boil. Simmer until the fruit has softened, stirring frequently, and adding extra water as needed to prevent sticking – but no more than 600ml/1 pint. Pour in the sugar, stirring slowly over a low heat until it has all dissolved, then bring rapidly to a rolling boil.

As an alternative to stoning, leave the fruit intact and skim off the stones with a slotted spoon as they float to the surface, before adding the sugar. Make sure you find them all – you don't want broken teeth! This recipe can also be used for plums, but add 4 tbsp lemon juice to the fruit, if using dessert varieties, as these are low in acid.

Greengage jam

1.8kg/4lb greengages, stoned
1.8kg/4lb sugar

Put the fruit into the pan with 300–450ml/½–¾ pint water. Use the lower amount of water if using ripe fruit, and the higher figure if the gages are firm. Crack ten or so stones, extract the kernels and immerse in boiling water for a couple of minutes, until the skins can be rubbed off easily. Add the kernels to the fruit, and bring slowly to the boil, then simmer until soft. Add the sugar and bring to a rolling boil, then to setting point.

Marrow and ginger jam

1.4kg/3lb marrows, peeled, deseeded and diced into sugar-lump-sized pieces
1.4kg/3lb sugar
40g/1½oz crystallized ginger, finely chopped
2 tbsp lemon juice

Put the marrow, sugar and ginger in a pan, and leave for 24 hours. Stir well (while trying to keep the marrow cubes intact) over a low heat, until the sugar has dissolved. Add the lemon juice and boil to the setting point.

Raspberry jam

This is one of the simplest and quickest of all jams to make, requiring equal amounts of fruit and sugar. The fruit breaks down extremely easily, and the jam soon reaches setting point. It's not a strong set, however, as raspberries don't contain a great deal of pectin, so to improve the set, add another 225g/8oz sugar and 150ml/¼ pint pectin stock.

1.4kg/3lb raspberries
1.4kg/3lb sugar

Put the raspberries into a large pan and crush them with a wooden spoon. Heat gently until they begin to boil, then add the sugar and stir over a low heat until it is all dissolved. Boil rapidly, until the setting point is reached.

Rhubarb jam

Rhubarb does not contain acid or pectin, so either use jam sugar or, if using granulated sugar, add pectin stock.

> 1.4kg/3lb rhubarb, cut into chunks
> 1.4kg/3lb jam sugar (or 1.4kg/3lb granulated sugar with 300ml/½ pint pectin stock)

Put the rhubarb in a large pan and bring to the boil, then simmer until tender. Add the sugar or pectin stock and boil rapidly, until the setting point is reached.

Strawberry jam

> 1.8g/4lb strawberries
> 1.8kg/4lb jam sugar (or 1.8kg/4lb granulated sugar with 300ml/½ pint pectin stock)

Use small, slightly unripe, strawberries, or cut larger ones into smaller pieces, add the sugar or pectin stock and bring to the boil, stirring gently to avoid smashing the fruit. Add the sugar and bring to a rolling boil. Use the same quantities if making strawberry conserve.

Making conserve

Fruit conserve is jam that contains whole, or largish, pieces of fruit. It's ideal for berried fruit, and others with soft skins, but it's not possible to make conserve with hard-skinned fruit, such as blackcurrants, damsons and gooseberries. Making conserve is very similar to making jam, the chief difference being that the sugar is added at the start of the recipe.

1. Put the fruit and sugar in a pan along with any extra pectin or acid, if required. Leave for up to two hours, while the sugar draws out the juice.

2. Heat slowly, stirring continuously, as the sugar dissolves, taking care not to damage the fruit. When the sugar has dissolved fully, bring to the boil slowly, without stirring, and test for the setting point.

3. Wait for a short time for the conserve to cool, then stir gently to even out the fruit throughout the pan. Pour into jars and seal.

An alternative way of making conserve, which is suitable for strawberries or other berries, is to heat the sugar with pectin stock until it has dissolved, then add the berries and stir gently. Leave to stand for half an hour, then return to the heat and cook for another 5–10 minutes, until the setting point is reached.

Apricot conserve

>   1.4kg/3lb apricots, stoned and halved
>   1.4kg/3lb sugar
>   6 tbsp lemon juice

Carefully mix all the ingredients together in a suitable cooking pan, and leave to steep for 20 minutes. Cook on a gentle heat, stirring continuously, until the sugar has dissolved, then turn up the heat and gradually bring to the boil. Add cracked kernels (see greengage jam recipe, page 278), if desired.

Making jelly

Strong-flavoured fruits that have high levels of acid and pectin, such as crab apples, gooseberries, loganberries, redcurrants and quinces, make the best jellies.

1. Prepare the fruit as for jam, and cook for up to an hour, until it has softened completely, for the pectin to be released fully. Submerge hard fruits, like apples, in water until they're just covered, but use only a little water, or none at all, with berries. Cover the pan while this is happening, to reduce evaporation (use kitchen foil if you don't have a lid).

2. Sterilize a jelly bag in scalding water, squeeze dry and set up on its stand. (Traditionally, a square piece of muslin was used, each corner attached to the leg of an upturned stool.) Spoon, or pour, in the pulp – you may need to do this in stages – and let it drip into a bowl. This can take anything from an hour to overnight. Don't attempt to speed things up by squeezing the bag, or the juice will turn cloudy. Wait until the pulp is completely dry. (If you want to extract more juice, you can add water to the pulp, boil for another hour, and repeat the process, but this is only possible with high-pectin fruits).

3. Measure the total amount of juice and pour it into the preserving pan. Heat until boiling, add 450g/1lb warmed sugar for every 600ml/1 pint juice, and stir over a medium heat until it has dissolved. Bring rapidly to the boil, and test for the setting point; the longer you leave it, the darker it gets.

4. Scrape any scum from the surface, and pour into jars while still piping hot. It should set quickly.

Mint jelly

900g/2lb whole unpeeled cooking apples, cut into chunks

sugar, as needed (see point 3 above)

30ml/2 tbsp wine vinegar

40g/1½oz fresh mint, finely chopped (but not so fine that it bleeds green)

Put the apples into the pan with 600ml/1 pint water. Bring to the boil and simmer for 1 hour, or until soft. (Crush any remaining lumps with a potato masher.) Strain through a jelly bag and collect the juice. Repeat, using 300ml/½ pint water, and add the juice to the original. Add the sugar and wine vinegar and bring to the boil for 5 minutes or so, until setting point is reached. Stir in the mint, ensuring that it's well distributed throughout the jelly, and pot while still hot. This recipe works well for other herbs, like rosemary, sage and thyme.

Quince jelly

900g/2lb whole unpeeled quinces or 'japonicas', chopped

juice of 3 lemons (optional)

sugar, as needed (see point 3 above)

Put the quinces in a pan with 900ml/1½ pints water. If the fruits are unripe, add an extra 600ml/1 pint water. Bring to the boil and simmer until the fruit is reduced to a pulp. If the quinces are over-ripe, add the juice from three lemons. Strain through a jelly bag, add sugar according to the formula above, and boil until the setting point is reached.

Redcurrant jelly

900g/2lb slightly unripe redcurrants
sugar, as needed

Put the redcurrants and 300ml/½ pint water in a pan. Bring to the boil and simmer until they're reduced to a pulp. If the redcurrants are fully ripe, don't add any water; if not, add around 300ml/½ pint water, just to stop the fruit burning. Strain through a jelly bag, add 450g/1lb sugar for every 600ml/1 pint juice, and bring to the boil, until setting point is reached.

Making low- and no-sugar jams and jellies

Although it's possible to make jams and jellies with smaller amounts of sugar by reducing every 450g/1lb sugar in standard recipes to 340g/12oz or even 225g/8oz, they will not set, or keep, as well as the traditional versions.

There are three storage options:

- Pour into suitable containers, refrigerate at once, and eat within three to four weeks.

- Pour into suitable containers, allowing headroom for expansion, and freeze.

- Pour into sterilized Kilner jars, replace their lids loosely, then put into a water bath full of boiling water (see page 269). Maintain the temperature at 88°C/190°F for five minutes, then take out the jars and tighten the lids. Check the following day that a vacuum has been formed.

If you wish to make jam without using sugar at all, you could experiment with apple juice (fresh, or as a concentrate). You'll need to use pectin stock to supply extra acid and pectin, or you might try using gelatine as a setting agent (vegetarians and vegans could use agar flakes, made from processed seaweed, instead). We don't have a great deal of experience of making no-sugar jams ourselves, but here is a recipe to try.

Sugar-free blackberry and apple jam

1.8kg/4lb blackberries
340g/12oz cooking apples, peeled, cored and chopped
600ml/1 pint apple juice
300ml/½ pint pectin stock

Put the blackberries, apples and apple juice in a saucepan and simmer for an hour. Add the pectin stock and boil until the setting point is reached. Bottle in sterilized Kilner jars (see above), or freeze.

CHAPTER 15

Pickles, relishes, chutneys, sauces and ketchups

Most vegetables and fruits can be turned into savoury preserves, using different combinations of brine, vinegar, sugar and spices, according to the recipe. There are no hard and fast rules. These preserves are amongst the nation's favourite foods – it's impossible to imagine a 'ploughman's lunch' without pickle or piccalilli – and they're great fun to make. So what's the difference between them?

- When vegetables and fruits are left whole, or in large pieces, and immersed in vinegar, they're called 'pickles'.

- If vegetables and fruits are grated, or chopped, and left uncooked or cooked only lightly, they're known as 'relishes'.

- When they involve spicy, sweet and sour mixtures of diced fruits, vegetables and herbs, cooked at length with vinegar and sugar, they're called 'chutneys'.

- If they're similar to chutneys, but sieved and processed into smooth, thick, piquant liquids, they're called 'sauces' (if they contain various mixtures of ingredients) or 'ketchups' (if they major on one ingredient). Some lumpy sauces ought to be called 'pickles' by rights.

Equipment

You'll need a large enamel-coated, stainless-steel or aluminium preserving pan. If it is an enamel pan, make sure it is not chipped, as the acid in the vinegar will corrode the pan. Vinegar attacks copper, brass, iron and zinc, so pans made from these materials are unsuitable. Don't use metal utensils, for the same reason; choose nylon sieves and wooden spoons instead. Almost any glass jar or bottle that has a lid with a plasticized sealing strip around the inner edge is acceptable. Metal lids are best avoided, unless they're lacquered, or plastic coated, or have a cardboard inner disc to protect them from splashing. Wide-necked preserving jars, similar to those used for bottling, are also suitable.

Ingredients

As well as the fruits and vegetables themselves, you will also need salt, vinegar and sugar. It is worth paying a little extra to get top-quality ingredients.

Salt

Salt is necessary, because it draws out water from the vegetables, making them firmer. At the same time, it penetrates the tissues, acting as a preservative. It also prevents the moisture in the vegetables from diluting the vinegar, thereby reducing its strength. There are various types of salt to choose from. Table salt contains anti-caking chemicals to allow it to flow easily, but these can darken pickles and make them cloudy, so this is not recommended. Fortunately, reasonably priced fine sea salt, harvested from the French Atlantic coast, is available from good wholefood shops and delicatessens (see Resources, p.306). You can buy unrefined sea salt, as collected from the marshes of Essex, and the shorelines of Cornwall and Anglesey, which has a subtle flavour, but it's expensive when bought in large quantities. Alternatively, you could try a natural, unrefined rock salt, like Tidman's.

Salt is traditionally used in pickling, as either a dry or wet brine. The dry-brine method involves sprinkling salt liberally over the vegetables, until they're completely covered, and then leaving them for a period of time, often overnight. This is particularly appropriate for vegetables that have a high moisture content, like cucumbers and marrows. The wet-brine method involves immersing vegetables for a similar length of time in a solution of 55g/2oz of salt per 600ml/1 pint of water. In either case, the salt is drained off and the vegetables are rinsed thoroughly in cold water.

Vinegar

Vinegar, which contains acetic acid, is a good preservative, because moulds and bacteria prefer a slightly alkaline environment and dislike acid conditions. The acid content should be at least 5 per cent, but need not be as eye-wateringly high as the 10–30 per cent found in the spirit vinegars that pubs use in their jars of pickled onions.

There are various types of vinegar available. Malt vinegar is still commonly used in pickles, on account of its relative cheapness. It's a product of the brewing industry. Use brown malt vinegar for most vegetables, and distilled white vinegar (which is usually slightly stronger at 6 per cent acetic acid) for fruits and some vegetables, like red cabbages or beans, where it's important to keep the colour. On the Continent, vinegar is usually made from wine – hence red wine and white wine vinegar. These, along with cider vinegar, have a more delicate flavour than the malts. Our own favourite is Aspall's Organic Cyder Vinegar, which we use most of the time.

Spiced vinegar

The flavour of any vinegar is improved by spices, which you add yourself, unless you buy 'pickling' malt vinegar, which already contains them. There are no fixed rules about which spices to choose. Cinnamon, mace, cloves and allspice frequently appear in pickling recipes, but your choices will depend on your personal taste. They must be used whole, however, not ground, or the vinegar will turn cloudy.

Put about 7g/¼oz of each of the above spices into a muslin bag, along with half a dozen peppercorns and 15g/½oz of bruised root ginger. Drop this into 1.2 litres/2 pints of wine or cider vinegar (ideally in a glass demijohn) and leave for six to eight weeks, shaking the contents from time to time. If you need spiced vinegar at short notice, you can miss out the prolonged steeping and just boil the vinegar with the spices (loose, or in a muslin bag) for 10 minutes. As a general rule, it's better to use too few spices, rather than too many, but you'll soon find a combination that's just right for you.

If your taste runs to something hotter, include mustard seeds or dried chillies, and if you want to add something more aromatic, use coriander seeds. Some condiment companies, like Schwarz, sell packets of mixed pickling spices, which cuts down the expense. Steenbergs stock a good range of organically grown spices (see page 306).

Sugar

Any type of sugar is acceptable, but many pickling and chutney recipes lend themselves to the use of brown sugar, and we usually opt for an unrefined, organic demerara.

Making pickles

1. Select tender young vegetables, raw, or lightly cooked, according to the recipe. Discard any tough stems or leaves. Leave whole, or chop into appropriately sized chunks.

2. Immerse thoroughly in salt, using wet or dry brine, as appropriate (most recipes state wet brine), and leave to cure. After the required time has elapsed, drain off the brine and rinse thoroughly in cold water.

3. Pack the vegetables into sterilized jars (which were washed with boiling water), then leave in a cool oven, 140°C/275°F/gas 1 until required. Leave around 2.5cm/1in headroom at the top. Drain off any liquid residue.

4. Pour spiced vinegar into the jars until the pickles are completely submerged – some vinegar will evaporate in store, so give a good 1cm/½in covering. Tap the jars while you're doing this, to eliminate air bubbles. Replace the lids and tighten.

5. Label and date all jars, and store them out of the light in a cupboard, preferably somewhere cool and dry.

When pickling fruits, replace the salt with sugar. It's usually added to the spiced vinegar, and the fruits are then gently cooked in it until they have become soft. Sugar is often used in recipes for vegetable pickles when a sweet and sour taste is required.

Sweet pickled onions

Remove the outer skins of pickling onions, or shallots, and immerse them in wet brine for 24 hours. Drain the salt away, and rinse several times with clean water. Pack the onions into warm, sterilized jars. Heat sufficient spiced vinegar to cover the onions completely and dissolve 1 tbsp of sugar in every 600ml/1 pint of vinegar. Pour over the onions and seal.

Pickled gherkins

Lay washed, but unpeeled, gherkins in a flat dish and sprinkle salt over them, until they're coated. Leave overnight, for the salt to penetrate the flesh. Drain and rinse well. Pack into jars with a couple of bay leaves. Fill with cold spiced vinegar, and seal.

Pickled garlic

Break the garlic bulbs into cloves, and peel. Pack into a warm jar with 1 teaspoon of black peppercorns and several bay leaves. Add 80g/3oz sugar to 300ml/½ pint spiced vinegar and bring to the boil, stirring until dissolved. Pour over the garlic and seal.

Pickled beetroot

Boil beetroots in their skin in salted water – 1 tbsp salt per 600ml/1 pint water – until they're slightly undercooked, then peel and slice them. Add 1 tsp black peppercorns and 30g/1oz peeled and sliced root ginger to 600ml/1 pint cider vinegar, and boil for 10-15 minutes. Strain off the spices and leave until cold. Pour over the beetroot and seal.

Pickled pears

Peel, core and quarter the pears. Add 2kg sugar to every 1.25 litres spiced vinegar (2lb per pint) in a pan and bring to the boil, stirring until all the sugar has dissolved. Add the pears and simmer until tender. Drain off the syrup (but retain it) and pack the fruit into jars. Return the syrup to the boil and reduce it slightly until thicker. Pour over the pears – give a good covering, as the fruit will partially absorb the syrup, and you may need to top up – and seal.

Making relishes

On the progression from pickles to chutney, relishes lie somewhere in between. They always contain vinegar, like pickles, but sugar is almost always added as well. Making relishes involves more preparation – the fruit or vegetables are chopped into much smaller pieces, for example, and they're usually cooked (though this isn't essential), although not for as long as chutney. Relishes can be eaten straight away, unlike chutney, which is best matured for a month or so.

Beetroot, cucumbers, celery, chilli peppers, sweet corn and tomatoes make good relishes, along with fruits such as apples, cherries, damsons and rhubarb. Horseradish is another favourite ingredient. Relishes may be hot and spicy, sweet and sour, or any combination of these.

Acid cherry relish

225g/8oz sugar

350ml/12fl oz cider vinegar

170g/6oz onions, finely chopped

900g/2lb unstoned morello cherries

1 tsp ground cinnamon

1 tsp ground allspice

grated zest of 1 orange

Heat the sugar with the vinegar in a pan until the sugar has dissolved. Blanch the onions for 2–3 minutes (see page 255), then drain and add to the syrup. Mix in the cherries and the rest of the ingredients, and simmer while the syrup reduces and thickens. Pot into warm jars, and label with the warning 'contains stones', to avoid broken teeth or choking.

Sweet corn relish

450g/1lb sweet corn (about 4 cobs)

1 small onion or shallot, finely chopped

vegetable oil, for frying

1 red chilli, deseeded, pith removed, and chopped

55g/2oz sugar

150ml/¼ pint cider vinegar

1 tsp dry mustard powder

Boil the sweet corn for 4 minutes and strip off the kernels. Fry the onion gently for a few minutes in the oil in a saucepan, until soft but not brown. Add the remaining ingredients and blend together. Bring to the boil and cook for 20 minutes. Pour into warm jars and seal.

Tomato relish

900g/2lb ripe tomatoes

2 onions, finely chopped

30g/1oz salt

2 celery sticks, chopped

1 large red pepper, deseeded and chopped

225g/8oz sugar

200ml/7 fl oz cider vinegar

2 tsp crushed mustard seeds

Skin the tomatoes (immerse in scalding water for several minutes until the skins slide off) and chop finely. Leave them in a bowl overnight with the salt, then drain. Mix the celery, pepper, sugar, vinegar and mustard seeds together. Stir in the tomatoes and onions, until all the ingredients are mixed thoroughly. Pour into jars and seal.

Making chutneys

Chutney is one of the most versatile of foods, a perfect accompaniment to curry, cold meats, cheese and salads. The word derives from the Hindi *chatni*, meaning 'strongly spiced', but your chutney doesn't have to be like that. One of the great joys of chutney making (apart from making good use of your surplus produce) is the possibility of infinite experimentation. Vinegar, salt, sugar and spices are all essential ingredients, but after that the choice is yours. Although apples, tomatoes, gooseberries, plums and rhubarb frequently figure in chutney recipes, there's scarcely a single fruit or vegetable that could not merit a place.

1. Always use the best ingredients, and mince or chop them finely.

2. Choose brown sugar, if you want dark-coloured chutney, and white sugar for light-coloured chutneys.

3. Bruise, or crack, whole spices, to release their flavours, and tie in a muslin bag to add to the pan.

4. Use white wine vinegar, cider vinegar or distilled white vinegar to make light-coloured chutney.

5. Sugar dissolves more easily when warm, so put it briefly in a low oven before adding it to the pan. The longer sugar is cooked, the darker the chutney becomes, so, when sweetening light-coloured chutneys, add the sugar towards the end.

6. Cook tougher ingredients, like beetroot, to soften them before adding to the rest of the ingredients.

7. Simmer the ingredients for one to two hours to achieve a uniform taste and texture. However, you should also use your discretion and remove from the heat when the desired consistency is reached. Avoid adding extra ingredients towards the end of the cooking, because this can unbalance the flavour.

8. Don't cover the pan – the chutney thickens by evaporation. Stir regularly, to prevent the chutney from sticking to the base of the pan.

9. Pot into sterilized, warm jars, then seal, label and date. Store somewhere cool in the dark. Check from time to time, for contamination.

10. Leave for one or two months before tasting, to allow the chutney to mature. It should keep for two or three years if stored correctly.

Apple chutney

1.8kg/4lb cooking apples, peeled, cored and diced
900g/2lb onions, finely chopped
750ml/1¼ pints vinegar
2 tsp mixed pickling spices (in a muslin bag)
112g/4oz raisins
1 tsp cayenne pepper
675g/1½lb sugar

Put the apples, onions and 300ml/½ pint water in the preserving pan. Bring to the boil and simmer for 15 minutes. Add half the vinegar, the pickling spices, the raisins and the cayenne pepper, and continue cooking until the mixture has softened. Pour in the sugar and the remaining vinegar, stirring until the sugar has dissolved. Bring back to the boil, then simmer slowly on a gentle heat, to reduce it until smooth.

Green tomato chutney

1.8kg/4lb green tomatoes, diced

450g/1lb cooking apples, peeled, cored and finely chopped

560g/1¼lb onions, finely sliced

600ml/1 pint vinegar

450g/1lb sugar

225g/8oz raisins

30g/1oz salt

8 dried red chillies, bruised

15g/½oz root ginger, bruised

Put all the ingredients except for the dried chillies and ginger in a preserving pan. Tie the chillies and ginger in a muslin bag and add to the mixture. Bring gently to the boil. Simmer, stirring frequently, until the chutney has thickened to the right consistency. Pour into warm jars, and seal.

Peach chutney

900g/2lb ripe peaches, peeled, pitted and chopped

336g/12oz sugar

168g/6oz raisins

750ml/1¼ pints vinegar

30g/1oz fresh root ginger, grated

1 lemon, minced or finely chopped

1 green pepper, deseeded, cored and chopped

1 tsp cayenne pepper

Mix all the ingredients together in a preserving pan and bring to the boil, simmering until the right consistency is reached. Pot into warm jars, and seal.

Pumpkin chutney

- 900g/2lb pumpkins, peeled and diced
- 900g/2lb sugar
- 600ml/1 pint vinegar
- 225g/8oz onions, finely chopped
- 55g/2oz fresh root ginger, grated
- 112g/4oz sultanas
- 2 tsp mixed pickling spice (in muslin bag)
- 4 red peppers, deseeded, cored and diced
- 3 garlic cloves
- 2 tbsp salt

Mix all the ingredients together in a preserving pan and bring to the boil. Cook until soft, stirring frequently, until the right texture is achieved. Pot into warm jars and seal.

Sauces and ketchups

As an alternative to pickles or chutney, you can convert surplus produce into sauces or ketchups. The ingredients are pretty much the same as for chutneys, with vinegar, sugar and spices included as preservatives, but sauces and ketchups are usually tangier, and they're sieved, to make them more pourable. Most chutneys convert readily into ketchups: simply use slightly less sugar in the recipe, sieve the end result, and reheat with extra vinegar.

If you are making fruit sauces or ketchups, opt for strong-flavoured fruits, like plums or blackberries. Sauces made with fruit are sufficiently acid to survive in store without further treatment, but sauces and ketchups based on tomatoes run the risk of fermenting, so they must be sterilized, as for syrups, at 88°C/190°F for 10 minutes. If in doubt, sterilize.

The classic British brown sauce is a mixture of tomatoes, shallots, chopped dates and up to thirteen different spices, which are cooked in a little water until soft, passed through a sieve, re-heated and reduced.

Apple sauce

This recipe goes well with pork.

450g/1lb whole cooking apples, finely chopped
15g/½oz butter
1 tbsp sugar
½ tsp ground ginger

Put all the ingredients in a pan with 150ml/¼ pint water. Simmer until soft. Rub through a sieve to remove the solids, then pour into warm bottles and sterilize for 10 minutes.

Gooseberry ketchup

This recipe goes well with mackerel.

1.35kg/3lb gooseberries, topped and tailed
less than 115g/4oz sugar
less than 300ml/½ pint spiced vinegar
ground cloves, to taste

Simmer the gooseberries in a pan with 300ml/½ pint water until they've softened into a purée. Rub through a nylon sieve, and add 55g/2oz sugar and 300ml/½ pint spiced vinegar for every 600ml/1 pint purée, along with the ground cloves. Bring to the boil and simmer until you achieve the right consistency. Pour into hot bottles and seal.

Mint sauce

This sauce goes well with lamb. When using the sauce, dilute with a little boiling water, into which sugar has been dissolved, to sweeten.

Wash and dry young tips of mint, then chop. Pack loosely into sterilized jars, cover completely with distilled white vinegar and seal.

Plum sauce

This goes well with duck

1.8kg/4lb unstoned plums, flesh cut roughly

225g/8oz onions, roughly chopped

112g/4oz currants

600ml/1 pint spiced vinegar

7g/¼oz fresh root ginger, finely chopped

30g/1oz salt

225g/8oz sugar

Put the plums, onions, currants and half the vinegar in a pan. Bring to the boil and simmer until the mixture has softened. Remove from the heat and press the pulp, including the stones, through a nylon sieve. Return to the pan and add the rest of the vinegar, the ginger and the salt. Stir in the sugar until it has dissolved, then bring back to the boil and simmer for up to an hour until it has reduced sufficiently. Bottle and seal.

Tomato ketchup

This goes well with lots of things! We use it spread on toast as a fat-free alternative to butter when we have scrambled eggs. It's also a great source of the protective phytochemical, lycopene. If you prefer your ketchup hotter and spicier, add several chopped fresh chillies (still containing their seeds).

1.8kg/4lb ripe tomatoes, chopped

450g/1lb cooking apples, peeled, cored and finely chopped

225g/8oz onions, finely chopped

1 tsp mixed pickling spices

600ml/1 pint distilled white vinegar

140g/5oz sugar

salt and ground black pepper

Put the tomatoes, apples, onions and spices in a pan, and simmer (don't add any water) until the mixture has the consistency of a thick paste. Rub the pulp through a nylon sieve. Return to the pan, add the vinegar and sugar, and stir until dissolved. Bring to the boil, then simmer until thickened. Add salt and pepper to taste. Pour into hot bottles or jars and sterilize.

CHAPTER 16

Juices and syrups

You can extract juice from fruit quite easily, mechanically or in a steamer. Adding dissolved sugar converts juice into a delicious syrup, to be used as a cordial, in milkshakes and smoothies, or poured over ice cream. Yummy!

Equipment

The simplest way of extracting juice from small amounts of fruit is with a juicer. Hand-operated devices exist – mainly for pressing oranges or for juicing wheatgrass – but most machines on the market are electrically powered. Centrifugal juicers are the most popular, and these shred the fruit (or vegetables) into pulp, and spin it at high speed to extract the juice. Masticating juicers, which tend to be more expensive, 'chew' or mince the contents, prior to squeezing out the juice. A third sort, of which the Mehu Liisa is the best known, uses steam to extract the juice. They can also be used for blanching vegetables, prior to freezing.

Ingredients

Always select fruits at their peak of ripeness, when the juice is in its most easily extracted form, and wash them thoroughly. Peel apples (and other thick-skinned fruits like melons and citrus), and chop into chunks, including the core. If you're using a mechanical juicer, de-stone cherries, plums and other stone fruit. Finally, check thoroughly for any signs of mould, or other diseases, and either cut out any affected areas or remove the offending items.

Making fruit juices

If you don't have a mechanical juicer, you can extract juice in a similar way to that used for making jellies. Put the fruit (or vegetables) in a large preserving pan with a small amount of water – sufficient to prevent the fruit from sticking. Soft fruits, like raspberries and strawberries, need no extra water, but cherries, gooseberries, peaches and others that are firmer require around 300ml/½ pint water for every 1kg/2¼lb of fruit, whilst apples, currants, plums and damsons need double this amount.

Cook the fruit gently, crushing it with the back of a spoon, or potato masher, as it softens until it has turned into a purée. If the mash is in danger of drying out, add a little more water. Spoon the purée into a jelly bag (see page 273) and leave it overnight to drip into a bowl. (If a little cloudiness is acceptable to you in your juice, a little judicious squeezing will help it on its way!) Pour into clean bottles and store in the fridge for immediate use, or freeze or bottle for long-term storage.

If you have large quantities of apples, or other fruit, that you wish to process on a regular basis – perhaps for making cider or wine – it may be worth investing in a fruit crusher and press (see page 306 for suppliers of juice-extraction equipment). Juice is squeezed out of crushed fruit by pressing it between two plates, operated manually by means of a screw thread. This works well for apples, pears, grapes, blackberries and raspberries, but is less successful with currants, blueberries, plums and quinces, which are best extracted using heat.

Whichever method of extraction you use, you'll be left with a quantity of dried pulp. Put it on the compost heap if it contains stones, pips or anything else that is inedible. You may be able to use pulp from an electric juicer as a filler in thick soups, stews or casseroles, but bear in mind that most of the goodness will have been extracted along with the juice. Steam juicers produce an even more unappetising pulp, which is best discarded.

Making vegetable juices

Carrots, celery, cucumbers and beetroot, along with tomatoes, are the most popular candidates for juicing, but other vegetables may be processed in a liquidizer, or juicer, to make refreshing and nutritious drinks. Preparation usually involves little more than washing, chopping and/or grating. Try blending fruits and vegetables: combinations such as apple, carrot and celery, or tomato, cucumber, carrot and parsley go well together.

Making fruit syrups

The best syrups are made from fruits that retain most of their flavour after extraction – fruits like blackberries, blackcurrants, raspberries, strawberries and loganberries. To make a syrup, add 225–340g/8–12oz of sugar, according to taste, to every 600ml/1 pint of juice. Heat gently for a short time until the sugar has dissolved, taking care not to let it boil, or it may turn into jelly! Pour into bottles and store in the fridge, where it should keep for a couple of months. For longer-term storage, it must be frozen or bottled, as follows.

Storing juices and syrups

Freezing is the easiest method of preserving juices and syrups, which should keep for at least 12 months. Almost any plastic container will do, but remember to leave headspace into which the liquid can expand when frozen. Alternatively, cut off the top of a plastic drinks carton, insert a heavy-duty polythene bag, and pour in the juice. This will freeze into the shape of an easily stackable brick. Individual cubes of syrup can be made in ice trays or, even better, poured into plastic moulds and turned into ice lollies!

Bottling is also an effective method of preserving juices and syrups (see page 266). Re-use or buy swing-top bottles, although any glass bottles with screw tops will do, as long as they have rubber or plastic seals around the inside edge. Glass preserving jars can also be used, of course.

Wash the bottles thoroughly and sterilize in boiling water. Fill with juice or syrup to within 2.5cm/1in of the rim and replace the lids loosely. Snap shut the metal fastenings on the lids of swing-top bottles, because they're designed to expand, to let steam escape. Stand the bottles in a sterilizer, or any suitably deep container, so they're not touching each other (or the base), and fill with cold water to their necks. Bring the temperature up to 77°C/171°F and maintain for 30 minutes. Remove from the heat and screw the caps tight.

If you're using a Mehu Liisa, or other steam juicer, you can skip this procedure because the juice is extracted at sterilization temperature, and can be bottled there and then. Fill the bottles right to the top, forming a meniscus at the rim, then screw tight (this is a two-person job). Catch any spilt juice in a bucket, and return it for reprocessing. The juice shrinks as it cools in the bottle, forming an impenetrable vacuum between the top of the liquid and the cap.

Stored somewhere cool and dark, bottled juices and syrups will keep for upwards of a year. Check them from time to time, and get rid of any that have mould growing inside the neck.

CHAPTER 17

Flavoured oils and vinegars

Flavoured vegetable, fruit and herb oils and vinegars are simple to make, a delight to the eye, and have a terrific taste. The most popular use herbs, and can vary from subtle to richly aromatic. Others capture the powerful flavours of garlic and chillies. Whether drizzled over salads, used as a base for mayonnaise and dressings or used to add a subtle flavour to many dishes, they're a versatile and tempting addition to the larder.

Flavoured oils

The basic technique for making flavoured herb oils requires little more than steeping leaves in the oil for a week or two, to let the flavours infuse, after which time it's strained and bottled. Choose good-quality oil – the sort that you might use for dressing salads, which will absorb, but not overpower, the essence of the herbs. Soya, groundnut, grapeseed and corn oils are all acceptable as a base, as is mild olive oil. Infused extra-virgin olive oil can be too strongly flavoured for some tastes, but it's great to dip freshly baked bread into. Avoid walnut, sesame and other similar oils, because of competing flavours. Oil is a poor preservative and turns rancid in contact with air. Sterilizing compromises the taste, so make small quantities, keep for only a few months, and store in the fridge once opened.

Thyme oil

Pick a generous handful of fresh thyme and gently bruise it – a rolling pin is ideal. Put in a bowl, and pour over sufficient oil to cover the leaves. Cover and leave somewhere cool for two weeks. Strain and bottle, adding a sprig or two of fresh thyme for effect. This recipe can be used for most culinary herbs, either singly or in mixtures.

Chilli oil

Heat your chosen oil in a pan with 115–225g/4–8oz chopped dried chillies, and cook for a few minutes until the oil has coloured and the chillies have ceased sizzling. Don't allow the oil to smoke. Remove from the heat, add 1 tsp of black peppercorns, and allow to cool. Strain – first through a sieve, then through a jelly bag. Pour the oil into sterilized jars.

Infusing vinegars

These are made by steeping herbs, fruits and vegetables in vinegar, in the same way as for flavoured oils. Most culinary herbs can be given this treatment, but basil, mint, rosemary, sage, tarragon, thyme and lavender are especially popular. Soft fruits, like raspberries, blackberries, strawberries and blackcurrants, also make excellent vinegars. Vegetable vinegars are less successful, other than those made with celery, cucumbers, chillies and garlic.

Choose white wine vinegar, cider vinegar or distilled white vinegar (which are all neutral in colour and less intense than malt vinegar), for all but the strongest-flavoured subjects. Sweetened fruit vinegars make a mildly astringent adult drink, especially when mixed with tonic water and ice, and can also be used to flavour desserts. The natural acidity of vinegar is anathema to most spoilage organisms, making it a much more effective preservative than oil. Flavoured vinegars should keep for up to a year in a dark cupboard.

Herbs are at their best when picked just before they flower. Gently bruise them with a rolling pin, put in a wide-necked jar, pour over the vinegar and replace the lid. Leave for a couple of weeks, stirring or shaking the contents each day. Strain through clean muslin, or a jelly bag, and pour into sterilized bottles.

Pick soft fruit on a dry day, when fully ripe, and crush gently in a bowl. To every 900g/2lb of fruit add 600ml/1 pint of vinegar. Red wine vinegars can be used with berries, but they will darken the fruit. Cover and allow to stand for three to five days, shaking or stirring the contents several times a day. Strain through muslin, or a jelly bag, and boil in a pan for 10 minutes. Leave to cool, then pot into warmed sterilized bottles. For a sweeter effect, add 225–450g/8oz–1lb of granulated sugar to each 600ml/1 pint of strained vinegar, prior to boiling. Fortify with a tot of brandy in each bottle, if desired.

Chop, split or grate vegetables that are to be infused in vinegar, then treat as for herbs.

Garlic vinegar

Peel and slice six fat cloves of garlic and put in a jar. Boil 600ml/1 pint cider vinegar and pour over the cloves. Cover the jar and leave for three to four weeks, shaking it from time to time. Strain and re-bottle.

Raspberry vinegar

Add 900g/2lb fresh, lightly crushed raspberries to each 600ml/1 pint cider vinegar or white wine vinegar. Leave for three days, stirring several times a day. Strain as above, and measure the liquid. Pour into a pan and add 225g/8oz sugar (more if you have a sweet tooth!) to each 600ml/1 pint. Bring briskly to the boil, stirring until all the sugar has dissolved. Pour into sterilized bottles and seal, adding a few fresh berries, if wished. Victorian ladies swore by raspberry vinegar as a pick-me-up, and as a cure for colds and sore throats.

Tarragon vinegar

Bruise approximately 55g/2oz fresh tarragon sprigs and immerse in a jar containing 600ml/1 pint white wine vinegar. Cover and leave for three weeks. Strain and pour into sterilized jars, adding a sprig or two of fresh tarragon for decoration.

Resources

Books

AFRC Institute of Food Research, *Home Preservation of Fruit and Vegetables*, HMSO, 1989

Baker, Harry, *Growing Fruit*, Mitchell Beazley, 2004

Bartholomew, Mel, *Square Foot Gardening*, Rodale Press, 2005

Bleasedale, J.K.A., P.J. Salter and others, *The Complete Know and Grow Vegetables*, Oxford University Press, 1991

Buczacki, Stefan and Harris, Keith, *Collins Guide to the Pests, Diseases and Disorders of Garden Plants*, Collins, 1981

Cherfas, Jeremy; Fanton, Michael and Jude, *The Seed Savers' Handbook*, Grover Books, 1996

Cunningham, Sally, *Asian Vegetables: A Guide to Growing Fruit, Vegetables and Spices from the Indian Subcontinent*, Eco-Logic Books, 2009

Goldman, Amy, *Melons for the Passionate Grower*, Artisan Books, 2002

Goldman, Amy, *The Compleat Squash*, Artisan Books, 2004

Goldman, Amy, *The Heirloom Tomato*, Bloomsbury, 2008

Grigson, Jane, *Jane Grigson's Vegetable Book*, Penguin Books, 1980

Hickmott, Simon, *Growing Unusual Vegetables*, Eco-logic Books, 2003

Larkcom, Joy, *Oriental Vegetables*, Frances Lincoln, 2007

Li, Thomas, S.C., *Vegetables and Fruits: Nutritional and Therapeutic Values*, CRC Press, 2008

McCance, R.A. and Widdowson, E.M., *The Compositions of Foods*, Food Standards Agency, 2002

McVicar, Jekka, *Jekka's Complete Herb Book*, Kyle Cathie, 1994

Patten, Marguerite, *Jams, Chutneys, Preserves, Vinegars and Oils*, Bloomsbury, 1995

Romans, Alan, *The Potato Book*, Frances Lincoln, 2005

Stickland, Sue, *Heritage Vegetables*, Gaia Books, 1998

Magazines

Grow Your Own. Tel: 01206 505979. www.growfruitandveg.co.uk
Kitchen Garden. Tel: 0844 826 7812. www.kitchengarden.co.uk

Organizations

Garden Organic. Tel: 024 7630 3517. www.gardenorganic.org.uk
The Royal Horticultural Society. Tel: 0845 260 5000. www.rhs.org.uk
The National Society of Allotment & Leisure Gardeners. Tel: 01536 266576.
    www.nsalg.org.uk
Landshare. www.landshare.net
Freecycle. www.freecycle.org

Seed suppliers

Alanromans.com. Tel: 01337 831060. www.alanromans.com
The Chilli Pepper Company. Tel: 015395 58110. www.chileseeds.co.uk
The Garlic Farm. Tel: 01983 865378. www.thegarlicfarm.co.uk
Heritage Seed Library. Tel: 024 7630 3517. www.gardenorganic.org.uk
Nicky's Nursery. Tel: 01843 600972. www.nickys-nursery.co.uk
The Organic Gardening Catalogue. Tel: 01932 253666.
    www.organiccatalogue.com
The Real Seed Catalogue. Tel: 01239 821107. www.realseeds.co.uk
W Robinson & Son Ltd. Tel: 01524 791210. www.mammothonion.co.uk
Seeds-by-Size. Tel: 01442 251458. www.seeds-by-size.com
Seeds of Italy. Tel: 0208 427 5020. www.seedsofitaly.com
Simpson's Seeds. Tel: 01985 845004. www.simpsonsseeds.co.uk
Tamar Organics. Tel: 01579 371087. www.tamarorganics.co.uk
Thomas Etty Esq. Tel: 01460 57934. www.thomasetty.co.uk
Thompson & Morgan. Tel: 0844 5731818. www.thompson-morgan.com
Edwin Tucker & Sons Ltd. Tel: 01364 652233. www.tucker-seeds.co.uk

Organic plant suppliers

Delfland Nurseries. Tel: 01354 740553. www.organicplants.co.uk
Jekka's Herb Farm. Tel: 01454 418878. www.jekkasherbfarm.com

Fruit nurseries

Bernwode Fruit Trees. Tel: 01844 237415. www.bernwodefruittrees.co.uk
Chris Bowers & Sons. Tel: 01366 388752. www.chrisbowers.co.uk
Brandy Carr Nurseries. Tel: 01924 291511. www.brandycarrnurseries.co.uk

Keepers Nursery. Tel: 01622 726465. www.keepers-nursery.co.uk
Reads Nursery. Tel: 01508 548 395. www.readsnursery.co.uk
R.V. Roger Ltd. Tel: 01751 472226. www.rvroger.co.uk
Rougham Hall Nurseries. Tel: 01359 270577. www.roughamhallnurseries.co.uk
Sunnybank Vine Nursery. Tel: 01981 240256. www.sunnybankvines.co.uk
The Dorset Blueberry Company. Tel: 01202 874737. www.dorsetblueberry.com
Walcot Organic Nursery. Tel: 01905 841587. www.walcotnursery.co.uk

Gardening sundries

Defenders. Tel: 01233 813121. www.defenders.co.uk
    (*biocontrols, traps, barriers*)
The Gardeners Shop. Tel: 020 8777 4332. www.thegardenersshop.co.uk
    (*tools, sacks, clothing, nets, etc.*)
Garden Systems. Tel: 01473 400101. www.ecpgroup.com
    (*drip irrigation and other watering equipment, rainwater harvesting*)
Green Gardener. Tel: 01493 750061. www.greengardener.co.uk
    (*biocontrols, wildlife gardening specialists, natural pest control, gardening
    sundries*)
Harrod Horticultural. Tel: 0845 218 5301. www.harrodhorticultural.com
    (*netting, greenhouse equipment, raised bed kits, compost bins, etc.*)
Heritage Garden Traders. Tel: 01989 720 178. www.heritagegardentraders.co.uk
    (*apple stores, cucumber straighteners, rhubarb forcers, etc.*)
Hibbitt of Oswestry. Tel: 01691 656152. www.hibbitt.co.uk
    (*apple stores, apple presses, traditional cloches, etc.*)
Implementations. Tel: 024 7639 2497. www.implementations.co.uk
    (*exquisite copper garden tools*)
CLM Keder Greenhouses Ltd. Tel: 01386 49094. www.kedergreenhouse.co.uk
    (*bubble design, insulated-walled greenhouses*)
Northern Polytunnels. Tel: 01282 873120. www.northernpolytunnels.co.uk
    (*polytunnels, tunnel cloches, fruit cages*)
Smith Bros (Quinton) Ltd. Tel: 0121 557 0077. www.woodenpackaging.co.uk
    (*tea chests and other wooden storage boxes*)
The Organic Gardening Catalogue. Tel: 01932 253666.
    www.organiccatalogue.com
    (*huge range of organic gardening sundries, including Procol wood preservative*)
Two Wests & Elliott. Tel: 01246 451077. www.twowests.co.uk
    (*greenhouse and garden equipment*)

Food preservation equipment

Ascott Smallholding Supplies Ltd. Tel: 0845 130 6285. www.ascott.biz
    (*jars, bottles, equipment, etc.*)

Freeman & Harding. Tel: 01322 351315. www.freemanharding.co.uk
  (*bottles and jars*)
Lakeland Ltd. Tel: 015394 88100. www.lakeland.co.uk
  (*food containers, bottles, jars, etc.*)
Peter Denyer Services. Tel: 01372 372611. www.kilnerjarsuk.co.uk
  (*replacement rubber rings and lids for obsolete Kilner jars*)
UK Juicers. Tel: 01904 757070. www.ukjuicers.com
  (*juicers and dehydrators*)
Vigo. Tel: 01404 892101. www.vigopresses.co.uk
  (*fruit presses and crushers*)
Wares of Knutsford. Tel: 08456 121273. www.waresofknutsford.co.uk
  (*bottles, jars, equipment, etc.*)

Food preservation ingredients

Aspall. Tel: 01728 860510. www.aspall.co.uk
  (*organic cyder vinegar*)
Billington's. Tel: 01733 422386. www.billingtons.co.uk
  (*unrefined and organic cane sugars*)
Goodness Direct. Tel: 0871 871 6611. www.goodnessdirect.co.uk
  (*unrefined sea salt*)
Steenbergs Organic. Tel: 01765 640088. www.steenbergs.co.uk
  (*organic pickling herbs and spices*)

Be inspired!

Visit the following places to see fruit and vegetable growing at its best.

Audley End House, Essex. English Heritage. Tel: 01799 522842.
Barnsdale Gardens, Rutland. Tel: 01572 813200. www.barnsdalegardens.co.uk
Brogdale Orchards, Kent. Tel: 01795 536250. www.brogdalecollections.co.uk
Knightshayes Court, Devon. National Trust. Tel: 01884 254665.
Lost Gardens of Heligan, Cornwall. Tel: 01726 845100. www.heligan.com
Normanby Hall Country Park, Lincs. Tel: 01724 720588.
  www.northlincs.gov.uk/normanby
Ryton Gardens, Coventry. Tel: 024 7630 3517. www.gardenorganic.org.uk
Tatton Park, Cheshire. National Trust. Tel: 01625 374400.
West Dean Gardens, West Sussex. Tel: 01243 818210. www.westdean.org.uk
Wimpole Hall, Cambs. National Trust. Tel: 01223 206000.
Wisley Garden. Royal Horticultural Society. Tel: 0845 2609000.

Index